FANTASY AND FEELING
IN EDUCATION

WITHDRAWN

FANTASY AND FEELING IN EDUCATION

by Richard M. Jones

HARPER COLOPHON BOOKS
Harper & Row, Publishers
New York, Evanston and London

To Karen

Acknowledgments

Those who have a voice in what is said in this book are just numerous enough to mention. I hope I remember them all.

First there were: Frederick Burkhardt, Jerrold Zacharias, Henry Bragdon, Robert Feldmesser, John Fischer, Francis Keppel, Harry Levy, Elting Morison, Stephen White, James Killian, and Carroll Newsom.

Then there were: Robert Ascher, S. O. Biobaku, Frank Brown, William Bunge, David Driscoll, Gerald F. Else, Edwin Fenton, Ernestine Friedl, Francis Friedman, Joseph Greenbaum, Mark Harris, Robert Havighurst, Alan Holmberg, Sister Jacqueline Grennan, Charles Keller, Norton Long, Martin Mayer, Saul Mendlovitz, Franklin Patterson, Leften Stavrianos, Joshua Taylor, William Warntz, Rowland Mitchell, Kevin White, Robert Greenway, and Susan Smullin.

Then there were: Robert Adams, Charles Brown, George Homans, Gilbert Oakley, Douglas Oliver, Morton White, Karen Hagen, Quentin Brown, Robert Young, Sally Polakoff, Edwin Dethlefsen, Ann Venable, Stephen Casner, Deborah Goodwin, James Hathaway, Harry Hines,

Florence Jackson, Hyman Kavett, Alice Liebman, Svetlana Rockwell, Chris Samples, Robert Samples, Diane Taylor, Alexandra Grannis, Nona Plessner, Charlotte Ward, Barbara Graf, Peter Wolff, Susan Sager, and Donna Kelso.

Then there were: Blythe Clinchy, Linda Brooks, Courtney Cazden, Kari Krasin, Elli Miranda, David McNeill, Eleanor Murray, Anne Ryle, Betty Stewart, Richard McCann, Linda Braun, Chris Speath, Gloria Cooper, Mary Henle, and Helen Kenny.

Then there were: Peter Dow, Annette Kaysen, Timothy Asch, Frances Brooks, Anita Gil, Amy Greenfield, Hans Guggenheim, Susan Phelps, Michael Sand, Paul Schmidt, Malcolm Slavin, Robert Trivers, Patricia Asch, Henry Atkins, Betsy Dunkman, David Martin, Catherine Motz, Cam Nadeau, Kathy Sylva, Marilyn Clayton, Babette Whipple, Barbara White, Clark Abt, Asen Balikci, Irvin De Vore, William Kessen, Richard Rosenbloom, Joseph Glick, James Gallagher, Blanche McLane, Anne Scattergood, Roger Wales, Phyllis Stein, and Elena Werlin.

Then there were: Anita Mishler, Sylvia Farnham-Diggory, Celeste Amenta, Nancy Bogg, Eileen Cutler, Barbara Hafner, Roberta Heimlich, Jonina Herter, Judith Kaye, Joanne Kipsher, Dorothy Nider, Louise Weston, Marguerite Capuzzo, Barbara Carlson, Cleo Flynn, Joanne Grossman, Muriel Hanley, Donald Koeller, John Lelocas, Natalie Mays, Joan McQuiston, Joseph Quinn, Helen Rooney, Albertha Toppins, Anne Marshland, and Lawrence Fuchs.

And then there were: Thomas Battaglia, Paul Bloomquist, Jean Brown, Olive Covington, Thomas Fitzgerald, Holly Heap, Mildred Kanare, Kent Kincaid, Dorothy Martinson, Dominic Matteo, Jo McFarlane, Henry Moss, Dennen Reilley, Roger Schlueter, Mary Schmale, Robert Seitz, Gordon Taylor, Judith Thomas, and Harriet Katz.

I must of course single out Jerome Bruner—the "heavy"

of the piece—and so I do, with much affection and continued admiration.

From the first, and finally, there was Evans Clinchy to whom I want to say: You were the biggest man of all, in many more ways than the obvious.

Contents

The Endicott Conference

Recent reckonings of what children *must* learn in school are prompting reconsiderations of what children *can* learn in school. Most notable in the resulting work of curriculum reform is the participation of university scholars. For the first time, the intellectual elite of one generation is involving itself substantially in the early public schooling of the next generation. The resulting infusion into elementary and secondary classrooms of new curricula ("new math," "new physics," "new biology," and soon "new social studies") has already altered the formats of teacher training and certification.

The emphasis of this influence is on instructional *materials*: syllabi, texts, films, documents, exercises, etc.—as it should be. Corresponding experimentation with new instructional *methods*, which the new materials often vaguely demand but cannot themselves supply, has not been proceeding apace. In this, the discipline of "educational psychology" has proved embarrassingly sterile, due to its traditional emphasis on achievement rather than on process, on the practical rather than on the possible.

Heinz Werner drew our attention to this imbalance in 1937, and accurately predicted its consequences, i.e., that it was a good position from which to measure educational deficiencies but not from which to define, much less cultivate, educational excellence (86). But no prescriptions accompanied Werner's diagnosis, and, before Sputnik, there was little pressure on teachers to explore the possible. By 1960, however, we were all ready to listen and my colleague, Jerome Bruner, was ready to prescribe. The reaction of the American educational community to Bruner's "The Process of Education" has been phenomenal (9). Only ninety-two pages in length, and in a genre usually viewed dimly by schoolmen (a conference report), it has come in a few years to rival Whitehead's "The Aims of Education" as the book most *re*-read by most teachers. How to account for the appeal of this book, which has earned its author recognition as spokesman for the "new educational psychology"? The answer is that the book represents the most advanced research in the psychology of cognition, is written with care and style by a master researcher, and was published at a time when many teachers and school principals were under increasing pressure to explore new ways of engaging the minds of children, while having previously been pained to learn that "educational psychology" bore little relevance to what actually transpired in classrooms.

Unfortunately, Bruner has sought in "The Process of Education" and its subsequent companion pieces (10, 11), to found the new educational psychology on an exclusively cognitive base. This would not warrant urgent concern were Bruner's influence merely that of an eminent psychologist. Psychology is a discipline in which it is still difficult to achieve both eminence and catholicity, and teachers have grown accustomed to making their own peace between divergent authoritative positions. However, American educators have welcomed Bruner's directives so unreservedly that his influence has come to carry something verging on political weight. There is the danger, then, that the very revolution that has received so much of its impetus from Bruner's hand will stall for lack of optimum confluence. In short, references to what has come to be known in curriculum reform circles as "the gospel according to Saint Jerome," while they may remain good-humored as regards the man, could become something less than a joke as regards the movement.

In what follows I shall try to indicate how Bruner's advances toward a theory of instruction, made as they have been by half-steps, have revealed possibilities for the taking of full steps; that is, for the coordination of cognitive moves with emotional and imaginal ones. In this I shall follow my friend's example in choosing to leave basic theoretical debts uncited. Thus, it may be seen more clearly that the views taken here seek not to oppose what Bruner has brought to pedagogy but seek rather to bring to Bruner's views their due complements.

Let it first be said that the one-sidedness I shall emphasize was not without its provocation from the other side. Psychoanalysis had done some sniffing in schoolhouses prior to Sputnik. This consisted largely in the setting up of clinical enclaves in schools. Sometimes by way of the front door, through which it was sought to practice preventive psychiatry, i.e., to diagnose mental disorder early and to render treatment on the spot. Sometimes by way of the back door, through which a range of objectives were pursued, from improved social adjustment to the conducting of less boring English classes. Both were essentially grafting operations. That is to say, neither approach aspired to bring psychodynamic principles and methods to bear on the educative process itself. Schools happen to be where the children are, where one can get at them for a variety of right purposes which need not be directly relevant to formal education. Certainly it is as advisable to use schools as places to prevent schizophrenia and to better the resolutions of family conflicts as it is to use them as places to prevent poliomyelitis and to instill good driving habits.

There are now a small minority of school systems whose staffs include a cadre of teachers and counselors skilled and practiced in the clinical arts of diagnosis and referral, and with whom normal children have learned to consult in times of healthy emotional crisis. There are also a small minority of school systems whose openness to the mental health professions has been abused. Through the front door, to take the most disreputable case, by psychiatrists in search of the most lucrative referrals; and through the back door, by teachers who view themselves as psychiatrists and who find children handy objects on which to practice self-deception. In between, there are many well meaning and well trained members of the teaching and clinical professions who can count among their better professional moments the time they learned to respect each other. But the respect of teachers for clinicians is usually superimposed upon a fundamental mistrust. A variety of causes are at work here: differences in status, disparities of income, outright snobbishness, and so on. The primary cause, however, is the clinician's characteristic lack of involvement in the teacher's realm of expertise, the educative process. For a clinician to exercise his skills, the pupil must be converted into a patient, however temporarily. He or his parents must be prepared to view certain behavior or certain attitudes as sick, whatever the euphemisms used against stigmata. Otherwise it might not be seen as appropriate to consult a doctor. Some teachers, recognizing the values of the clinician's objectives, and impressed by the delicacies of his skills, become practiced at lending a hand in the conversion process. But clinicians in schools are part-time help; they treat and leave. There is almost never occasion for professional exchange, for the teacher to enlist the help of the clinician in the instructional process, which to any honest observer would be as recognizably valuable and as impressive in the delicacies of skill required.

A true story will illustrate how this alternate form of monocularity has compounded the difficulties of bringing pedagogical and clinical views into concert in educational settings. In the summer of 1962 a two-week conference was held at the Massachusetts Institute of Technology's luxurious Endicott House to consider the possibilities of reforming the humanistic and social studies in the primary and secondary grades. Some of the nation's ablest scholars were in attendance. Included were Frederick Burkhardt, president of the American Council of Learned Societies, James Killian, president of M.I.T., and Professors Francis Friedman, Robert Havighurst, Alan Holmberg, Francis Keppel, Norton Long, Leften Stavrianos, Franklin Patterson, Elting Morison, and Jerrold Zacharias, to name only some of the most prestigious. Martin Mayer has described the proccedings of the Endicott conference in his "Social Studies in American Schools" (64). Suffice it to recall that the atmosphere of the meetings was one of compelling erudition; each prepared statement was a scholarly document; the comments from the floor were prose pieces; even the quibbling was noteworthy.

On the day I was asked to present my views, there had been some consensus that one of the weaknesses of the extant social studies curricula was its omission of 99 per cent of its temporal sphere. Social studies did not begin, it was agreed, with the Babylonians. At what earliest point in time we could all agree to locate the beginning of the subject might stir some debate, but certainly not later than the emergence of Australopithecus, the small-brained, tool-using biped whose remains Professor Leakey was then notably digging from Olduvai Gorge. Moreover, since Bruner, whose writings formed part of the conference's background reading, saw much pedagogical efficacy in having children discover knowledge for themselves, why not make up kits of replicas of the bones and stones that Leakey was excavating and let the children reconstruct prehistory at its source? It seemed a fine way of launching the subject and had the added merit of exposing children to the concepts and methods of the behavior sciences along the way. A young professor from Cornell took to this idea with particular enthusiasm, suggesting the inclusion of field trips to the local dump, the better that children might understand the enactive aspects of gathering archaeological evidence.

To this level of brain-storming discussion I tried to raise my thoughts: I applauded these potential enrichments of elementary social studies. They assured me that Educational Services Incorporated,* the organizing agency of the conference, really meant to answer Bruner's call for converting our increasingly complex cultural heritage into elementary curricula that would be no less pedagogically viable for being intellectually honest. I was sure that had I as a grade-schooler been offered the kinds of lessons which these suggestions conjured in the imagination I would now be not only a better scientist but a better man. It was therefore with hope that such suggestions would find wide ways into classroom practices, and not be aborted in their pilot runs, that I wished to place before the meeting certain considerations to which my particular training made me attuned: the standards of intellectual

* Now, Education Development Center, Inc., Cambridge, Massachusetts.

honesty to be brought to schoolrooms by a curriculum of this nature would be unprecedented. If we succeeded in committing teachers to these standards, we would, I thought, be obliged to succeed as well in committing them to similarly unprecedented standards of *emotional* honesty. Grade school children, we could be sure, were going to respond to replicas of bones and teeth and broken skulls, to "digs" in other people's graveyards and garbage heaps, with a range of emotions and images that would both pose special problems and introduce special opportunities into the instructional process. If the venture was to be as successful as it deserved, it would, I judged, be well to plan as early as possible to train teachers to handle these problems and to exploit these opportunities. The new challenges would reside not only in presenting such materials to children in ways that would not be noxious but also in presenting them in ways that would enlist the children's predictably rich emotional and imaginal responses in the enlivenment of their learning.

I was about to add that the challenges would be made the more difficult by the fact that most clinical research was still preoccupied with understanding how to enlist such emotions and fantasies in the kinds of *un*-learning processes associated with psychotherapy, and had as yet little to offer teachers in the way of guiding pedagogical innovation. But before I could amplify this note of caution, one of the nation's most prestigious scientist-educators rose to urge the assembly to disregard my remarks, as they represented for him the narrowness of vision he had learned to expect "from psychiatrists." "Unless they can render their data into indices of pathology and sickness," he said, "they are helpless before it." He urged the membership therefore to be "man enough" not to be diverted from its task by these "psychophantisms."

So, I thought, it has come to this: the clinician says "emotions" and "fantasy" and the educator hears "pathology and sickness." As regards the etiology of these misperceptions my own conscience was clear, but I could not deny that guilt by professional association was deserved.

My critic had exempted Professor Bruner by name from "the psychiatrists." Therefore, feeling myself to be no match for my antagonist, I phoned Bruner that evening, described the situation, and suggested he might render a timely service to a cause I knew him to value if he would come out to Endicott House to set the matter right. He agreed to come the next morning. Knowing Bruner's persuasiveness before the lecturn and knowing that the points I had tried to make were fundamental ones, I approached the next session whistling.

The book before you, I now recognize, was conceived on that morning. Bruner was at his best, which is an event to behold. He reviewed the findings of the latest research in cognitive development as these might be applied to curriculum reform in the social studies. He emphasized the importance of designing educational materials that would engage optimal sequences of the enactive, iconic and ratiocinative modes of representing knowledge. It was a first-rate Piagetian talk. But the controversy of the preceding day was not reopened. And so the project was launched by the predicted half-steps. The materials for honest elementary social studies curricula would be produced, the films made, the texts written, the games invented, the heuristics devised and the lesson plans formulated. These would be immeasurable improvements over the materials then available to teachers of social studies, and by these virtues they would arouse such interests of children in themselves and in their species as would create uncommon opportunities for pedagogical innovation in general. And then the time would come when these opportunities would be at best missed and at worst misused for lack of teachers trained to notice them.

CHAPTER TWO

The Challenge of the "New Social Studies"

It is six years since the Endicott Conference. The materials for a pioneering fifth-grade social studies course have been designed, and are currently being tested and refined in experimental classes. These are described in Bruner's latest book "Toward a Theory of Instruction" under the title, "Man: A Course of Study":

> The content of the course is man: his nature as a species, the forces that shaped and continue to shape his humanity. Three questions recur throughout:
>> What is human about human beings?
>> How did they get that way?
>> How can they be made more so?
> We seek exercises and materials through which our pupils can learn wherein man is distinctive in his adaptation to the world, and wherein there is discernible continuity between him and his forebears. . . .
> In pursuit of our questions we proceed to explore five subjects, each closely associated with the evolution of man as a species, each defining at once the distinctiveness of man and his potentiality for further evolution. The five great humanizing forces are tool making, language, social

organization, the management of man's prolonged child-hood, and man's urge to explain his world. (11, pp. 74–75)

In order to bring these five dimensions into the kinds of inwardly induced articulation which are known to support some of the most lasting and buoyant of the learning processes, materials have been designed which show evidence of these humanizing forces at various points of contrast to modern man along the evolutionary con-tinuum: preliterate man, as represented by the Kalahari Bushman and the Netsilik Eskimo; lower primates, as represented by the free-ranging Amboseli baboon; and various sub-primate fauna (salmon, herring gull, caribou, etc.). There is tentative thought of including at some future date materials on the Australopithecine man-ape based on the Olduvai excavations.

Let us begin with a typical day in the pilot phase of "Man: A Course of Study." The scene is an experimental summer-school classroom consisting of twenty fifth-grade boys and girls (unselected except by their wish to attend a free summer school and their parents' approval), a master teacher, a coordinating teacher, three assistant teachers, a film projectionist, and various observers of this writer's stripe. For the past three weeks the children have been studying the world and ways of the Netsilik Eskimo. This by means of various textual and source materials, exercises, demonstrations, slides, tape recordings, and films taken on location at Pelly Bay in Northern Canada by one of ESI's expert camera crews—all composed under the supervision and guidance of Professor Asen Balicksi of the University of Montreal, a specialist in Netsilik ethnography.

The children have some acquaintance with the ecology of these people, the harshness of their Arctic environment, their dependence on the caribou, the seal, and the salmon.

They know something of their primitive, ever so resourceful, technology. They have recently learned something of the structures distinctive of Netsilik family and societal life, including those stemming from and leading to the practices of female infanticide and senilicide. They have begun to show signs of empathizing with the Netsilik, the unique problems they faced, and the unique solutions they found. There are signs, too, that the children are beginning to appreciate the outlandish ways of the Netsilik as variations on themes which all men share, and not as further variations on the palliative themes of previous social studies classes, i.e., that people are merely different.

In short, the course is going well. Later in the week, they are to be introduced to some of Netsilik cosmology and related aspects of social organization; for example, the practices of magic and shaminism and others of the distinctive forms that the regulation of aggression has taken in this society, where survival has precluded the niceties of institutionalized authority, while leaving room nonetheless for the expression of "what is human about human beings."

This morning the children are to take up the technology strand again, to learn more of what the Netsilik hunter knows, does, and uses in order, in his distinctively human way, to adapt the naturally selected regularities of the ringed seal to the cultured irregularities of man.

There is a further aim: the children are to develop their "cognitive skills," to perceive intelligently and with a purpose, to categorize, classify, and generalize with an imposed objective, and to do all this with objectivity. They are to view an authentic color film, superbly photographed and imaginatively edited, of a group of Netsilik men hunting the ringed seal from their winter camp. Flashbacks to igloo life among the waiting women and babies have been deftly edited into the film in preparation for future lessons. The children are to bend this morning's viewing of the film to the purposes of filling the cells of a 3 x 3 chart: What must the Netsilik (1) know (2) do and (3) use, in order to (1) find (2) kill and (3) retrieve a seal?

Enter Mr. Donald Koeller, the master teacher. In his own winter work he must, by Massachusetts statute, meet twenty-five classroom teaching hours weekly. He is a man who loves his work as only a man can who does it better than most. He is on his own version of a busman's holiday: under the largesse of experimentation he need only teach for two hours today and has had two days to prepare his lesson. The verve and skill with which he conducts the lesson is every bit the equal of the patience and skill with which Zachary (the hunter) catches his seal. Mr. Koeller gives the class its assignment: "This morning I want you to use your brains and your eyes. We're going to see a film of Zachary and his winter companions hunting seal. Remember how important it is to all of them and their families that a seal be caught soon. There can be nothing else for them to eat this time of year. It's kill or starve. Now, you will see some things that you've never seen before, things you'll want to turn your eyes from. But you must look closely to answer the questions we're going to take up after the film: what does Zachary know, what does he do, what does he use, in order to find a seal, kill a seal, and retrieve a seal? You don't have to like everything you see, but I want you to understand it." It is impossible to convey in print the excitements of such a class, the moments when the children were about to tune out and were instead tuned in by Mr. Koeller's movements of body, his stagings, his sense of timing, his persistence and love, and by his having had time to bring all these to pitch. It was a virtuoso performance.

Here are this observer's notes taken during the viewing of the film:

1) Re nakedness of male baby playing in igloo with mother and grandmother: children are agape; not sure they are supposed to see this.

2) Re breast feeding scene: girls whisper inaudible secrets to each other.

3) Re mother giving fish eye to baby (who eagerly swallows it): children moan, groan, squirm.

4) Re baby pushing grandmother off balance, grandmother laughingly hitting head against wall of ice: children delighted.

5) Re blood-filled breathing hole after spearing of seal and matter-of-fact skuring of the nostrils, and labored pulling of dead seal out of red hole in white ice: children audibly distressed, look to teacher as if to say: do you really mean for us to see this? Child: "Does it have to be so bloody?" Teacher: "That's part of hunting. Pay attention." (Child reassured, screws up courage, and looks—proudly.)

6) Re men cutting and eating raw meat: "Ugh!"

And here are some excerpts from the evaluation conference that afternoon:

Unit Coordinator: "It was good. The chart helps, especially when you let them fill in the cells as their thoughts come to them and not by a prescribed sequence."

Master Teacher: "It was a ball! They didn't want to, but they used their heads. What I liked was the din of learning in the room, not only about Netsilik technology but about how to think."

Assistant Teacher: "And at the end they were loving it!"

Assistant Teacher: "They resisted seeing the film a second time ('Oh, all that blood again') but they seemed disappointed when you stopped it in the middle. Is it that they're repulsed or fascinated by the gory parts?"

Master Teacher: "The gory parts didn't get in the way. I wanted them to think—not feel."

Assistant Teacher: "God, that bloody hole!"

Unit Coordinator: "Well, what do we say to ESI? The film serves the purpose at this point, I think, and it can be shown again when we get into the family. They seemed to want to talk about the baby and they finally got to see a live grandmother."

Assistant Teacher: "That's all very well, but I was thinking during the film that I'd lose them. Their stomachs were really turning during the gory parts. Mr. Koeller was so involved in the hunting techniques, and he got the kids so involved, that they got over their revulsions, but I'm not sure I could ever do it. I'd have had mayhem on my hands and been thinking more of classroom management problems than of cognitive skills and how to use the chart."

Subject Matter Specialist: "No doubt they learned a lot about tool use and that's what we set out to teach them, but I too find myself thinking about all that emotional hubub during the film. They were visibly disturbed at many points. You got them over it and back to the lesson nicely, but wasn't there an awful lot being bypassed? Was that good or bad? What does the psychologist say?"

Psychologist: "They learned a lot about technology. On that we're agreed. And they had a good exercise of the cognitive skills involved in concept attainment: focused observation, identification, categorization, classification, generalization, analytical thought, objectivity, and the rest. Good. They also had a healthy exercise in the emotional skills necessary to support such cognitive activities: control, containment, postponement."

Master Teacher: "That's right. The kids aren't so finicky that they can't look at the world as it really is if you give them a good reason and hold them to it."

Psychologist: "From which I gather we are about to heave a sigh of relief that 'the gory parts' and the attendant images didn't obtrude on the lesson, and let it go at that?"

Assistant Teacher: "Isn't that enough?"

Psychologist: "Is it enough to put your money in the bank? Don't you want to remember which bank, so you can collect the interest? Tomorrow, or next week, or next month we're going to want these children to exercise another kind of cognitive skill, to think not only analytically and objectively, with an eye to solving the problems we pose for them, but to think intuitively and subjectively with an eye to posing problems for themselves. And for that we are going to want them to indulge their imaginations, their offbeat thoughts, a different order of cognitive skill presuming different orders of emotional skill: expression, sharing, use. We've prepared them for that by teaching them control. So far so good. People can't express, share, or use emotions that they can't control. But we're only halfway there, and if we forget where we helped them to leave their emotions we shouldn't be surprised if later they can't find the images that went with those emotions."

Psychometrist: "Are you suggesting we take time out to conduct a group therapy session?"

Psychologist: "I'm suggesting we remember where Mr. Koeller directed these children to stow their imaginations this morning: in their well-contained emotional reactions to the sight of a baby's penis, a bloody hole, and the swallowing of an eye. When we want them to think sensitively and with feeling, whether in respect to mythology or child rearing practices or what have you, we needn't devise any special new hardware. We need only provide relevant ways for them to share what they obviously put away for safe keeping this morning."

Let us consider this lesson and the meeting that followed it from the longer perspective of hindsight. Consider first that the next objective of the course was to highlight certain facets of paleolithic social organization as exemplified by certain Netsilik myths and customs. Bonds of trust between kin and non-kin are not strong among the Netsilik, who live most of the year in small family units. Yet to hunt the seal effectively in winter, many men must coordinate their efforts, requiring that they and their families live together in a confined winter camp. Scarcities of food, space, and privacy keep tensions high and conflicts frequent. Having no recourse to institutionalized patterns of extra-familial authority the Netsilik have come to regulate their periodically heightened mistrusts, jealousies, covetings, suspicions, and rivalries by an interweaving system of ritualized food sharing, gaming partnerships, taboos, magic and shamanistic practices. The children are to be brought to perceive these as more than the expressions of an exotic and quaint people from another land. It is intended that by comparing the Netsilik's ways of regulating human conflict with our own ways the children may begin to deepen their comprehension of their species, of what makes all humans human.

Now consider that when such objectives have proved elusive in the past the instructional process which sought to achieve them can usually be shown to have lacked a crucial element: significant and believable points of comparison between unfamiliar worlds, as brought to the child by the instructional materials, and familiar worlds, as brought *by* the child *to* the instructional materials. This is to say no more than the Piagetian truism that children adapt to knowledge by accommodating it *and* by assimilating it. It is important to bear in mind that in order for this

fundamental Piagetian principle to generate optimal pedagogical power the elements of significance and believability
must accrue to both the unfamiliar and the familiar
spheres. It is also important to bear in mind the part of
this principle on which Freudian psychology has placed
emphasis: the points of comparison which are potentially
the most significant are sometimes not immediately believable, and must first be *made believable*. In other words,
children must sometimes imagine reality the better to test
it.

There is concensus among contemporary critics of
traditional social studies curricula that they have emphasized the familiar to a fault, in misguided pursuit of the
child's supposed "readiness," and have proceeded to com-
pound the imbalance by limiting the unfamiliar to trivia.
Recent innovations like "Man: A Course of Study" have
gone a long way toward eliminating trivia from curricular
materials. However unfamiliar these new materials may be
to the children they are significant. The challenge to the
teacher who introduces these materials is that of finding
points of comparison in the familiar sphere that are equally
significant. Many teachers are adept at perceiving what
such significant and relevant familiarities might be, but
hesitate to follow their professional nose for one or both
of the following reasons: (1) their professional training has
committed them to judge these familiarities as incredible
and threatening to the children; (2) their professional
training has omitted the skills of cultivating imagination,
which is after all the faculty upon which we all depend
to make the incredible credible.

In summary then, when curricular points of contact
between familiar and unfamiliar worlds do not generate
pedagogical sparks it is probably the case either that the
instructional materials are insufficiently significant and

believable, or that the instructor has underestimated or alienated the children's abilities to create credibility, that is, to *make* beliefs.

For example, on the day following the lesson in Netsilik seal hunting technology the children were asked to speculate on the kinds of things the Netsilik might have conflicts about in the winter camp. They responded admirably: "Not enough food," "Not enough room," "Not enough knives," "Not enough women," "Not enough heat," and so on. They were then asked what kinds of conflicts were familiar to themselves. There followed such answers as: "When you don't get what you want," "When you want to see one thing on TV and your sister wants to see something else," "When your brother teases you," "When your father comes home tired," "When you don't want to go to bed." The standard items which children in Newton, Massachusetts have learned that their adults will countenance as appropriate expressions of conflict by children in school.

The teacher of this lesson knows children, and sensed that they were supplying their own equivalents of previous social studies lessons about the friendly postman, but he had not been trained to be as insistent on the cultivation of emotional and imaginal skills as on the cultivation of cognitive ones. And so the lesson proceeded: "And now we shall read a Netsilik story, which tells of one of the ways that they settle their kinds of conflicts. The story is called "Evil Magic." * First we'll read it, then we'll act it out; and then I want you to compare the ways the Netsilik settle their conflicts with the ways we settle ours."

---

* The story tells of two hunting partners one of whom aspires to the other's wife, and seeks to do him in by stamping out his footprints in the snow, only to be provoked by guilt and fear into confession and reconciliation.

The children read dutifully and then went through the motions of acting out what they had read. Afterward one brave child asked: "Why are we studying the Eskimos?" For the rest, there had been a bull session and then a reading lesson and then a drama lesson—with nothing in between that was sufficiently believable or make-believable to stimulate the kinds of questions about "Man" that the course is designed to raise. And, in fact, in this instance, it raised none.

Meanwhile another teacher, Miss Joanne Grossman, had designed this lesson plan, which unfortunately there was no time to test:

1) Remind the children of the seal hunt film and the feelings they had suppressed in response to it. Categorize these: embarrassment, envy, disgust, fear, pity, etc.
2) Have each child compose a play, write a story, or paint a picture about a conflict involving one of these feelings.
3) Discuss and categorize *our* conflicts: too much to learn, too many children, crime, war, divorce, etc.
4) Query: "How do we settle our conflicts?" Fathers, principals, courts, laws, United Nations.
5) Now ask what causes Netsilik conflicts: Not enough food, not enough room, not enough knives, not enough women, not enough heat.
6) How do the Netsilik settle their conflicts? Expect the children not to be able to go beyond "Fathers" since they have not yet been given sufficient information to answer the question.
7) Introduce the "Evil Magic" story and return to No. 6.

Had the children been afforded this lesson, or one like it, they might have had the benefit of sharing and using the emotions and images they had previously had the opportunity of controlling; not only, and this is a point to which I shall return, for the sake of their mental hygiene, but for the purpose of themselves constructing significant and credible points of comparison between modern and paleolithic societies. Bear in mind that conflicts over TV sets, sibling teasings, tired fathers, bedtime, etc. while admittedly of much personal significance to the children, were remote from the objective of the lesson, which was to deepen the children's comprehension of Man—not family life in Newton, Massachusetts, nor family life in Pelly Bay, but "Man." Moreover, it was obvious that the emotions involved in the discussion of TV sets, teasing, etc. were far less deeply felt than those the children had experienced together in their classroom the day before. The virtue of Miss Grossman's pedagogical strategy lay precisely in providing the children with opportunities to express these emotions while channeling them immediately and with relevance into the teaching of the next lesson.

That the more promising of these two lessons was not tried can be attributed to this writer's inability, under pressure of production deadlines, to provide the needed perspective. Retrospective must therefore do: Here was a trained and experienced teacher, with plenty of time to prepare his lesson, luxuriously staffed and equipped with instructional materials devised by some of the nation's leading scholars. He taught a superb lesson, getting as much mileage from the materials and from the children as most experienced teachers would consider *practical*. It was not, however, I submit, all that was ultimately *possible*. Clearly, there were possibilities being created by these materials for engaging the minds of children in unusually involving ways—ways which we have all too glibly in the past left to the so-called "artistry of teaching." Artistry was doubtless the only recourse when teachers were equipped with the kinds of happy little Eskimo films that you and I had to suffer in grammer school. But this is what I meant when I said that Bruner's half-steps have created opportunities for the taking of full steps. Bruner has persuaded schoolmen that the effectiveness of teaching materials is in proportion to their authenticity. "A lie is still a lie—even if it sounds like a familiar truth" (10, p. 124). Thanks to Bruner's influence then, ESI did not send mere picture-takers to Pelly Bay. It sent Asen Balicksi, who knows his Netsilik, and Robert Young, who knows his camera. And when it came time to compose a film for use in classrooms no educators were consulted; the job went to a professional producer of films, Quentin Brown, who knows that the cutting room floor is no place to leave the truth.

This film * and others like it will soon be available for mass distribution in the schools. Many teachers will not show it for lack of confidence in their ability to control the emotions it stirs—their own as well as the children's. That is another problem. The first claim on our attention should be that many teachers like Mr. Koeller will jump at a chance to make these films part of their routine stock of teaching tools and will get out of them only a portion of the teaching power that is in them.

The crux of this issue is not obscure. Only in the vicinities of schoolrooms do we make it so. Normally, the human mind and the human heart go together. If not normally, may we say optimally? We are witnessing a revolution in pedagogy which is committed to honest dealings with the minds of children. It follows, therefore, that we may also enjoy more honest dealings with the

---

* "Winter Sea-Ice Camp," Part 1A (Cambridge, Massachusetts: Educational Development Center, Inc.).

hearts of children. Not that this *necessarily* follows, nor that it should always be made to follow. Admittedly, there are times for *dis*passion in schoolrooms; but teachers need no reminding of this. They do, however, need reminding that there are also times for passion in schoolrooms.

I wish to direct the attention of teachers, therefore, to two half-truths which have become ingrained in the assumptive reflexes of some curriculum designers and which, if allowed to persist as such, must reduce the effectiveness of the new social studies curricula by exactly the other half, thus subverting the new possibilities into the same old practicalities. The two half-truths were implicit in the evaluation conference described above. They may be stated as follows:

1) Emotions and fantasies can obstruct learning.
2) Expression of emotions and fantasies can have cathartic benefits.

The first half-truth was implicit in the general relief experienced by Mr. Koeller and his staff over the fact that although emotions were running high these did not, under his skillful hand, get in the way of the lesson. The second half-truth was implied by innuendo in the remark about giving the children a group therapy session.

Now, it is true that emotions and fantasies can obstruct learning *when they are uncontrolled.* Uncontrolled emotions and fantasies obstruct almost all aspects of learning. The other half of this truth is that the control of emotion and fantasy is substantive in one kind of learning (the attainment or discovery of knowledge) and preparatory to another kind of learning (the formation or invention of knowledge). In respect to the latter, however, control of emotion and imagery, while necessary, is not sufficient. This is where the second half-truth needs completion: it is true that the expression of emotions and images can carry cathartic benefits. In themselves these should, admittedly, be of secondary concern to teachers, and afforded the children only when there is time for kindness. Of primary concern to teachers should be the pedagogical half of this truth: the construction of knowledge, as distinct from the attainment of it, presumes freedom and skill in the sharing and use of controlled emotion and imagery. We say then that the children are involved, are making the lessons their own, are aroused, excited, interested, original, inventive, and so on. I shall return to these points in detail in a later chapter. Here I wish only to emphasize the obvious. A child cannot, of course, learn to share and use what he has not learned to control. Beyond the matter of control, however, the teacher has the option of instructing the child or leaving him to his own devices.*

To the professional eye the issues involved in exercising the option of when to leave the sharing and use of affect and imagery to the children's inner life and when to deploy it into the instructional process, while complex, need not be unclear. It is at this juncture that my observations have led me to locate the most urgent need for teacher development programs, if curricula like "Man:

* In exercising this option, inexperienced teachers have traditionally found the issues blurred by several layers of polemics generated by various vested specialists, ranging from educationists to politicians, whose responsibilities require that they judge what goes on inside of classrooms from outside of classrooms. It has been heard, for example, from one quarter, that teachers should teach children, not subjects; and from another quarter, that schools should not be turned into clinics. And, should a teacher, grown weary of boring the children, risk upsetting them, she is almost sure to hear certain righteous remarks about respecting children's privacy!

A Course of Study" are to have optimal effects on the educative process. For if ever a course was designed to create special opportunities for engaging the softer, more precious reaches of children's minds, it is "*Man* (italics mine): A Course of Study." Yet, at this writing, ESI is still largely committed to the strategy of assuming either that the materials will somehow suggest to teachers how the emotions and images they arouse can be made pedagogically relevant, or that there are enough naturally gifted teachers around to do the trick by way of inherent artistry. Nevertheless, it is obvious to anyone who observes teachers at work (1) that instructional materials cannot convey instructional skills, especially skills that have been made counter-intuitive by the rationalist biases of traditional teacher training programs, and (2) that the most gifted of teachers in this respect, those whose intuitions carry them beyond the controlling of emotions and fantasies to their sharing and relevant use in mastering the subject matter— and such teachers are fewer than we like to think—cannot usually say how what they do works as it does, and so are hard put to teach their colleagues how to improvise accordingly.

CHAPTER THREE

Meeting the Challenge

Some will say that the kinds of innovations called for in the preceding chapter should be attempted by only the most experienced teachers. We are thus fortunate to observe what two young teachers * were able to improvise in the way of taking the full step.

The scene is the same, one week previously: same children, same course, same staff. The aim is to bring the class to thinking significantly and credibly of the effects of the harsh Arctic environment on Netsilik patterns of social organization. It happens that some of the most distinctive and dramatic features of Netsilik social organization are the direct consequences of institutionalized senilicide and female infanticide. A film had previously been shown of a Netsilik family on the move in which an old woman was barely able to keep up. The children had shown concern, but their discussion had been steered into other directions. Courage in hand, and over the resistance of some of her colleagues, Miss Amenta eschews the practical in favor of exploring the possible: "I'm not sure why the Netsilik were chosen to exemplify primitive societies, but I am sure we can't say anything that is true of their social organization if we avoid these nasty details."

* Miss Celeste Amenta and the same Miss Grossman.

She proposed and offered to conduct the following lesson plan:

1) Summarize the conditions of an Arctic winter.
2) Review the "winter trek" film. Who was walking last? Why wasn't the old woman's family worried about her?
3) Have the class read the tale of Kigtaq.

KIGTAQ

In seasons when seal hunting is bad the Netsilik have to move constantly from place to place. The winter becomes a hard one, not only for the hunters themselves, but especially for all the old people. The treatment of the old people, of course, varies in different families. Here, as everywhere, there are helpful and sympathetic sons and sons-in-law, or hard-hearted ones, and the fate of the old people lies in their hands.

A move from one hunting place to another is like a whole migration. Men and women have to carry along everything they possess. True, this is not much, but when clothing, sleeping skins and household utensils are piled up on the small, often miserable sledges, there is no room for people to sit. The sledges move off in a long procession over the ice to find a good camp with deep drifts for building snow huts. Men and women have to help the dogs to pull the loads. When they arrive at a place where good hunting may be expected, they stop and pitch camp.

They move slowly across the ice. Children who can must be able to keep up with the sledges. The only ones who have great difficulty are the old worn-out men or women. They come plodding behind, bent with rheumatism. No matter how slowly the group moves, they are usually unable to keep up and do not arrive at the camp until the snow houses are finished.

In one camp there was an old woman by the name Kigtaq. She was the mother of a woman named Terigssaq who was married to Arfeq. When Terigssaq and Arfeq moved from camp to camp she was often left behind out on the ice in midwinter, dressed only in a thin inner jacket and no thick, warm outer coat. Even in bad weather she often had to sleep cut on the ice because she had not caught up with the others. The other people in the camp said, 'She was not dead yet and life was still sweet to her.'

The Netsilik were asked whether it was not wicked of Arfeq that more care was not taken of the old woman. To this Samik answered, 'No one here among us wishes harm to old people. We ourselves might be old some-day. Perhaps there are those among us who think Arfeq might take more care of his mother-in-law, particularly by giving her better clothes.

'Others excuse Arfeq because he has been so unlucky in his hunting that he has barely been able to get furs for his wife and his children. They think he must first and foremost attend to them, for not only are they more closely related to him, but they have their lives before them and they might live long. There is no future for an old worn-out woman.

'Then again, there are others who think that Arfeq should allow his mother-in-law to ride on his sledge, or at least go back for her when he has built his snow hut. But he has only two dogs and with his wife he has to help drag his sledge from place to place. If he is to be at the breathing holes next morning at the proper time to get food, he cannot travel backwards and forwards between the old and the new camp to save an old woman. He has to make the choice between helping one who is at death's door anyhow, and allowing his wife and children to starve. This is how it is, and we see no wickedness in it.

Perhaps it is more surprising that old Kigtaq, now that she is no longer able to care for herself, still hangs on as a burden to her children and grandchildren. For our custom up here is that all old people who can do no more, and whom death will not take, help death to take them. They do this not merely to be rid of a life that is no longer a pleasure, but also to relieve their nearest relatives of the trouble they give them.'

4) Query: What are the different Netsilik attitudes on the treatment of Kigtaq.
5) Allow the children to express their opinions of these attitudes.
6) Query: Is there only one way of thinking or behaving in a given society? Do we all think alike on a given issue? Do the Netsilik all think alike on a given issue? If we understand their environment, the difficulties it presents for survival, we can better understand how their feelings about some things differ from ours. But, as we have seen, even within this environment, there are individual differences; people behave and believe and feel differently.
7) We've seen how the Arctic winter affects some Eskimos. Now we'll turn to how the Eskimos use their environment to help them survive.
8) Introduce film on igloo building.

The children went through this lesson very much on tiptoe. The implications of the key line in the Kigtaq tale

("For our custom up here is that all old people who can do no more, and whom death will not take, help death to take them") were not lost on them. Neither, however, did they lose the hint of the instructions: to quickly include these implications among their growing list of "ways in which people differ," and then to hasten on to a cozier topic—in this case, the niceties of igloo building.

Here are some of this observer's notes on the class:

1) Children perk up at reference to "winter trek" film and plight of grandmother. Formerly unsatisfied curiosities on this point are obviously still available.

2) Reading of Kigtaq tale is labored. Children more than usually frustrated by the hard words. Teacher wisely reads the story aloud.

3) At the phrase: ". . . help death to take them" several children exchanged subdued glances which have the effect of saying "Yes, I heard it too."

4) Mixed reactions of relief and disappointment to instructions re listing Netsilik and "own" differences of opinion:

Netsilik	*"Own"*
"Finish moving, but go back for Kigtaq"	"If you give her warm clothes, the others will be cold"
"Give her warm clothes"	"They should all chip in and give her some more clothes"
"Let her ride on sled"	"Who's more important, the old woman or possessions?"
"She could take her own life"	"You'd think they'd have some feelings"

Netsilik	*"Own"*
"Don't go back: wife and child need food"	"If they don't catch some seals, she'd die anyway of starvation"
	"They should go back to get the old lady because some day they too will be old"
	"After all she's their mother"

The responses are relevant and promising but lifeless and offered grudgingly.

5) Teacher on the ropes. Discussion dying. Igloo building lesson a total loss. Children's minds are elsewhere.

A post-class conference was about to give Miss Amenta a gold star for effort (the controversial issue having at least been faced) and to move on. But Miss Amenta would have none of it. She was thoroughly disappointed, felt the children were potentially there, and that she had lost them: "Not so fast. What did I do wrong?"

Master Teacher: "We tried to do too much in one lesson. The igloo building should have been left for tomorrow."

Unit Coordinator: "The reading was too difficult. We'll have to fix that. And the key line was too subtle. Some of the children didn't seem to get its full import."

Psychologist: "They got it all right, but they didn't get a chance to do anything with it."

Miss Amenta: "The drama wasn't there. I felt like I was dehumanizing the children, asking them to be objective before they were ready. Some of the talkers wouldn't talk and that made the silent ones doubly uneasy. And that awful silence at the end! Where were their questions?"

Unit Coordinator: "I thought you were right in asking them to talk about Netsilik opinions rather than their own, that it would make it easier for them, but it didn't work out that way."

Psychologist: "That's where the lesson went astray. Celeste is right. We were asking for objectivity before they'd had a chance to exercise their involvement with some powerful subjective images. After all, as Jerry said, 'it's their mother' who was left out there to die. And Billy's 'You'd think they'd have some feelings.' He's right and what are those feelings? Let's *begin* with ours and end with theirs, rather than the other way around."

Master Teacher: "Wouldn't that be harder on them?"

Assistant Teacher: "I think it was harder on them this way. Like we dangled something juicy in front of them and then took it away."

Psychologist: "Right. We're interested in teaching them cognitive and emotional skills as well as the subject matter. What emotional skills would they have learned this morning if they followed our example? 'Here's a story about a useless old lady who's expected to commit suicide. Get it? Now let's see how they build an igloo.' What else could the children have learned from this, but how to deny or isolate feelings? Admittedly denial and isolation are emotional skills and sometimes very handy. But were they the ones we wanted them to use in this lesson?"

Psychometrist: "Yes, but do we want to get them bogged down in their own feelings so early in the course? Do we want to spend the time necessary to deal with such strong emotions before they have any empathy for the society they're studying? They don't yet appreciate the harshness of the environment nor the difficulties of surviving in it. I still think it's too soon to bring up the whole topic."

Psychologist: "If we want the children to empathize with the Netsilik winter environment, we had better figure out a way for them to experience temperatures of 40 and 50 degrees below zero. But if we want them to empathize with the *people* who live in that environment we're on the right track by confronting them with emotionally charged issues they can locate in their own lives. Hell, these children are not strangers to the problems a senile person can raise in a family. Some of them live in families who have used the same solution—abandonment. But let's slow down and do this right. We're treating it all like a hot potato to be dropped at all possible speed. In fact it's the best opportunity we've had yet to teach about 'man.' "

Miss Grossman: "I agree with that. Until this morning these kids haven't really cared a darn about this course. Every day in the individual interviews I ask what problems the Netsilik have and it's always 'food, clothing, and shelter; food, clothing, and shelter.' We don't need Jerome Bruner to design a curriculum to teach children that Eskimos have problems with food, clothing, and shelter. But this morning I got: food, clothing, shelter *and grandmothers!* I agree with Celeste that the lesson was poor, but I'll settle for it for openers. Next I'd look to hear: 'food, clothing, shelter, grandmothers, and babies.' And then 'food, clothing, shelter, grandmothers, babies, and too few wives.' I mean if all ESI wants to do is provide better materials for teaching the same dry old stuff then why bother with experimental try-outs at all?"

Unit Coordinator: "It sounds like you'd be willing to try a lesson on infanticide tomorrow."

Miss Grossman: "I'll try it if we can answer Celeste's question: what did she do wrong this morning? I too felt the kids were potentially there and that we lost them."

Psychologist: "Miss Amenta did one thing wrong. She stuck to the lesson plan instead of following her own good professional ear. You say, Celeste, you felt you were dehumanizing them in asking them to be prematurely objective about the story. What would you have preferred to do?"

Miss Amenta: "Well first I'd have liked the story to have more dramatic appeal. It wasn't just that the reading level was a bit over their heads. Maybe if ESI would make a slide-tape with drawings, interesting voices, and music or sound effects. Something that would pull the children into the key line rather than just letting it flit across their attention. Then I'd want the children to do something with their own reactions before listing the Netsilik reactions. After this morning I'm not sure I'd trust the discussion medium, although I do think they'd have offered their own reactions if I'd asked for them. But if discussion didn't work then some other expressive medium—art or creative writing or play-acting. Something that showed the kids I was interested in them first and the Netsilik second. And *then* I'd go to the Netsilik, and their harsh environment, and their problems, and so forth. Finally I'd like to end with some comparison exercise that required the children to be objective not only about the Netsilik but about themselves."

School Principal (a rare one) *: "Yes. Couldn't we put a feather in our collective caps if we could set these youngsters to rationally considering *our* society's problems with overpopulation, birth control, increasing life span and old age, before they have to vote on them."

Unit Coordinator: "Yes, in *your* school, in Newton. But what about the average teacher in the average community in Kansas? What's she going to do about the Birchers in the P.T.A.?"

Principal: "Not use the course. According to Bruner we're to see what's possible, not what's practical."

Miss Grossman: "If I'm going to do a lesson on infanticide tomorrow morning, could we get back to the point please? What do you think of Celeste's plan?"

Psychologist: "I think it's a sound one, provided the expressive exercise is designed to do more than let off emotional steam. We want that steam to power the children's mastery of the subject. But I think that's what she had in mind for the comparative exercise at the end."

* Mr. Henry Atkins.

Miss Grossman: "Well, it's too late to find an infanticide story, but there is something I'd like to try following Celeste's strategy—on one condition: no observers tomorrow, except the people in the room right now. Last week I myself was violently against exposing the children to any of this, and I don't want to try it with that kind of opposition looking over my shoulder."

Next morning, under protection of a "No Visitors" sign, Miss Grossman begins the class:

Teacher: "I think the desks got in the way of your discussion with Miss Amenta yesterday. So today I want you up front here with me so we can talk more freely with each other." (Teacher sits on floor under blackboard and children sit huddled around her.)

Teacher: "I'm going to tell you something else about the Netsilik today that may be just as puzzling to you as what you learned yesterday in the story of Kigtaq. But first I want to hear everything that you've learned so far about the Netsilik that you remember."

Student: "They live in the ice and snow."

Student: "It's almost always winter there where they live."

Student: "They don't have much food."

Student: "They only have skins for clothing."

Student: "They build igloos out of ice for shelter."

Student: "They're very smart the way they do it too. They know about heat rising and things like that."

Student: "They have to hunt and fish."

Teacher: "What else do you remember?"

Student: "They leave the old women behind if they can't keep up because the father has to build the igloo and he has to get up early in the morning to hunt seal or they'll all starve."

Student: "When a Netsilik grandmother is too old she 'helps death take her.'"

Teacher: "Yes, that's right. What other kinds of people have you seen in the film?"

Student: "Children."

Teacher: "Yes. Now we're going to see a short film showing what it's like in the igloo when the father is out hunting. We'll see some of the things that must be done in the igloo, and that only the mother can do, like keeping the lamp lit."

After film showing:

Teacher: "What do you think of the people in the film?"

Student: "Was the baby a girl or a boy?"

Student: "They all have long hair. It's hard to tell."

Teacher: "What are some adjectives you would use to describe the people in the film?"

Student: "Very cold."

Teacher: "No, the *people.*"

Student: "Hard working."

Student: "Happy."

Student: "Smiling."

Student: "They help each other."

Student: "In the igloo the baby has no clothes."

Teacher: "The Netsilik, then, *look like* warm and happy people. Yesterday we found out that their lives weren't always filled with happy things."

Student: "Yes."

Student: "The old lady."

Teacher: "Are *we* always happy?"

Student: "No."

Teacher: "Would you like always to be happy?"

Student: "No."

Teacher: "Why not?"

Student: "It'd be boring."

Teacher: "Sometimes things happen which make us unhappy that we don't understand. Can you think of any things like that?"

Student: "When someone dies."

Student: "A relative who dies."

Student: "It's hard to move in the snow and the old grand-mother would slow them down."

Teacher: "What does the father do for the family?"

Student: "Protects the family."

Student: "Brings the food."

Student: "Kills it."

Teacher: "How do we get our food?"

Student: "From stores."

Teacher: "Can a Netsilik family run out of food?"

Student: "If the hunting isn't good, they might run out."

Teacher: "What happens then?"

Student: "They starve."

Teacher: "Anything else if the hunting isn't good?"

Student: "They freeze; no skins."

Teacher: "Who else would suffer if there were no food and no skins?"

Student: "The baby."

Student: "If the hunting isn't good, there wouldn't be food for the baby."

Student: "If it was just a little baby, they'd give it the last of the food."

Teacher: "Do you think so?"

Student: "Yes."

Student: "Sure."

Teacher: "You mean that's what *your* father and mother would do. Who is the most important member of the Netsilik family?"

Student: "The father."

Student: "Yes."

Teacher: "Who would be next?"

Student: "The mother."

Student: "The baby."

Student: "No, the mother."

Student: "No, the baby."

Teacher: "Well, all human beings are important. But for the Netsilik, the most important members of a family have to be the father and the mother. Why is that, do you suppose?"

Student: "Without the father they'd starve."

Student: "Without the mother they'd freeze."

Teacher: "Now let's suppose that the hunting isn't so good and the mother has a small child like Alexei and another little baby is born."

Student: "Give the baby to another family that didn't have any children."

Teacher: "That's what the Netsilik *try* to do. In fact, Umay-apek, the boy we saw last week, was adopted. His parents had no children and arranged to take the next *son* of another father and mother who already had a *son*."

Student: "What if it had been a girl?"

Teacher: "That depends. If the father is a good hunter, they might keep her for themselves."

Student: "What if there *are* no families with no children?"

Teacher: "Then there is a difficult decision: whether to keep the new baby, or to abandon it and hope that another family will take it for their own. That is their custom."

Student: "Do they just leave it there until another 'troop' comes?" (The children had just completed a unit on baboons.)

Student: "What happens if another 'troop' doesn't come?"

Student: "Do they put clothes on it first?"

Student: "They must leave it outside so it will cry so another family will hear and come to get it."

Teacher (timidly): "What would happen if no one came to get it?"

Student: "It would starve."

Student: "Freeze."

Student: "It would die."

Teacher (confidently): "Yes, how do *you* feel about that?"

Student: "Oh!"

Student: "It's mean."

Student: "They're cruel."

Student: "The baby has a right to live."

Student: "The grandmother 'could do no more.' But they're taking away the baby's *future* life."

Student: "If there is an older daughter, say fifteen, couldn't she help to take care of it?"

Student: "Don't they have any feelings?

Teacher: "What feelings would *you* have?"

Student: "They said it wasn't wicked about the grandmother. But with the babies it's wicked."

Student: "It's worse than eating fish eyes."

Student: "How can they do it?"

Student: "But the baby doesn't know it."

Student: "They shouldn't get married if they're going to do that to the babies."

Student: "Does it hurt to freeze?"

Student: "They're stupid."

Student: "Why do they live there?"

Student: "They'll be sorry when they don't have good hunters to take care of them when they are old."

Teacher: "This has been a very good discussion. Now I'd like to tell you something. When I first heard about this custom that the Netsilik have, I almost had a sick feeling much like you had: 'It's mean, it's cruel, it's stupid.' Then I found out something else that made a difference. The Netsilik don't really like to abandon babies, but they believe a baby has no soul until it has a name. So what might they do to help their feelings out?"

Student: "Not name the baby if they're going to abandon it."

Teacher: "Right."

Student: "Then they're not murderers. But why do they have to live there in the first place?"

Student: "But if there is an older girl in the family, say fifteen, couldn't she mate up with a boy and take the baby?"

Student: "They could put the baby in an orphanage; *we* do that."

Student: "They could put the grandmother in an old persons' home too. *We* do that."

Teacher: "Yes. What do *we* do if the mother and father cannot support a baby?"

Student: "Give it to some other people."

Student: "Put it in an orphanage."

Student: "Not have it."

Student: "Get an abortion."

Student: "But the girls here are the same as the boys when they grow up. They can do the same things. I have a lady doctor."

Student: "If they were twins, would they keep the boy and leave the girl outside?"

Student: "If they were both boys, would they have to keep them both?"

Student: "The mother is just as important as the father."

Student: "The boys will grow up to hunt and they won't starve."

Student: "What happens if the mother dies after the baby is born and it's a baby girl?"

Student: "If they don't keep some of the girls, who will keep the flame going?"

Student: "What happens if they abandon all the girls?"

Student: "If they adopt a baby, then have one of their own, which will they keep?"

Teacher: "They will not abandon a child after it is named. The older one would, of course, have a name. Which reminds me. Why are we studying Eskimos?"

Student: "It's about 'Man.' "

Student: "What is human."

Student: "How we got this way."

Student: "Mr. Bruner said it was about 'the family of man.' "

Teacher: "Yes, and man has language and so gives names to his children. We've learned that the baboons communicate but do not have language. Later on we'll study the differences between communication and language. As you can see, to some Netsilik girl babies, language can make *all* the difference."

Miss Grossman heaves a well-earned sigh of satisfaction and instructs the children further: "When you return from your dance class we're going to find some other ways of thinking about the Netsilik family—the problems they face and how little room they have in which to face them."

Meanwhile, without benefit of such imaginative regular classroom teaching as Miss Amenta's and Miss Grossman's, the dance teacher, Miss Amy Greenfield, had previously been moved to write this memorandum:

I am growing increasingly disturbed over how the new films must be affecting the children in their regular classes. I have no objection to helping them to express their feelings about violence and death through the medium of the dance. Sometimes they do it beautifully. But the theme is becoming monotonous. Is there no way to channel these interests into thought and fellow-feeling *in* the classroom, before they come to me?

I would like to think that I have something to *add* to this curriculum and not that I am merely being used as a random outlet for unused feelings.

. . . Film has the power to exaggerate—the face, the hands, the body, the emotion. Thus the focus of the great documentary films has always been on basic activities, simplicities of being in nature. . . . The exaggerations of the media have always been modulated, however, by the use of black and white and by narrated interpretations, both of which remove the viewer from actuality and offer a point of view. The new films are in vivid color and are silent.

I presume these features are in the interests of authenticity and I must not quarrel with them. But the children who come to me from your classrooms are not yet trained anthropologists, looking for details of the what and how of the tools being used. As yet they have nothing to vitiate the vivid registration of their senses that an animal has been killed. Moreover, you are apparently giving them nothing with which to assimilate these facts or with which to make them credibly remote. Else *I* as their dance teacher could sometimes have other images with which to work. Everyday it is violence and death.

What have we come to when we act as though a child is not made curious and aroused by the sight of a naked baby at a mother's breast or the breaking of a dead seal's back? When we see a beautiful actress in the cinema do we come away talking about the shape of the knife with which she ate or the kinds of shoes she wore or the way her hair was arranged? No, we remember the act of eating and its particular emotional significance in the setting of the drama, the expression of her hands, the way she walked, the beauty of her ankles, her facial expression, etc. Perhaps on third or fourth viewing we focus on technological details. How can you deny that a young child who sees the breaking of a seal's back will remember this longer and more deeply than the method of retrieving the animal, the season of the hunt, or even the difficulty of finding a seal hole. You must have found a way because I hear you complaining that the children are uninterested in your classes. My complaint is that they are *too* interested in mine. It is always death or violence—sometimes beautiful, but it is boring me.

Miss Greenfield had no complaints about Miss Grossman's class. The children, she reported, were strangely desirous of instructions in dancing *per se*. What had we done? Was it possible someone had read her memorandum?

Upon their return from dance class, the children were given a half hour in which to either compose a Netsilik story about life in the winter or to make a collage representing their views about life in an igloo. Most chose to do collage. As interested and industrious a group of children as one would want to see in a schoolroom.

Then:

Teacher: "At the end of our discussion this morning you had so many questions I couldn't answer them all. Some of them I didn't know the answers to and I'd like to look them up. So while you were in dance class I made this question box. In the time remaining I'd like those of you who didn't get your questions answered, or who have thought of another question, to write them out on the slips of paper that Miss Amenta will hand out. Then we'll spend a few minutes every day trying to answer the questions in the box. (*All* of the children respond.)

The questions read as follows:

Why would they pick a boy over a girl, because a girl can start to help at five years of age and a boy starts to work at least at ten years of age?

What do they do in case of two male twins?

If the mother and father died could a girl and boy survive?

Who gets fed first?

Are we going to compare what we learn?

What is the name of a girl Eskimo?

Why do the Netsilik people follow their food on that specific course?

Would they let an old person die without caring for her?

If the hunting season was good but the Eskimo family were not good hunters would they keep an infant boy when they had another infant girl?

Are there many Eskimos living now?

Why are we studying Eskimos?

Why do I hate you teachers?

If the hunting season isn't good, will the family die?

How long is it before they wear clothes?

When an Eskimo has two female twins, and another infant, would she abandon one or both of them, if the hunting season was not good?

Would the Eskimos let a five year old go without a name?

Would the Eskimos abandon a five year old without a name?

What kind of food do the babies eat?

Does the father get married again after his wife dies (when he still has kids)?

What if they had two boys?

Suppose an Eskimo lady had three babies and she died after they were born. What would the father do?

A small boy really isn't as important as a girl because there wouldn't be any boys if there weren't any women to bear them.

How shall we evaluate these two experiments? Traditionally, evaluation of new lessons, materials, and methods is conducted as a separate enterprise and kept at a purposeful distance from the heat of the classroom. This in the questionable interests of experimental rigor. Psychometrists are called in to find out what the children know before and after the lesson or program at issue. The emphasis on achievement again, and the same cultivation of ignorance as regards process. As Bruner has observed, this is like collecting military intelligence after the war is over. But there is a better reason for eschewing such impositional approaches to evaluation. Teachers know that the proofs of well-composed and conducted lessons are more often found in the questions raised than in the answers given. Moreover, one has only to spend some time as a professional outsider in an elementary school to know that children will share their answers with almost anyone who asks the right questions; but they will only share their questions with their own teachers—and then only if they love them. After all, their is little risk in giving an answer; it is either right or wrong and that is usually the end of it. But to share a question is often to invite inspection of one's tenderer parts. Like other loving acts this is not something we do with strangers.

So, here we have twenty-two questions from twenty-two children, earned in two days by two teachers. What can these questions tell us about the *process* of education? It is obvious on the face of the questions that their composers are generating points of comparison between themselves and a primitive society which are significant and believable (or on the way to being made believable). More important however, the points of comparison being generated are relevant to the stated objectives of the curriculum. Strictly so. One of the ways the curriculum is planned to help children learn what it is that makes man human, and how we got that way, is to set them thinking about the interrelations between ecology and social organization under paleolithic and modern technological conditions. God forbid we should hear fifth grade children thinking in just these terms. But how about: "When an Eskimo has two female twins, and another infant, would she abandon one or both of them, if the hunting season was not good?" Indeed I would submit these twenty-two questions as proof positive of Bruner's now famous dictum that "any subject can be taught to anybody at any age in some form that is honest and interesting" (10, p. 124). Let us dwell, however, on the *processes* that achieved these questions. These are rather neatly revealed by the naturally controlled experiment described above: the subject matter, materials, and classroom conditions were almost identical in both instances. Moreover, Miss Amenta and Miss Grossman are equally gifted teachers. Bear in mind also that at the time of the experiment they were also only moderately experienced. Yet in one instance the children evinced superficial involvement and boredom, the lesson ending in questionless silence; while in the other instance, the children evinced spirited concern and involvement, the lesson ending with so many significant, credible and relevant questions that the teacher was moved to improvise a special procedure to preserve them.*

I think we may be permitted the conclusion that while the materials, classroom conditions, and native teaching talents involved in both these lessons may have been necessary to the results achieved, they were not sufficient. We may also be permitted to suggest that what provided the sufficient factor was an approach to emotions and images which was present in the second instance and absent in the first. In the second instance the children were instructed—not permitted, but instructed—to control, express, and use the emotions and images which had been stimulated by the materials. In that order, and with the teacher's professional help at each step in the sequence. In the first instance the children were merely allowed to exercise their

---

* For days afterward the children insisted on the "question box period."

affective and imaginal skills *if* they possessed them, and *if* they chose to use them, but were only instructed to control them.

It is such action researches as these, in their cumulative effects, that have led me to focus on the cultivation and deployment of affect and imagery as the skills most urgently needed by teachers of the new curricula in the social studies. I can best make this point by correcting a misimpression left by Bruner in his latest book.

In discussing the cosmology or "world view" dimension of "Man: A Course of Study" Bruner writes:

> But it is also necessary that the children "feel" myth as well as understand it—for it is different from "explanation" or "narrative." We have found that this requires much care in the teaching. At least two methods have been used, each with what seemed to be striking effect in gripping the children's imagination. In one, . . . the children are introduced abruptly to Eskimo society by a film of the family of Zachary, Marta and their four year old son Alexei. . . . It is one in which they are jigging through the spring ice for salmon, and catching a good share, until a howling gale arises and the film comes to a close. It is particularly useful as an "introduction" to Netsilik life, at once full of humanity and the wildness of the terrain and weather. There follows an extended discussion of seals, and how much of what they wore and lived in and used in daily life was derived from the seal. Following this, there is a short film of Zachary, technically extraordinary, stalking a seal on the ice, creeping up on it slowly and with evident guile, hoping to harpoon it before it can get back into the water through its breathing hole. Zachary fails. The children try their hand at writing a dream that he might have had that night. They need a fair amount of encouraging to avoid the "slick" dream pattern of the mass media. Why did Zachary

miss? With his beautiful skill and tools and experience,
why did the seal get away? Let the dream be about that.
The stories and illustrations are sometimes startling, very
often "myth-like," always dramatic. Only after these are
the children introduced to Nuliajik, the myth of the origin
of seals, the Eskimo orphan girl who tried to climb on the
raft and was refused, her fingers cut off and turned to seals,
and left with an ever unfulfilled sense of vengeance against
humanity, holding back the seals over whom she exercised
domination.

We were struck by how strongly the children sensed the
mythic qualities of the Nuliajik tale, how much (through
their own efforts) they had become adept at judging an
imaginative "explanation." Some still preferred their own
stories to Nuliajik, but no matter. . . . (11, pp. 91–92)

In this account, and others like it, Bruner takes care
to use his great clarity of pen when describing the materials,
but he is content to use generalities like "a fair amount of
encouraging" when describing the teaching, thus suggesting
it is the materials rather than the teaching which most de-
serve clarity. Yet the effectiveness of the lesson he describes, which so impressed us both, was the result of a
particular method of teaching.

It happens that the same lesson had previously been
tried by the same teacher with a similar group of children
with the single exception that a preparatory myth writing
exercise had been included in the sequence where later the
dream construction exercise had proved so productive. The
children had been confused and uncharacteristically hesi-
tant. As in the revised sequence they had grown fond of
Zachary, Marta, and Alexei; had been duly impressed by
their resourcefulness and had begun to comprehend the

total dependence of these people on the seal. They too had been moved by Zachary's failure, and they too were gripped by the myth of Nuliajik. But connectives between all this and themselves eluded the children, and so the essence of myth eluded them. Myths remained exclusively characteristic of people "from olden times." When asked to compose myths themselves they resorted, as Bruner says, to genres more familiar to their own schooling: explanation or narrative. As we approached this lesson with the second group of children it was suggested that they might not have believed the teacher really meant for them to bring their own fantasies into the lesson. They might therefore need some instruction in how to do this. Dreams were composed in an idiom similar to that of myths. Surely the children could remember a dream or two, as models to work from. Why not instruct them to compose a dream around Zachary's failure, and then get on to myth composition?

The lesson was then planned and conducted by Miss Catherine Motz, Mrs. Kathleen Sylva, and Mrs. Elena Werlin much as Bruner describes it. I shall only add to his account a sample of the children's productions, in illustration of the pedagogical power that lies in asking children to make their own beliefs:

One day millions of years ago volcanoes blew rock and boulders filled with seals into the sea. When the rocks hit the surface they broke. All the seals got loose for their first time. They all swam to Alaska and the North and South Poles. The seals started to eat and eat. First they ate the plants in the water. Then the plants grew taller and began to grow out of the water. Then some seals turned into Eskimos that lived on ground. And they killed many other seals to eat. They forgot they were killing their own people. (Roger) See Figure 1.

A long time ago people died and they were buried all together in one graveyard. Practically every night seals used to come out of the graves on the dot of midnight. And they slithered out of the graveyard through the fence and into the water. In the daytimes people used to look at the graves and the earth was moved away and the coffin was wide open. One day because of the force of gravity something strange happened. The moon hit the earth and the seals got confused as to which was earth. They climbed up onto the moon. Then the moon went back to its normal place. The next thing the Eskimos knew they saw seals slithering through the sky and back down into the Arctic Ocean. The moon kept going up and down for some strange reason and some days when the Eskimos were hunting the seals were slithering through the sky. They couldn't catch them because they weren't there. (Ronald) See Figure 2.

Zachary started to fall asleep and he saw a kind of blurry band of seals. He was sneaking up on them and all of a sudden they disappeared. His mind started to get clearer that there must be some power that puts them there. Maybe it's a witch, he was thinking. It could be my wife. But why would my wife take them away? He soon found out that his wife was mad at him. He was thinking why and he said in his dream: "I know. I'll be more kind to her. Now that my mind is clear I know that my wife is sometimes mad at me. When she is she will not put the seals there. She knows that I have worked very hard to catch food for the family and I think that my wife is the witch. When the seals are there that means that my wife is not mad at me. And when there are no seals that means that she is mad at me.

"I will try to be much nicer to her than I usually am because we need food for our family. I think that next time

Figure 1

Figure 2

Figure 3

Figure 4

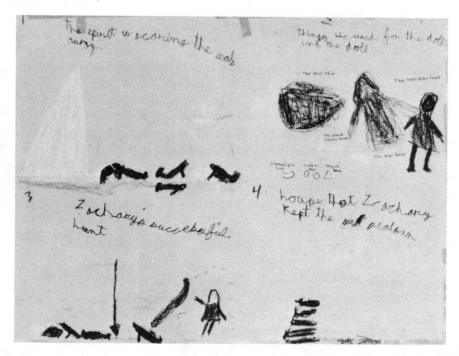

I will try my best and I will always use the same tools because I think my tools are working well, but it is the way I behave with my wife that counts."

He will probably wake up the next morning all blurry and in a way he feels better because he found out why the seals were there some days and why they were not there other days. (Jeremiah) See Figure 3.

He dreamed the spirits scared the seals away because sometimes they wanted him to catch them and sometimes they didn't. He said, 'I'll try to use magic powers—maybe carry a little doll that would scare the bad spirits away.'

He got some bones from a dead Eskimo and found a dead seal and got the bones and took a little portion of the skin. He wrapped the skin around the bones first. Then he made a little coat of the caribou and covered the whole thing except for the face. For the face he got the eyes from a small baby rabbit. For the nose he took a small baby seagull's beak. And for a curved mouth, the jawbone of a lemming.

He put the doll in his parka pocket, took up his spear, his polar bear skins, put on his snowglasses. He *knew* that he would catch a seal, and so he tried harder.

He found a group of seals. He aimed his spear at the biggest one and fired. He threw his spear right in front of the seal and the seal had to stop. Then he came up close and threw his knife at the seal. And he hit the seal and the seal died. Then he ran in front of the hole in the ice so the other seals couldn't get away and he killed a few other seals. And then he took some pups and then he took the dead seals and the pups home alive so that when they grew up they would always have meat.

He woke up and thought of his dream. Then he made a doll like in the dream. And he put it in his pocket. And he went out after the seals. He had success! Everything happened that happened in the dream. From then on he had some ambition because of the doll. So he was a lucky hunter. (Samuel) See Figure 4.

CHAPTER FOUR

Insight and Outsight

Some years ago I considered taking leave from university work in order to learn how to teach. The strategy was to take a position in a good elementary school where I could learn by doing and also have some professionals at hand for consultation. It required a license from the State Board of Education. I filed the necessary transcripts, and, in time, received notice that my papers were in order, with one omission: I would have to show that I had passed an approved course in educational psychology. In undergraduate years I had overenrolled in psychology courses and had in fact thought at the time that educational psychology was something that might safely be skipped.

It was an opportunity to sport with life: I phoned my correspondent to ask if the course in educational psychology offered at Brandeis University was an approved one. "Yes indeed," he replied, "We've heard good things about our Brandeis teachers." Savoring the words, I countered: "I'm happy to hear that because I have been its instructor these past six years and I have need to presume that I could pass my own course." What did I have in mind? I spelled out what I thought to be the easily resolvable dilemma. Alas, he was a humorless man: "Very unusual," he said. "I will have to think about it."

Further considerations led me to decide I had little

talent for teaching and had best stick to teaching teachers.

All of which is to alert the reader that the views on "educational psychology" to be found in what follows are biased from more than one direction.

Among the many occupational hazards of the teaching profession, one of the more insidious has been the requirement that one pass a college course entitled Educational Psychology. Insidious because the course is usually based on that body of theory and evidence known as the "psychology of learning." The reader who has not had experience with such a course will wonder what is insidious about that. Is not a teacher, after all, a husbander of learning, and if there is a psychology of it shouldn't she know what it is? If there was a psychology of *instructed* learning, yes. However, the briefest perusal of any text in the "psychology of learning" will reveal that *instructed* learning is given a singularly wide berth. This for the purpose of adherence to controlled scientific procedure. Ironic though it may sound, a trained investigator in this field would no more instruct a learner than he would fudge his data. In fact the designs of most learning experiments make instruction of the learner (i.e., coaching the subject) impossible; so if it appears that instruction did occur, then the investigator has either been guilty of poor design or he has indeed fudged his data.

I hasten to say that I value the literature of "learning psychology." It is very enlightening as regards three questions:

1) How do other animals adapt to their environments outside the influences of their instincts (e.g., conditioning experiments)?

2) How do humans adapt to *impoverished* environments (e.g., experiments in learning nonsense syllables)?

3) How do humans adapt to the "average expectable environment" as a function of normal maturation (e.g., the developmental studies of Werner, Gesell, Piaget, etc.)?

Insofar as he is a student of adaptation in all its forms, a psychologist wants to know these things. A teacher, however, must find them systematically unrelated to her specialty. The first she must find extraneous, since she doesn't instruct animals. The second she must find irrelevant because she is committed to enriched environments, not impoverished ones. And the third can be relevant only to the extent she is content to be an "average expectable" teacher.

In my opinion Jerome Bruner should be awarded one of the American Psychological Association's medals for this one of his many achievements: while president of that unwieldy establishment, a position he had earned as one of America's foremost "learning" psychologists, he stood to say: *Our educational psychology has little to do with education.* Specifically, he noted that the psychology of learning had necessarily to be *descriptive,* while a psychology of education should ideally be *prescriptive.* He went on (I will paraphrase): Would any psychologist dispute Jean Piaget's eminence in the psychology of learning? Then: would any psychologist begrudge Piaget his experimental prerequisite— the random encounter? And then: do you send *your* children to schools for random encounters? The message dawned: psychologists need a theory of learning, yes. But teachers need a theory of *instructed* learning. And that we did not have.

Undertaking to make a bond of his word, Bruner then published "Toward a Theory of Instruction" (11). This will be a historic book because it is the first one. However, it omits much. In particular, it says little about imagination, that aspect of the human learning process which is uniquely human and which most often goes uninstructed in our schools.

How shall we conceive of imagination within a theory of instruction—observing the requirement, of course, that our formulations be conceivable to instructors? First, imagination is not an extra feature of a person's psychological makeup, not something a person has or does not have. Nor is it something we acquire. In common parlance we sometimes say that this person "has a lot of personality" and that that person "has little personality." What we mean is that this person is more free to express his personality, and that that person is less free to do so. Similarly with imagination: we all have it; some of us are more free to use it than others; and all of us find it more accessible under some conditions than under other conditions.

Our understanding of imagination should therefore include (1) an appreciation of its ubiquity, and (2) knowledge of the conditions that vary its availability.

The ubiquity of imagination resides in the fact that human beings *perceive* the world symbolically. Our everyday, conscious, adult experiences tend to obscure this fundamental feature of human existence. The common sensing of our imaginations is rather that they come into play *after* perceptual events, i.e., that we perceive the world as it unalterably is, and then, in occasional moments of idleness or sport, alter it, as we say, in the mind's eye. It was Freud's most significant contribution to our understanding of ourselves that common sense misleads us in this matter, that in fact we alter the world, change it, play with it, make it up and over constantly, when awake and asleep, in every perceptual, cognitive, and recognitive event, whether extraceptively framed or intraceptively framed. That the worlds we thus individually perceive and remember generate sufficiently common beliefs to support human community is due to our capacity for consciousness and for the instruction of consciousness—our uncommon, or "made beliefs," coexisting in unconsciousness.* This is no more than to restate the fundamental axiom of psychoanalytic theory, which made Freud at once so controversial and so persuasive, that the major portion of significant human experience is unconscious. There is no suggestion here that, in appreciating the parts that unconscious experiences play in human life, we demean the crucial participation of conscious experiences. There is only the implication that man can never become so civilized as to become unimaginative.

Later Freud sought to systematize this axiom with his formulations of the systems Unconscious, Preconscious, and Conscious; and with his formulations of the primary and secondary symbolic processes, as successively influenced by bodily cues at various stages of maturation. (See Chapters six and seven.) Piaget was then to reformulate the same views and to substantiate them with his many empirical observations.

The same fundamental axiom has since been confirmed from a variety of clinical and experimental sources: Silberer's studies of the hypnogogic state (77), Poetzel's studies of dreaming (71), Kubie's studies of the hypnotic state (57), Werner's studies of microgenetic perception (85), Klein's studies of subliminal perception (51), Paul's studies of serial reproduction (67), and the many recent studies of "sensory deprivation" and "consciousness expansion"—to name only those that come immediately to mind.

Susanne Langer has categorically stated the point as follows:

* I intend the descriptive rather than the dynamic connotations of the term.

> Symbolization . . . is the starting point of all intellec-
> tion in the human sense, and is more general than thinking,
> fancying, or taking action. For the brain is not merely a
> great transmitter, a super-switchboard; it is better likened
> to a great transformer. The current of experience that passes
> through it undergoes a change of character, not through
> the agency of the sense by which the perception entered,
> but by virtue of a primary use which is made of it imme-
> diately: it is sucked into the stream of symbols which con-
> stitutes a human mind.
>
> Our overt acts are governed by representations whose
> counterparts can nowhere be pointed out, whose objects
> are "percepts" only in a Pickwickian sense. (60, p. 45)

The reader who wishes to confirm for himself that his
conscious world is but a strategic, and not always representative, sampling of his many unconscious worlds may
readily do so. He may offer to participate in one of the
aforementioned researches, each of which includes in its
design some way of effecting atypical instruction of consciousness. Or, he may simply remember his dreams, those
private showings of our invented worlds which are arranged
for us four or five times nightly by the psychophysiological
metabolisms of sleep.

Now, consider imagination in the context of "learning
psychology." How do the other animals learn? That is, how
do they adapt to their environments when not governed
exclusively by their instincts? They do so by having their
responses conditioned by their environments. A dog
salivates in response to the smell of food. Let the dog regularly hear a particular sound in the presence of the smell
of food and he will come to salivate in response to that
particular sound. We say that his salivary response has been
conditioned to the sound. A species' capacity for having its

responses thus conditioned has survival value. The ecologies of dogs can change slightly, even within the life span of an individual dog. The dog's capacity for having his responses conditioned to these changes is the reason dogs range more widely on the planet than do clams.

We, of course, share our forebears' capacity for having our responses made more flexible in this way. But this is not the kind of learning we put children in schools to cultivate. Rather, we school our children the better that they may develop their distinctly human capacity to condition their stimuli. That is, to use their imaginations, and thus to contribute to their culture. Our predecessors' actualization of this capacity is what created the culture in which our children find themselves in the first place. Moreover, the culture we are currently passing along is changing so rapidly that it can surely soon be said of an individual child that if he is not equipped to contribute to his culture, he is not properly equipped to live in it.

To what do we refer when we speak of the human animal's distinct capacity to condition his stimuli? We refer to the fact that it is in his first nature to perceive symbolically, to respond to his responses, as well as to stimuli. He may then rest content with this or that stimulus, as modified in his head, or he may proceed to change it to fit the way it appears in his head. There are particular sounds in my life that sometimes cause me to salivate too, but it is as impossible for me to proceed to simply eat as it would be for a dog to ask for a napkin. For me there is: when, where, with whom, and possibly, might it not suit the taste to leave the steak in the freezer and go out for some steamed clams? As humans, in other words, we must live imaginatively in even the most habituated events of our lives. This is what makes us the naturally selective animal.

As a species, we are actually twice removed from the laws and comforts of "natural selection." Not only do we live in privately modified versions of the world but, for us, the world was put there, interposed between us and "nature," by preceding generations of our own species!

We call this invented world our culture. In fact, it is the health of this cultured environment, in respect to ourselves, and no longer the health of ourselves in respect to the natural environment, which measures our adaptation as a species—an evolutionary turn of no small significance, as Julian Huxley has noted (36); and of no small responsibility, as Loren Eisley has noted (22).

Young teachers tend to shy away from the perspectives of evolution. They are often putting their husbands through medical school and feeling insignificant in their jobs. To be asked to contemplate their place in the universe seems an additional assault on their egos. Yet, it is sometimes illuminating to speculate on the possible counterparts in cultural evolution of the basic forces which move and regulate organic evolution. What is the cultural counterpart of organic mutation, for example? Is it not new ideas? And what is the cultural counterpart of the organic vicissitudes of genetic variation? Is it not conflict between differing new ideas? And what of natural selection itself; what is its counterpart in cultural evolution? Is it not education, their own profession? The analogies are hardly credible, but they do sometimes make their point by way of being no less *in*credible than a teacher who sees insignificance in her job. One teacher even fetched farther: "I've been thinking about those counterparts you spoke of. You didn't give one for catastrophe in organic evolution—when a whole species becomes extinct." Yes? "Well, it's sort of improbable," she said, "but, then, so is the extinction of a species. Suppose one generation of teachers was somehow steered completely wrong, say by some kind of John Dewey type who happened to be insane, or something, so that there was one generation of completely misguided teaching. And suppose this happened to coincide with the invention of some drug, or something that made children completely obedient. Suppose, in other words, our culture had just one generation of totally bad teachers and totally good children. That would be the end of us, wouldn't it?" Improbable, yes, but —by evolutionary criteria—conceivable!

It is not in the interests of clarity when speaking to adults of imagination to leave illustrations to unaided introspection. I shall therefore conclude these remarks on the ubiquity of imagination with some excerpts from Piaget's systematic and painstaking observations of young children:

> *Observation 95.* As early as 1;4(15) * X., after simulating certain needs, burst into laughter, thus showing the first signs of symbolic play similar to that of J. whom at 1;3(12) made a pretence of being asleep. At 1;9(29) X. put an open box on top of another and said: "Sitting on pot." At 2;1(9) her dolls dirtied themselves: "But must ask for pot." Scenes connected with the toilet were frequently reproduced during the following weeks. At 2;7(9) she laughed at an adult with a biscuit sticking out of his mouth and indulged in pleasantries it would be difficult to quote. On the other hand, at 3;6(10), here feces were compared to a finger, a mouse, a rabbit, etc., or were even personified and given ladies' names.
>
> From about 2;6 to 3;6 these games were associated with all kinds of symbolic fantasies and games in which all sorts of objects had excretory organs, not only animal toys, but little cars, planes, cups, sticks, etc. At about 3;6 there were questions about the morphological differences be-

* One year, four months, and fifteen days of age.

tween the sexes, and remarks which were sometimes serious and sometimes playful as to the possibility of making anatomical characteristics uniform. At 3;6(2): "I think the mountain hanging here grows and turns into a little long thing with a hole at the end for water to come out, like boys have." And at 5;8(0): "Why do boys need a long thing for that? They could do it through their navel. Zoubab (an imaginary character) makes water through her navel." And at 5;8(1), after saying that boys could do it through a gate, X. played at nursing Zoubab who was ill: "I'm making her make water through the bars."

Y., at 3;3(12), looking at two male statues: "It's a good thing they've got two things for water to come out; if they hadn't they'd quarrel."

Observation 96. We must now give examples of all the games connected with family relations in which the affective tendencies which give rise to them are to some extent outside the child's consciousness. At 2;0(4) X. reproduced meal-time scenes with her dolls, in the course of which she exerted more maternal authority over her children than she herself was accustomed to experience. At 2;7(27) she played at being the mother of her younger brother, born a short time before. At 2;8(0) she identified herself with this baby brother, and imitated his attitudes and voice. Subsequently, from 3;6 to 5;0, she reproduced whole scenes of family life, playing all the roles in turn. At 5;9(16) she played at being in bed for a confinement, then declared that a certain doll was her "because it came out of my inside." At 5;8(5), being for the moment on bad terms with her father, X. charged one of her imaginary characters with the task of avenging her: "Zoubab cut off her daddy's head. But she has some very strong glue and partly stuck it on again. But it's not very firm now."

After 3;3 Y. often played at being a boy. At 4;2(11) she made up a story of a little boy "who laughed when his father died. But after he was buried, he cried and they had to comfort him. I wouldn't have had to be comforted because I'm a big girl. Afterwards he became a father. He became a father all of a sudden, without noticing. He didn't know he had. He was sleeping in a bed, as small as that, by his mummy, and then in the morning his mummy said to him: "Your bed is much too small for you." His legs were much too long and fat. He was big all over. He had become a father suddenly during the night, because his mummy had given him a spoonful of potato. And then he had a little sister who became a mummy too, suddenly, without noticing it."

Observation 97. The part played by games dealing with birth is particularly noteworthy. We have already seen X.'s game at 5;9(14). At 3;3(28) Y. said of her doll Nicholas, "When he was born he stayed for a long time inside me; he had sharp pointed teeth and afterwards they became smooth." At 3;6(2) she pretended that her son Nicholas's head was in her head, etc. At 3;9(13) someone was arguing with her: "No, don't do that. You know I have a little baby inside me and it hurts him." Then, when the person had gone: "You know, when my little baby is born, he'll kick him and knock him down." At 3;10(17) she explained to her doll which wanted to be inside her again: "No, you're too big now, you can't." In contrast to this, at 3;10(24) Y., who wanted to become a boy, said to her father: "I want to go back inside you, and then when I come out I'll be a little baby again. I'll be called Y. (the masculine form of her name) because I'll be a boy." (69, pp. 173–74)

The richness of imagination exemplified in these accounts will wane as the children grow toward adulthood. The comparative extents to which this erosion of novel imagery is the function of maturation and/or education is, at this time, a very moot question in developmental psychology.

We do know something, however, of the two conditions which are likely, at all ages, to suffuse the convergent thoughts of our conscious lives with the divergent images of our preconscious * lives. Herbert Silberer has coined the terms *apperceptive deficiency* and *apperceptive insufficiency* to describe these two conditions (76). The reader who is more at home with standard psychoanalytic terminology may prefer to think in terms of their corresponding ego functions: defensive regression and strategic regression, respectively.

Apperceptive deficiency refers to situations in which a person finds himself mentally off his game. He is unable to maintain rational mastery of intellectual achievements which are normally routine for him, and falls back, as it were, on their prerationative approximations. He may be fatigued, or sleepy, or have had a few, or be in a fevered condition, or in an emotional conflict, or under influence of drugs, or in some other way have lost the fine edges of his optimal mental state. *Apperceptive insufficiency* refers to situations in which a person is at the top of his form, in full command of his optimal mental state, but who has momentarily assumed challenges which just barely elude his best intellectual efforts. He may then receive an assist from these same prerationative approximations. We sometimes call this "inspiration."

Silberer arranged to catch these passing prerationative assists on the fly, so to speak, by training himself to observe his reveries under a delicate blend of the two conditions. At the first signs of drowsiness he would set himself to contemplating some intellectual problem of which he was not yet quite master. When the elusive rational thought process

---

* The term is used in Kubie's sense, to be spelled out in a later chapter.

gave way to its imaginal sequel, he would alert himself to full wakefulness and ponder the two versions of what he called the "autosymbolic phenomenon."

> In a state of drowsiness I contemplate an abstract topic such as the nature of transsubjectively (for all people) valid judgments. A struggle between active thinking and drowsiness sets in. The latter becomes strong enough to disrupt normal thinking and to allow—in the twilight-state so produced—the appearance of an autosymbolic phenomenon. The content of my thought presents itself to me immediately in the form of a perceptual (for an instant apparently real) picture: I see a big circle (or transparent sphere) in the air with people around it whose heads reach into the circle. This symbol expresses practically everything I was thinking of. The transsubjective judgment is valid for all people without exception: the circle includes all the heads. The validity must have its grounds in a commonality: the heads belong all in the same homogeneous sphere. Not all judgments are transsubjective: the body and limbs of the people are outside (below) the sphere as they stand on the ground as independent individuals. In the next instant I realize that it is a dream-picture; the thought that gave rise to it, which I had forgotten for the moment, now comes back and I recognize the experience as an "autosymbolic" phenomenon.
>
> What had happened? In my drowsiness my abstract ideas were, without my conscious interference, replaced by a perceptual picture—by a symbol. (77, p. 198)

Other examples follow:

> I think of human understanding probing into the foggy and difficult problem of the "Mothers." (Faust, Part II)

Symbol: I stand alone on a stone jetty extending out far into a dark sea. The waters of the ocean and the dark and mysteriously heavy air unite at the horizon.

Interpretation: The jetty in the dark sea corresponds to the probing into the difficult problem. The uniting of air and water, the elimination of the distinction between above and below, would symbolize that, with the Mothers, as Mephistopheles describes it, all times and places shade into each other so that there are no boundaries between "here" and "there," "above" and "below." It is in this sense that Mephistopheles says to Faust: "Now you may sink!— I could just as well say: rise." (77, p. 202)

I am trying to think of the purpose of the metaphysical studies I am about to undertake. The purpose is—I reflect— to work my way through ever higher forms of consciousness, that is, levels of existence, in my quest after the basis of existence.

Symbol: I run a long knife under a cake as though to take a slice out of it.

Interpretation: My movement with the knife represents "working my way through." To clarify this apparently silly symbol I must give a detailed explanation. The symbol-basis, that is, the relationship which makes the picture here chosen usable for autosymbolic representation, is the following. At the dining-table it is at times my chore to cut and distribute the cake. I do this with a long and flexible knife, necessitating considerable care. It is particularly difficult to lift the slices; the knife must be carefully pushed *under* the slice (this is the slow "working my way through" to arrive at the "basis"). There is yet more symbolism in the picture. The symbol is a layer-cake, so that the knife cutting it penetrates several layers (levels of consciousness and existence). (77, p. 203)

In opposition to the Kantian view, I am attempting to conceive of time as a "concept." Thus the individual time-span should be related to the totality-of-time as a particular mass of matter to the total-mass of matter of the same category. This attempt to force a problem into a preconceived scheme results in the following symbol:

Symbol: I am pressing a Jack-in-the-Box into the box. But every time I take my hand away it bounces out gaily on its spiral spring. (77, p. 204)

This is the stuff of metaphor and paraphrase—the substance of creative thought. Not the least provocative intimation of Silberer's studies is that our creative thoughts are often thus composed of both our weakest and our strongest lights.

I shall now try to follow that intimation to its best pedagogical conclusion. Over the years, consulting with producers and teachers of new curricula, and being especially concerned to exploit the potentials of these curricula for stimulating creative thoughts in classrooms, I have come to regard as the most futile of last words: "Oh, but that would threaten the children!" For example, it was a fellow psychologist, I am embarrassed to report, who objected most strenuously to the infanticide lesson, because, she said: "It could do lasting harm to the children." Remember what an exceedingly instructive and strengthening lesson it turned out to be.

What is it, then, that does psychological harm to children? Is it images? Of course not, else Piaget's children would be walking wrecks. Is it emotions? Likewise not, else the pupils of Miss Amenta and Miss Grossman would have plagued Miss Greenfield with even more themes of violence and death, and hardly returned with twenty-two relevant questions about the subject matter. Is it provocative stimuli? No, again, else most children would long since have been done in by their televisions. Besides, as has just been described, humans are just not that bound to stimuli. One state of mind does psychological harm to children: anxiety. Or, more precisely, the defensive excesses of thought, feeling and behavior which we tend to develop against chronic expectations of anxiety.

It should not be for naught that psychologists can speak with more authority about anxiety than about any other single psychic state. And yet we continue to permit ourselves to be intimidated by prospects of "threatening" children with stimuli—as if we didn't well know the difference between threat and anxiety.

Let us review what is known about anxiety. I shall speak only a little loosely in the interest of orienting the review toward a theory of instruction. We know the *range* of anxiety in evolution: it is almost unique to Homo Sapiens; certainly it is not as prominent in any other species. We also know its *preconditions*. They are in fact the preconditions of being human: (1) our instincts, while strong, are not specific; (2) we languish in immaturity for an extremely lengthy period; (3) we must adjust our behavior to social environments of bewildering complexity; and (4) we are equipped with an oversized cerebral cortex which incessantly constructs hypotheses about the ambiguities attending these—hypotheses as to what our instincts of the moment are seeking, hypotheses as to what our social circle of the moment will condone, hypotheses as to what our competence of the moment will support. By virtue of being human, in other words, we are always imagining, and we are sometimes alone and helpless in the process. When we are all of these simultaneously—imagining *and* alone *and* helpless—we are in a state of anxiety.

Moreover, we know that anxiety differs from fear in having as its effective *cause* internal rather than external agents. And we know the general nature of these agents.

They are symbolic. We know most about the *effects* of anxiety, i.e., the spectra of misperceptions, misconceptions and misbehaviors for which elaborate nomenclatures have been devised which we need not go into here. Finally, I repeat, we know the variable conditions that are conducive to anxiety: aloneness and helplessness. The phenomenologies of these conditions vary with age and with need. At a certain age, or under the influence of certain needs, aloneness may be experienced in any situation not including the touch of skin; at another age, and under the influence of other needs, aloneness may result primarily from differences of opinion with someone who is important to us. Similarly, one may feel helpless before the challenge of one's shoelaces, quadratic equations or Newton's law. But anxiety will only follow when *both* these conditions confront an open imagination. If an openly imagining person is alone but not helpless, he may feel unhappy, sad, or aggrieved but he will not be anxious. If he feels helpless but not alone, he may develop feelings of inferiority, dependence or resentment, but he will not be anxious. If a person feels both alone and helpless but can insulate himself against his imagination, he may feel afraid, suspicious, or angry but he will not be anxious.

It follows that there are three general ways, this side of insanity, to avoid anxiety: (1) be less alone; (2) be less helpless; (3) be less imaginative.

In our official pronouncements in catalogues, and statements of principles we tend to emphatically eschew the third way of avoiding anxiety in schoolrooms. Rather, we are likely to hear ourselves say that as educators we want to have a hand in producing men as well as minds, and that to this end we wish to engage each student in a search for himself through providing opportunities to examine his imagination, his feelings, and his judgments. "In any schooling worth its salt," says one such statement, "an individual must have the opportunity to find out who he is as well as what he relates to . . . " (65).

In practice however, the third way tends to be the method of choice—granted, often unwittingly so. For example, witness this moment in a sixth grade arithmetic lesson:

Teacher: "And now can anyone tell me what infinity means?"
   (*silence*) What is infinity?"
Billy: (*pause*) "Uh, I think it's like a box of Cream of Wheat."
Teacher: "Billy, don't be silly!"

I was Billy's psychotherapist at the time. I knew him well and shall provide the detailed context of this interchange further along. For now, may I put it to you: is not infinity very like a box of Cream of Wheat?

What I wish to bring into focus here is that when we aspire to give school children opportunities to find out who they are as well as what they relate to, to exercise their imagination, feelings, and judgments, we are in fact saying that we intend to create conditions in the schools which will most certainly threaten the children, and which could make some of them anxious. The experienced teacher will recognize that it is this paradox from which have followed some of her proudest professional moments as well as some of her rankest hypocrisies.

I should like to say that I have only respect for a teacher who wilfully chooses to help her pupils avoid anxiety by way of helping them to avoid their imaginations. Such a course is often required by her mood, or by the mood of the class, or by the exigencies of the school schedule; in any event, it has the virtue of being above the board. All too often, however, what we find is the teacher falling into such a course by default, for lack of methods and materials which can help the children avoid anxiety by way of being less alone and/or less helpless *with* their imaginations.

How did we find out so much about anxiety? We did it by learning to heal its consequences in clinics, hospitals, and psychotherapists' offices. Let me illustrate: Billy had suffered a more than usual share of anxiety from the age of two. Among a series of ways he came to deal with his anxieties, two caused his adults to bring him to a guidance clinic: he read very poorly, although his IQ was high; and he was given to excesses of profanity, and other "attention-getting" behaviors, which made him a trial to his teachers. What was done for him? Billy was given a doctor who told him he would help him to read better, and be a better boy in school, by talking and playing with him in a special way once a week. He could say anything he pleased without limitation, and he could do anything that pleased him short of physical damage.

Billy took the hint; he played out variations on a single theme week after week. He would build a house of blocks, and then give it a make-believe family; a father and mother, a grandfather, an aunt, and a little boy. Something mysterious would always happen to the father. He would go on a trip and disappear, or he would be sent to the store by the mother and never come back, or he would contract a strange sickness that made it seem he was dead and then be buried by mistake, or he would have an argument with his wife and storm wildly out of the house—and disappear.

When Billy was two, his father had deserted the family, gone off with another woman, married her, and started another family, without benefit of divorce. His devoutly Catholic family could find no better solution to their resulting fear and shame but to surround the man's memory with a dense wall of secrecy and dissimulation. Divorce could have meant excommunication from the church; notoriety could have meant civil prosecution for bigamy. The mother, herself in her early twenties, had her own and the child's subsistence to think of, and therefore had to manage her humiliations in silence. For example, once when the school nurse asked Billy his father's occupation Billy said he would have to find out. This led to a crisis at home, and instructions that to future such questions he should say his father had died!

So Billy played out with his doctor imaginary version after imaginary version of what makes fathers leave families:

Therapist: "Well, Billy, that's an even stronger house you built this week. What are we going to make believe about it this time?"

Billy: "The boy is cranky. He just got over a cold and can't go out. 'Stop that boy's fidgeting now, woman, or you know I'll just pick up and leave this house forever.' That's the father saying that."

Therapist: "Billy always has the man of the house going away. Why is that?"

Billy: (engrossed in directing his cast) "Oh, I don't know. . . . 'There, that does it,' he says, 'I knew that rascal would break that dish if you didn't take it away from him. I warned you. Now I'm going and I won't be back' (Door bangs). Now the mother is crying. I'll have to get some water for the tears."

Therapist: "What's he going to do?"

Billy: "Oh, maybe he goes around the world on a tramp steamer. Maybe he gets lost someplace and gets sick and there'd be nobody to help him get better."

Therapist: "Pretty sad."

Billy: "Oh, I don't know."

Therapist: "What's the boy going to do?"

Billy: "I haven't thought about that yet."

Therapist: "I wonder if the boy thinks it was *his* fault that the father had to leave."
Billy: "Gee, aren't you the curious one? You know what happened to the cat! . . . Let's play something else."

Gradually the causes of the original anxieties come to light: Fantasies about what was wrong with him and/or his mother that caused his father to leave. Fantasies before which he was necessarily helpless for lack of information, and before which he was made to feel alone by the grotesque responses which met his requests for information.

What to do with the anxieties? One way, as it developed, was to flee from them by arranging never to find out what came at the ends of things—like stories, sentences, or long words. Thus the reading problem. Another way was to fight them by cultivating whatever forms of badness his young mind and body could aspire to—the strategy being that someone, sometime, might get so angry that he would tell him what was wrong with him. And then he would not have to wonder. Thus the behavior problem.

At the time of the Cream-of-Wheat-box episode, Billy and his mother had made considerable progress. The mother was taking a more selfish hold on her life and was standing up to her in-laws. And I had been able to tell Billy the sad but true story of his father, thus relieving him of some of the more fantastic of his speculations. In fact, he had left his last session consciously resolved to try harder in school, and he returned to relate the Cream-of-Wheat-box interchange in tones that said: "See, it's too late, Doc. I cried 'wolf' too often. Nobody will believe me now."

"Doc" had to do what the teacher would have been better equipped to do: "Billy, *how* is infinity like a box of Cream of Wheat?" "Well," said Billy, "think of a box of Cream of Wheat. It shows a man holding a box of Cream

of Wheat. Right? And that box shows the same man holding the same box. Right? And that box. . . . You can't
see them all, like you can't see infinity. You just know
they're all there, going on forever and ever."

It qualified as a creative thought, and having the confidence of its author, I sought the bottom of it. Billy re-
called that his mother used to put a bowl of Cream of
Wheat before him as she left for work mornings, and "I'd
sit there, kind of bored, all by myself, and make up . . .
stories about things. Maybe I used to look at the man on
the box when I was thinking of them."

"Stories about things," indeed! The boy couldn't have
experienced mathematical infinity, but, in a very related
sense, he had experienced emotional infinity. His depth of
longing for his father was infinite—if anything is—and here
was that very experience, composed of his weakest and
strongest resources, providing needed inspiration at a moment of fine intellectual pitch, high resolve, and tenuous
mastery of the subject matter.

I have told this story before and been accused of wanting to bootleg psychotherapy in the schools. "How was his
teacher to know all this, and what business of hers was it
anyway?" I detect prejudice in these questions, because they
beg their own answers: she could not have known all this,
but she obviously had no need to know it. And it was her
business only to the extent that infinity *is* like a box of
Cream of Wheat. I put it to you again: could anything in
a sixth grader's life be *more* like infinity than a box of
Cream of Wheat? Moreover, I do not think a doctor's
office is the best place for a boy to bring his creative
thoughts. He can get more out of them in school, as can
his classmates, not to mention his teachers.

The question remains whether Billy would have had
his creative thought without the special reduction in alone-

ness that his doctor had provided. I rather think he would have, as I rather think many of his "silly sayings" had included some such well-pearled grain of truth. It was, after all, his way of fighting, rather than fleeing, anxiety. But the question is neither here nor there, since there is no way to answer it.

It raises another question, however, which I want to take up next: In developing *instructional* methods of cultivating emotion and imagery, should we model our efforts after the more polished and practiced methods of psychotherapy? The answer I want to give to this question, and it will take some explaining, is: yes, provided we are very careful to reverse everything.

A therapist's first concern is anxiety. A teacher's first concern is learning, i.e., *human* learning, i.e., creative thought (some purists will reject the equation but much more evidence suggests it than disputes it). As we have seen, anxiety and creative thought are related as the two poles of a continuum. Their interrelations should be born in mind, but they should not be mistaken, one for the other. It follows that a therapist's methods seek to reduce aloneness and helplessness, and that a teacher's methods seek to increase the polar opposites: community and mastery. These interrelations can be schematized so:

$$(\text{imagination} + \text{aloneness} + \text{helplessness}) = \text{anxiety} \leftarrow \text{psychotherapy}$$
$$\updownarrow \qquad\qquad \updownarrow \qquad\qquad \updownarrow$$
$$\text{instruction} \rightarrow (\text{imagination} + \text{community} + \text{mastery}) = \text{creative learning}$$

It says that imagination plus aloneness plus helplessness produces anxiety, which may be relieved by psychotherapy. And that instruction may lead to imagination plus community plus mastery, which produces creative learning.

Consider now what it is that distinguishes all forms of psychotherapy, what they have in common, which sets them apart from other methods of tending human development. First, some special method is employed to make the patient's conscious life more receptive to his imagination. Administration of drugs, hypnosis, free association, reinforcement of dream recall, or, in the case of children, play—all designed to stimulate conscious imagination. Even the professionalized impersonality and noninvolvement of many psychotherapeutic approaches may be conceived as partially serving the purpose of stimulating imagination, insofar as this relieves the patient of the pressures of conventional attitudes.

The modus operandi of these methods can be articulated in a variety of theoretical frames. Freud would say that they encourage regression; Piaget, that they require organizations of schemata in which assimilation predominates accommodation; Silberer, that they invite the condition of apperceptive deficiency. Of primary concern to us at the moment, however, is not *how* these methods work, but *what* their purpose is. Do psychotherapists seek to induce mental order in their patients merely by helping them to be more imaginative? No, the strategy is to re-create the causes of the mental *dis*order, the better to treat these causes. And, since it is ultimately anxiety which causes all functional forms of mental disorder, we may say that the therapist seeks to arouse imagination in his patients in order to evoke one of the prime components of anxiety. If, in other words, the patient has previously felt alone and helpless with the feelings and images which these methods are designed to bring forth, he is likely to be threatened anew by anxiety.

Next, all schools of psychotherapy seek ways of reducing feelings of aloneness. The patient is given a certain amount of the therapist's time which he may consider as his possession. It is furthermore agreed that the patient's disclosures will be kept in strictest confidence, thus not only providing a previously unknown degree of safety, but perhaps offering a previously foresworn degree of intimacy. There are also the qualities of being good company to the patient, which every effective therapist perfects according to his style: listening, remembering details, correcting inconsistencies, learning the patient's mannerisms of speech, his preferred metaphors, and crypticisms—all designed to create a situation of comparative non-aloneness. Over time, the therapist comes to symbolize this situation in his person. Corrective emotional experiences are then possible: images which previously led to anxiety, because they could neither be used nor shared, can now at least be shared. They may bring shame, doubt, guilt, or some other normal emotion in their wake—but not anxiety. This is the measure of psychic economy which accounts for all forms of psychotherapy being able to count some successes despite wide differences of theoretical persuasion.

The theoretical differences among the various approaches to psychotherapy (Freudian, Jungian, Adlerian, Rogerian, etc.) cluster around the comparatively less critical question of whether and how to invest this saving, in helping the patient to also feel less helpless before his imagination. Traditionally, this has meant the cultivation of "insight," usually by some kind of interpretation; what has brought forth this or that image in the past; what situations bring it forth now; how it has been overgeneralized, misapplied, rashly acted upon; how it can be more aptly viewed in future, etc. The various schools of psychotherapy differ as to what kinds of insights are likely to prove most useful in this respect, and as to how such insights are best achieved in the therapeutic setting. But this is frosting. Experienced therapists of every school have seen some patients get well despite what their particular training would judge to be faulty or incomplete insight, and other patients remain ill despite possession of apparently all possible insight. Reduction of feelings of aloneness is the common denominator of all forms of psychotherapy.

Insight is only one way that images which no longer estrange a person can be put to use. The other way is by way of *outsight*: grasping, enlivening, enhancing, discovering, making one's own this-or-that datum in the real world— by virtue of gracing it with this-or-that private image. To see that infinity is like a box of Cream of Wheat is not an insight, but it is a very piercing outsight. It is, of course, awkward to say, in such instances, that we have been rendered less helpless before our imaginations. Better to say that we have gained greater mastery of our thoughts, and thereby of the world in which we live. As Robert Frost, in his disarmingly outsightful manner, said of coining figures of speech: "It is a sign that we are thinking."

Most contemporary experimentation in psychotherapeutic methodology (Angyal, Boss, Frankl, Goodman, Kaiser) seek to include in the therapeutic process methods which cultivate outsight, as well as insight. These are usually, on their face, *instructional* methods, their descriptions sometimes being more suggestive of teaching than of treating. No matter; if they defuse anxiety by way of leading patients to feel less helpless before their imaginations, either instead of or in addition to feeling less alone, a therapist may feel justified in employing them.

From the standpoint of including the findings of the therapeutic arts in a theory of instruction, it is interesting to note the point at which the above unorthodox therapeutic methods are most subject to criticism. It is the observation that the employment of such instructional meth-

ods, usually requiring as they do that the therapist take a
stand of judgment somewhere in the patient's real life,
sometimes endanger the climate of personal neutrality
which has traditionally served both to invite freedom of expression and to arrange corrective emotional experiences in
respect to chronic expectations of aloneness.

Useful controversy on this point will continue. It is
possibly the case however, that as far as the professional
tending of human development is concerned, we cannot
have it both ways; that we must undertake to teach or to
treat, and, if both are indicated, to conduct these procedures separately. Not, of course, that the two disciplines
cannot be richly suggestive to each other as regards refinements of their respective methods. Far from it.

We may now ask what it is that distinguishes all
forms of instruction, what *they* have in common which
sets *them* apart from psychotherapy, penology, pastoral
guidance, and other kinds of ministration to human development. Instruction, in all forms, also begins by appealing to the imagination. This is no less true for being so often
left to chance. Despite everything, children are likely to
encounter novelties in schools which challenge their sphere
of mastery, and therefore incite their imaginations, on some
regular schedule—except when systematically prevented
from doing so by misguided considerations of their "readiness." Indeed, the new curricula's most noteworthy contribution to pedagogy is the increased precision with which it
administers novelties to school children that are designed
to just barely elude their "readiness." Whether by chance,
or by design, however, all forms of instruction begin by
appealing to the students' imaginations. And it is notable
that they do so according to the converse of the psychotherapeutic model: in Freud's terms, by encouraging the
testing of unfamiliar realities; in Piaget's terms, by requir-

ing organizations of schemata in which accommodation slightly predominates assimilation; in Silberer's terms, by inviting the condition of apperceptive insufficiency.

The teacher's approach to the aroused imaginations of her students is also the converse of the psychotherapeutic approach. Where the therapist comes to call forth by his person expectations of sharing one's images, and sometimes using them, the teacher comes to call forth by her person expectations of using one's images, and sometimes sharing them: how to conceive a squared root, a declined verb, a balanced equation, the plural of "deer"; or the harshness of Arctic environment, or the nature of myth, or the varieties of human conflict regulation—or the meaning of infinity. Instructional methods, in short, give routine priority to gaining mastery of one's images, and this also by the converse of the therapeutic method: by means of cultivating outsight rather than insight.

Even the main controversy of contemporary experimental education is the converse of its counterpart in experimental psychotherapy: it asks the teacher if she might jeopardize her effectiveness in cultivating mastery and outsight to the extent that she also seeks to cultivate community and insight. There are some fine points here also, and useful controversy will continue to emanate from them.

I should like to state my own position in this controversy, in order to orient the reader to what he may expect in the way of bias through the remainder of this book. Fifteen years of experimentation and research in seeking ways to avail the educative processes of children's emotions and images has led me to adopt what I suppose must be called the conservative view. This will surprise those who may be familiar with my published work, which has consistently represented the opposite view (38, 43, 44, 45). I have courted dreams and daydreams in classrooms, devised "preconscious exercises" involving darkened rooms or closed eyelids, made confidentiality pacts and other such quasi-therapeutic agreements with groups of students, have interpreted their resistances, finessed their transferences (and the corresponding counter-transferences), engaged their silences, given assignments which required autobiographical introspection, improvised examinations which elicited involvement of the "primary process," and have in other ways tried to involve emotions and fantasies in the instructional process—by *following* the therapeutic model. That is, by applying the leverage on imagination that is afforded by conditions of apperceptive deficiency and expectations of community. I remain impressed by the results of these experiments, and gratified by the reports of other teachers who have adapted them to their own styles. But reservations have mounted apace.

First, students will do almost anything that is courteously asked of them by teachers, so the enthusiasm which these experiments have met in students is no clear sign of progress in pedagogy. Moreover, what transpires in many classrooms is so deadly dull that anything new is likely to meet with exaggerated enthusiasm. Secondly, the more successful of these ventures have been with college students studying psychology, and with very young children in whom emotions and fantasies need very little encouragement by special devices. I have therefore been hard pressed to reply to colleagues who have been interested to know how I would conceive these methods to be applicable in freshman anthropology, say, or sixth-grade history, or ninth-grade civics.

Thirdly, there has always been the gnawing suspicion that the gains in learning which followed from these procedures were secondary gains, resulting indirectly from reductions in the students' normal anxiety levels. People

learn better on their own when they are made more com-
fortable with themselves, but this could mean I *was* boot-
legging psychotherapy in the schools. If so, it seems to
have been worth the effort, but then I cannot strictly
count the successes as instructional in nature.

Fourthly, a teaching method can only be as useful as
it is acceptable to teachers, and teachers have tended with
discouraging regularity to be intimidated by these methods.
They have seen in them, however mistakenly, the need
to be on trained and experienced terms with "the mysteries
of the mind." "Maybe *you* can make them work, and
maybe *you* can train some of your students to make them
work, but I don't want to fool around with such things
without more training than I am likely to get." I am, in
fact, a trained psychotherapist, and, therefore, know the
limitations and simplicities of the craft. Hence, I am more
impressed with the mysteries and complexities of teaching.
Admittedly however, it would be carrying things to the
point of absurdity to suggest that teachers should receive
training in psychotherapy the better to appreciate the
greater complexities of teaching, by contrast.

Most persuasive, however, has been the time spent
with teachers of new curricula in the social studies. I have
been convinced that when a teacher is equipped with
documents, exercises, films, tapes and key queries, which
truly represent Man, which invite open-eyed identification
by the children with their species as it has really developed,
as it really behaves, and as it may really be imagined to
develop in the future, there is no need for *in*directly
appealing to emotions and images. The royal road is then
right under the teacher's feet. She has merely to know
how to stay on it. I am convinced, in other words, that
the subject matter of the social studies and humanities,
when artfully and honestly presented to the children, is

the medium of choice for starting the instructional process toward its objective of creative learning. It has the advantage of being at once more plausible to students, more credible to teachers, and even less subject to criticism by taxpayers who, although ready to find fault with "coddling the children," can see value in "threatening" them if this is clearly in the interests of "science."

Be reminded, however, that invoking the imagination is only the first step in the direction of creative learning. There remains the question, to be put to any comprehensive theory of instruction, of *how* to cultivate and deploy aroused imaginations, and their attendant emotions, in the interest of increased mastery of subject matter. Educational —not clinical—research must answer this question. Merely to state it properly has required a rather long way around the considerable advances made by clinical research in its closely related spheres of interest. The advantages that accrue to correctly stated questions come immediately into view, however, for we are now free to modify, adapt, refine, or even to copy the methods used by psychotherapists, because we have now more clearly defined the respective means and ends. If, as teachers, we employ the therapist's methods as means to the end of reducing anxiety, we are merely doing psychotherapy with students. Sometimes beneficial, but discourteous in being uninvited. If we employ these methods as ends in themselves, we embark on a course of ineffectual psychotherapy—not as risky as some fear, because being uninvited it is not likely to be followed. But, in any event, this is not a course of instruction. If, however, we can see ways to employ such methods, or the modifications of such methods, as means to the ends of instructing creative learning, we open new vistas in pedagogy. If the students indirectly acquire greater insight, and thus reduce their anxieties as a secondary gain, so much the better. But that is their business. Our business, at the beginning, and again at the end, is the subject matter of the social sciences and the humanities: our species, where we came from, where we are, where we may be going—using as our touchstone what the students can imagine, share, and use of their special acquaintance with these subjects, which is theirs by virtue of quite literally being first hand specimens of the subject matter.

CHAPTER FIVE

Critique of Bruner

The last chapter might well have concluded with these words:

> Children, like adults, need reassurance that it is all right to entertain and express highly subjective ideas, to treat a task as a problem where you *invent* an answer rather than *finding* one out there in the book or on the blackboard. With children in elementary school, there is often a need to devise emotionally vivid, special games, story-making episodes, or construction projects to re-establish in the child's mind his right not only to have his own private ideas but to express them in the public setting of a classroom.

But these are not this writer's words. They are Bruner's (14, p. 13). He had been speaking of how to stimulate thought in the setting of a school, and had concluded that this is best done by teachers who offer tasks which represent problems to be solved, rather than solutions to be memorized. He goes on to note that the progressive movement's emphasis on personalized knowledge had led to the banalities about the friendly postman, etc. and he suggests that there is more merit in children's discoveries of "kinship and likeness in what at first seemed bizarre, exotic, and even a little repellant" (14, p. 14). He concludes with an illustration:

> It has to do with Alexei who, with his father's help, devises a snare and catches a gull. There is a scene in which he stones the gull to death. Our children watched, horror struck. One girl, Kathy, blurted out, "He's not even human, doing that to the seagull." The class was silent. Then another girl, Jennine, said quietly: "He's got to grow up to be a hunter. His mother was smiling when he was doing that." And then an extended discussion about how people have to do things to learn and even do things to learn how to feel appropriately. "What would you do if you had to live there? Would you be as smart about getting along as they are with what they've got?" said one boy, going back to the accusation that Alexei was inhuman to stone the bird (14, pp. 14–15).

Well said, but while the illustration speaks to the pedagogical power of emotionally vivid *stimuli* (in this instance a very authentic film), it offers nothing to teachers in the way of guidance as to how they are to bring the children into controlled and productive ways of responding to their responses to these stimuli. The teacher is thus led to conclude that she has but to show the film, in order to bring about the kind of discussion described.

I cannot refrain from saying that I speak with some authority on these points, since it was I who devised the lesson which supplied my friend with his illustration. And two very accomplished teachers, Mr. David Martin and Mrs. Linda Braun, who made it work with the children. Therefore, claiming whatever squatter's rights may apply here, I will give the illustration its full context.

The youngsters were, once again, in pursuit of understanding the Netsilik. As reported:

> In the films, a single nuclear family, Zachary, Marta, and their four year old Alexei, is followed through the year—spring sealing, summer fishing at the stone weir, fall caribou hunting, early winter fishing through the ice, winter at the big ceremonial igloo. The children report that at first the three members of the family look weird and uncouth. In time, they look normal, and eventually, as when Marta finds sticks around which to wrap her braids, the girls speak of how pretty she is. That much is superficial—or so it seems (14, p. 14).

"But consider a second episode," says Bruner, and uses the illustration quoted above. A good deal had transpired between the superficial and the profound in this class. In fact, the children had been growing increasingly restive and unreachable as they were shown the films of spring sealing, summer fishing at the stone weir, and fall caribou hunting. Moreover, they had begun to develop attitudes toward the Netsilik which were the opposite of those the course was designed to instill. The Netsilik were coming to be seen alternately as savages with no hearts (and therefore too disagreeable to comprehend) and just one more distant society of which it can be said that "they have their customs, and we have ours" (thus, too trivial to comprehend). In other words, instead of cultivating deepened awareness of the humanizing forces at work in all human societies, we were dangerously close to teaching generalized attitudes of prejudice and apathy. Mr. Martin sought out a consultant to talk over what might be done to remedy the situation.

Was this behavior typical of the children? "No," they

were 'Newton children.'" What, then, did he sense the trouble to be? "The films!" . . . "The kids have had a daily diet of blood and cruelty, and the eating of fish eyes. I think they just want to holler 'Ouch.'" Why not let them? "I'm not sure I know how. . . . Besides, they're supposed to be thinking of Arctic ecology, and the advantages of social organization, division of labor, and so forth."

That very morning Mr. Martin had shown the film of the fall caribou hunt. It superbly depicts the advantages that accrue to the Netsilik as a consequence of social organization and division of labor in hunting the much needed caribou. The film opens with scenes of one group of hunters decoying two caribou into the water, where caribou are at great disadvantage. Further out at bay two other hunters are waiting in their Kayaks. Under these circumstances the caribou are clearly no match for the hunters. The hunters, just as obviously, do not press their luck. They do press the feelings of the viewer, however. If ever there was an unfair contest it is this! With red blood, drooping heads, and begging brown eyes to accentuate whatever experiences with unfair contests the viewer may be bringing to these scenes. Clearly, a couple of caribou must inevitably give themselves over to a couple of socially organized Homo Sapiens capable of dividing their labors! But, shades of Miss Greenfield, who would see this, unaided?

The children, as their teacher well knew, had every cause to be "restive." But why "unreachable?" What did Mr. Martin think? "I think they need to vent some steam before they can appreciate the points about social organization and division of labor." Why not let them, then? "How?"

We should first appreciate Mr. Martin's style of conducting a class. He is always very calmly on the move.

Within any span of five minutes, every child has tangibly felt his presence—the brush of a trouser leg, the tap of a finger, a palm on shoulder, or, when necessary, the firm grip of his eyes. All very soothing to the children. It says to them: there is little danger in this class of anyone getting out of control, so you can think as you wish. In this atmosphere the first signs of boisterousness in response to the films had merely required "None of that!", and emotional control held sway. This was inhibitory control, however, and Mr. Martin was now concerned that it was being carried too far. How to help the children to replace their *inhibitory* emotional skills with *regulative* emotional skills?

The following plan was devised: a short lesson on language would first be given in which the children would distinguish "instruction" messages from "feeling" messages. The teacher would then confront the children with a mock dilemma: someone had put it to him the day before that the Netsilik were, in fact, not human beings at all, but some other species! How would the class instruct him to answer that person? Then, assuming the children to be on the side of Netsilik humanness, they would be given an opportunity to share the feelings they had until now inhibited in respect to some of the more repellent aspects of Netsilik behavior. The children would then be given an opportunity to *use* these feelings by trying to empathize with Alexei in what was known to be the most repellent scene in the Netsilik footage: the stoning of the seagull. Finally, they would be shown a film of Netsilik children at more familiar kinds of play, and asked to contrast it with the seagull sequence.

Mr. Martin had one major obstacle to overcome before proceeding with the plan. To a man, his supporting staff of evaluators and researchers were opposed to it: the seagull sequence *was* inhuman and should be excluded from the curriculum. It would "push the kids too far"; the films they had seen already were "a bit much"; this one would surely convince them the Netsilik were not human! One lady threatened not to attend the class if Mr. Martin persisted in this "abusive" plan.

The children's responses are worth reporting in detail: (after the lesson on "instruction" and "feeling" messages)

Teacher: "Why is it good to be able to send 'instruction' messages?"
Student: "For planning."
Student: "The future."
Student: "The world wouldn't be right—parents wouldn't be able to tell children what to do."
Student: "For driving, like: 'Slow down here' etc."
Teacher: "Why is it good to be able to express feelings?"
Student: "If you're mad at someone you have it out with them."
Student: "It's nice to say when you're happy."
Student: "It feels good for *you* to say when you're mad."
Student: "Maybe you want to kill someone for playing badly in a game. If you say so, you're less likely to act violently."

Teacher: "Yesterday someone came up to me and said that these Netsilik were not human beings at all. I wasn't sure what to say to him. Can you tell me what to say?"
(A chorus of excitedly waving hands)
Student: "They look like us."
Student: "They have the same bone structure."
Student: "They don't look like animals."
Student: "You could test their temperature to see if it's the same."
Student: "They have spears."
Student: "They build homes."
Student: "They make clothes."
Student: "They use their brains. Animals have instincts."

Student: "They speak a language without using other parts of their bodies."

Student: "They can be killed . . . by a walrus."

Teacher: "Now I want you to write in your notebooks some things you've seen the Netsilik do that you found difficult to understand, or that *you* could never do."

EXAMPLES

"Clean a fish and get so bloody."

"Eat seal raw."

"Eat blood."

"Eat eyes."

"Why the Netsilik don't multiply more."

"How they can be so heartless?"

"Cut a seal open."

"How could they eat fish eyes? I know I would never eat a fish eye, or drink blood soup, or eat seal meat raw, or skin the seal the way they do. I would help skin one, but I would never do one myself."

"Spear caribou, when they can't fight back."

Teacher: "Now we're going to see two films of Netsilik children playing. The second one will be familiar to you, the kinds of play you engage in. The first film will be difficult to understand. So I want you to pay close attention in the first film to how the boy is *feeling* and how his mother is *feeling.*"

FROM NOTEBOOKS:

1) "I think the boy felt happy because in the film he seemed so happy when he killed it."

2) "I don't think the boy had any trouble killing the bird because he wants to be like his father, so he had to kill the bird. The mother was very happy and proud

because she saw that her son would not have any problem in killing something to eat. The way she smiled at him, as if she were saying 'Good work, son.' "

3) "I thought the boy had no feelings because he let the bird suffer. I think if he was going to be killed, they should kill him with a knife. I think the mother felt sorry because she was looking kind of sad when the boy was killing the bird."

4) "I think the boy was happy because it was sort of like a game to him and he was smiling as though it was fun. I thought the mother was glad they had the bird because she picked up the boy and swung him around and she acted as though she needed the food."

5) "I think the mother was happy for the son the way she kissed him."

6) "He felt proud of himself because he was killing the bird. She felt proud of her son because he was killing the bird and would soon be a fine hunter."

7) "I think the boy felt glad that he could really be like his father to kill a bird and then a seal. The mother, I think, felt proud of her little boy and that he was doing a good job of killing him."

8) "The boy felt happy and proud because that was probably the first he had killed. The mother was kind of sad to see the bird being crucified and struggling."

9) "I think the boy enjoyed killing the bird because he didn't cry about it and he looked happy. I think he liked playing with the legs because they were like toys. The mother was happy because she had some food for the family. She hugged her son when he brought her the bird. I felt sorry for the bird because it was suffering, but happy for the boy."

10) "He must have felt very happy because that might have been the first animal he caught, and the way the mother hugged the boy showed she must have been proud of him for the good work he did. I felt like I was

standing on my head. I felt awful because I was sad for the bird."

After the second film, a discussion followed:

Jerry: "I killed a bird once myself."

Billy: "Yeah, I was with him and it took us quite a while but we finally did it."

Emily: "I felt awful sorry for the bird in the film."

Elaine: "But we kill animals too, for meat, and nobody seems to mind."

Richard: "Yeah, how about slaughter houses and all those cows?"

Pat: "The Eskimo children seem to be loving children in the second film, especially the girl holding the dog."

Richard: "They were playing house in that film."

Audrey: "The first film showed a boy practicing to be a hunter, but the second one showed some children just playing."

Emily: "In the first film it seemed to me the boy was being sort of mean, but in the second film they were being very nice."

Jerry: "Don't forget they have to kill to live, though."

John: "Yeah, and in the second film they're not having to kill anything."

Jean: "We are all civilized in different ways."

Ellen: "Yes, but some of you kids are looking at these Eskimos from the way *you* see things, and not the way *they* see them."

It was in the course of this discussion that "Kathy" and "Jennine" engaged in the interchange cited earlier.

Let us take another example. Bruner begins his description of "Man: A Course of Study" with these inviting phrases:

. . . It is only in a trivial sense that one gives a course to "get something across," merely to impart information.

> There are better means to that end than teaching. Unless
> the learner also masters himself, disciplines his tastes, deep-
> ens his views of the world, the "something" that is got
> across is hardly worth the effort of transmission (11, p. 73).

There follows, eloquently, a description of the content
of the course, and of the materials that will carry this
content. As to pedagogy, we hear of the powers of the
contrast case, the benefits of "informed guessing," the
values of student participation and the advantages of stimulating "self-consciousness about thinking." A generation
of teachers has come to call the aggregate of these the
"self-discovery method,"—wherein one can sometimes observe the self, discovering, all right, but rarely the discovering of self.

What must the teacher conclude who was initially
led to expect guidance in teaching the course in such ways
as would help the student "master himself, discipline his
tastes, and deepen his views of the world?" Either that
Bruner said it and she didn't get it, and so it must be
beyond her. Or that since he refers exclusively to the
cognitive self, to *rational* tastes, and to *intellectual* views
of the world, he must mean that the emotional and evalu-
ative aspects of these processes will somehow take care of
themselves. Thus, the counter-reformational suggestion:
Do as always, only more so.

For calling Bruner on this way he has of sometimes
leading teachers up the more heady reaches of familiar
paths, John Holt got called a romancer of "no-think
thinking." Gordon Allport, who once called Bruner a
rationalist, was let off more easily—his being presumed to
be a case of preoccupation with an "appearance." With
some trepidation, therefore, I shall contend that Bruner's
impact on teachers has been that of a rationalist.

His over-emphasis on cognitive skills and curricular materials, and his corresponding under-emphasis on emotional skills and pedagogy have been generally illustrated in the foregoing accounts. Before going more specifically into these, I should like to bring attention to two other general imbalances in his writings on education. The first pertains to a preoccupation with that aggregate of human motives which have been variously termed "autonomous," "aggressive," "agentic," etc., to the seeming exclusion of another aggregate of human motives which various of our colleagues have termed "homonomous," "libidinal," "communal," etc. The second imbalance pertains to a preoccupation with the processes of "concept attainment," or discovery; to the seeming exclusion of the processes of "concept formation," or invention.

Neither form of exclusivism reflects deliberate choice. Doubtless they reflect the shape of one man's curiosity. As such, they would merit the respect of silence, were it not that the sweep of Bruner's pen sometimes conjures other shapes.

Intrinsic motivation is a more durable aid to learning than extrinsic motivation, says Bruner. Teachers should therefore wean the child whenever possible from a system of extrinsic rewards and punishments to a system of self-reward. In itself, this point is very well taken. Also emphasized is that Man's use of mind is dependent upon his ability to develop and use tools, instruments, and technologies. The main emphasis in education should therefore be placed upon skills—"skills in handling, in seeing and imaging, and in symbolic operations, particularly as these relate to the technologies that have made them so powerful in their human expression" (11, p. 34). These points are also, in themselves, well taken. In presenting "Man: A Course of Study" he has it that technology, social organization, language, education, and cosmology are the five great humanizing forces in that they amplify the human animal's powers and enable him to extend dominion over his environment.

> Man gains better technical control of his world through modern science than he does through mythic explanation; but in science and in myth, the same component processes or logical operations provide the base. It is in this sense that we try to make clear that man is equally human whether he uses a stone ax or a steel one, explains eclipses by astronomy or by spirits, murders with a gun or by the use of magic" (11, p. 88).

Again, very well taken.

But one looks in vain for the needed counterpoints. Teachers and children mean more to each other than can be expressed by reference to reward systems—self—or otherwise. Man's use of mind is certainly amplified by his tools and technologies, but so is his use of heart. People make myths and scientific theories, not only the better to explain their lives, but also the better to share them.

The situation recalls the need that Andras Angyal felt to rectify a common oversight regarding his original views on human motivation. Freud had reduced this subject to the aggressive and sexual drives. Harry Stack Sullivan had condensed the neo-Freudian dilutions of these into the *needs* for security and satisfaction. Robert White was yet to advance his distinction between effectance and libidinal *motives*. Meanwhile Angyal sought to skirt the controversy by viewing behavior in more general terms. He observed that all human acts seemed ultimately to be organized around two *trends*: the trend to master and the trend to belong. He spoke of these as the trends toward "autonomy" and "homonomy" respectively. Twenty years later he felt compelled to reinforce his formulations of homonomy, because a generation of psychologists had insisted on giving it short weight in their interpretations of his theory:

> Human behavior cannot be understood solely as a manifestation of the trend toward autonomy. Seen from another angle, human life reveals a basic pattern very different from self-assertiveness, from striving for freedom and mastery. A person behaves as if he were seeking a place for himself in a larger unit of which he strives to become a part. In the first orientation he is struggling for centrality in his world, trying to mold and organize objects and events, to bring them under his own control. In the second orientation he seems rather to strive to surrender himself and to become an organic part of something that he conceives as greater than himself. Processes concerned with procreation are evidence that even at the physiological-biological level the individual is integrated into super-individual units. At the cultural level, the person's conception of the larger unit to which he belongs, or to which he strives to belong, varies according to his cultural background and personal orientation. The super-ordinate whole may be represented for him by a social unit—family, clan, nation—by an ideology, or a meaningfully ordered universe. The objective existence of such super-individual wholes is a metaphysical question with which the empirical scientist need not be concerned. For the student of personality, the important fact is that the trend toward homonomy, the wish to be in harmony with the unit one regards as extending beyond his individual self, is a powerful motivating source of behavior. . . . Still, the tendency persists among theorists to view the second trend as less basic, as perhaps derived from the first in some circuitous way, or as being of lesser importance. I have been

asked by people who have discussed my concepts with me
whether I would not agree that autonomy was more important than homonomy. I am certain that the second trend is
quite as basic as the first. I do not consider it a super-struc-
ture, a luxury which comes only after all other needs have
been fulfilled. It is just as much a part of human existence
as the autonomous trend, at least in a fully functioning
human being. To ask which is more important makes no
more sense than asking whether hands or feet are more
important. From a psychiatric point of view, the second
trend is, if anything, more crucial, because if things go
wrong in our lives, we have more trouble in that area than
in any other. (4, pp. 15–16)

"I shall take the view," says Bruner, in his "The Course
of Cognitive Growth,"

. . . that the development of human intellectual functioning from infancy to such perfection as it may reach is shaped
by a series of technological advances in the use of mind.
Growth depends upon the mastery of techniques and cannot be understood without reference to such mastery. These
techniques are not, in the main, inventions of the individuals who are 'growing up'; they are, rather, skills transmitted
with varying efficiency and success by the culture—language
being a prime example. Cognitive growth, then, is in a
major way from the outside in as well as from the inside out.
(13, p. 124)

He does say "as well as," but one hears no more of the
"inside out!"

Let us turn to Bruner's special interest in the processes
of discovery and his inattention to the processes of invention. I was first made aware of this at a time when it

could best be attributed to the necessary constraints of research, and thought of no more. Neither Bruner nor I were then actively concerned with education. He had just published "A Study of Thinking" (20); and I, a series of articles on the thought mechanism of negation (40, 41, 42). I read his book with much interest, being especially struck by one finding:

> We know from careful studies of Hovland and Weiss, and from our own investigations of conjunctive categorizing, that subjects seemed not as willing or able to use negative information—instances telling what the concept is not—in the process of attaining a concept . . . (the negative instance) is not preferred, perhaps simply because it gives indirect information, perhaps for other reasons. (20, p. 180)

My initial reaction to this finding was one of surprise, as my own investigations had shown the thought mechanism of negation to be singularly useful in availing subjects of normally inhibited thought content, and one which they seemed almost grateful to have suggested to them by the experimenter's instructions (what is *not* going on in this picture, what could *never* be true of this or that, what is the furthest from a correct solution to Task X, etc.). I had summarized these findings as follows:

> "Under the influence of negation instruction, the content of subjects' responses, whether in projective test situations, or in interview behavior, or in the performance of cognitive tasks, is consistently less 'censored'—or more imaginative—depending on how we choose to appraise it." (42, p. 179)

The apparent contradiction between the two sets of findings was dispelled, however, by a closer look at the kinds of cognitive tasks Bruner and I were putting to our respective subjects. Bruner was putting tasks requiring engagement in concept-attaining cognition, a kind of categorizing which involves "a search for and testing of attributes that can be used to distinguish exemplars from nonexemplars of various categories, the search for good and valid anticipatory cues" (20, p. 233). In reference to processes whereby the subjects create fictive categories—classes of objects that have not been encountered or are clearly of a nature contrary to expectancy—Bruner coined the term "empty category," seeing it as "a way of going beyond the range of events one encounters to the sphere of the possible . . . or of the uncanny . . . the currency of art, fantasy, and dream; perhaps . . . the vehicle for exploring the ambiguous interstices of experience" (20, p. 237). Subjects who had been instructed to perform concept-attainment tasks tended to avoid this "empty" category.

> In general, it is as if information that results from "in-the-head" transformations is distrusted perhaps through an appreciation of the possibility of the errors one can make in such transformations." (20, p. 237)

I, on the other hand, was putting tasks requiring concept *forming* cognition, the creation of just such fictive categories or classes of objects that had not been encountered, or were clearly of a nature contrary to expectancy. In the performance of such tasks, the subjects characteristically found the thought mechanism of negation a singularly productive way of going beyond the range of their everyday experience. In retrospective support of Bruner's findings I had noted that subjects seemed loathe to employ the thought mechanism of negation until after they had had an opportunity to affirm the probable. In short, it appeared that negation was an aid to divergent thinking and a disruptive influence on convergent thinking. Consideration of the two sets of findings led to speculation that:

> . . . the consciously ideating ego is not prepared to afford disconfirming information, stemming from objective sources, the same strategic reception it is prepared to afford disbelieved information, stemming from subjective sources. From this point of view it might be that "in the head" transformations are not so much distrusted, on logical grounds, in the process of attaining concepts; as they are disruptive, on psychological grounds, in the dove-tailing process of forming concepts. Presumably it is the inventive act of forming concepts . . . that requires access to imaginal cues; and negation, not the negative instance, is presumably a key to such access. (42, p. 207)

I concluded that:

> . . . the cognitive mode of negation does for subjective thinking what rootedness in perceptual cues does for objective thinking: it binds the unconscious. The principle suggested by Bruner's work adds to this that negation and affirmation have specific instrumental roles in concept formation and concept attainment, respectively; and that the overall cognitive process will not casually submit to other arrangements. (42, p. 208)

So here we are, Bruner and I, still pushing what seem to be our favorite cognitive processes: the *attainment* of *probable* concepts, and the *formation* of *possible* concepts, respectively.

Let us focus more sharply on Bruner's more specific offerings: In fitting the findings of cognitive psychology for service in a theory of instruction, he begins with a list of six "benchmarks" about the nature of intellectual growth:

1) Growth is characterized by increasing independence of response from the immediate nature of the stimulus.
2) Growth depends upon internalizing events into a "storage system" that corresponds to the environment.
3) Intellectual growth involves an increasing capacity to say to oneself and others, by means of words or symbols, what one has done or what one will do.
4) Intellectual development depends upon a systematic interaction between a tutor and a learner, the tutor already being equipped with a wide range of previously invented techniques that he teaches the child.
5) Teaching is vastly facilitated by the medium of language, which ends by being not only the medium for exchange but the instrument that the learner can then use himself in bringing order into the environment.
6) Intellectual development is marked by increasing capacity to deal with several alternatives simultaneously, to attend to several sequences during the same period of time, and to allocate time and attention in a manner appropriate to these multiple demands. (11, pp. 5–6)

Note, first, the exclusive attention given to extrapsychic stimuli; the equating of symbolism with verbalism; the preoccupation with representational knowledge; and the oversight of *pre*sentational knowledge.

Of the "increasing independence of response from the immediate nature of the stimulus," he elaborates: "[The child] gains his freedom from stimulus control through mediating processes . . . that transform the stimulus prior to response" (11, p. 5). I thought, when I first read this, that it referred to man's distinctive predisposition to symbolize his experience. There was even hope of finding reference to such precise laboratory studies in cognitive psychology as those of George Klein and his associates, who are tracing some of the ways we transform both extrapsychic and intrapsychic stimuli, both in and out of the waking state, prior to and independently of responses to stimuli. Instead, one finds this qualifying statement:

> "A great deal of growth consists of the child's being able to maintain an invariant response in the face of changing states of the stimulating environment or learning to alter his response to the presence of an unchanging stimulus environment." (11, p. 5)

Indeed, a great deal of growth does consist of such mediating processes. We call these the processes of *adjustment*. They are essential to, but far from identical with, the processes of human learning—and hardly the best rallying point for prescribing new instructional possibilities.

As for growth depending "upon internalizing events into a 'storage system' that *corresponds to the environment*," the italics, which have been supplied here, suffice to reveal once again an acceptance of the limitations of an adjustment psychology. That we need not accept these limitations has been shown by a range of experiments from those of Silberer (77) through those of Klein (51) to those of Shevrin and Luborsky (75), all of which make it clear that we humans not only "store" our environments, but constantly, incessantly—often needlessly—*re*store them (39).

Again, yes, "intellectual growth involves an increasing

capacity to say to oneself and others, by means of words or symbols, what one has done or what one will do." But it would have been well to add that some of man's most distinctively human moments involve the capacity to express to himself and others what he has not done, or may never do, all the while he goes on dreaming. And I wish some way had been found to indicate that symbols are not synonymous with words. Words may be our most advanced symbols but we know how empty they can become when cut off from their non-verbal roots, i.e., from access to their pictorial, imaginal, metaphorical nutrients (see Chapter Nine). Aldous Huxley makes these points as follows:

> It is a matter of observable fact that all of us inhabit a world of phantasy as well as a world of first-order experience and a world of words and concepts. In most children and in some adults this world of phantasy is astonishingly vivid. . . . For them the world presented to their consciousness by their story-telling, image-making phantasy is as real as, sometimes more real than, the given world of sense impressions and the projected world of words and explanatory concepts. (35, p. 56)

> Children should be taught that words are indispensable but also can be fatal—the only begetters of all civilization, all science, all consistency of high purpose, all angelic goodness, and the only begetters at the same time of all superstition, all collective madness and stupidity, all worse-than-bestial diabolism, all the dismal historical succession of crimes in the name of God, King, Nation, Party, Dogma. Never before, thanks to the techniques of mass communication, have so many listeners been so completely at the mercy of so few speakers. (35, p. 48)

Increasing numbers of educated youths are making the same points on their "acid trips."

As for intellectual development depending "upon a systematic and contingent interaction between a tutor and a learner," this smacks of breathless understatement until it again becomes clear that Bruner is content to consider only the *transmitting* aspects of this interaction, "the tutor already being equipped with a wide range of previously invented techniques that he teaches the child" (11, p. 6). Admittedly, some of the early progressivists went too far in attending to the receiving aspects of the instructional process—to the point where some of them were heard to boast that they no longer taught subjects, only children—but the corrective will not be found in the other extreme. Rather, let the teacher, being equipped with her society's range of previously invented techniques and with expert knowledge and methods pertaining to their transmission, also be equipped with expert knowledge and methods pertaining to the inevitably transformative nature of the children's reception systems.

Similarly, there is no question that over the course of human growth language comes to serve as both a medium of exchange and an instrument for bringing order into the environment. But let us keep the full view. This is conveyed in a statement by George Klein, which he made in summarizing the implications of some of his studies of nonverbal, prerationative symbolic processes:

In considering the kinds of transformations to which incidental registrations are subject in the "waking state" and the vicissitudes of awareness from one state of consciousness to another, we touch upon matters that concern inventive and creative thinking. Someone's observation that to create a new order you have to destroy a familiar one seems to me a good characterization of inventive and creative thought. Awareness in the ordinary workday paradoxically serves an efficient and sensitizing and yet blinding function. Were this not so, our lives would have little stability. For the most part, conceptual contact with the objects, places and events we encounter takes place at the lowest common denominator of identity. The conceptual schema which dominate cognition in our jobs, our relationships with others, our encounters with objects have a proven utility; we therefore have a stake in them and we prefer to cling to them— as a principle of efficiency and economy. The thought forms dominating awareness provide us, at the least, with a relatively unchanging and *persisting* world of things—an unchanging background for the effective *control* of things. But the reality-adaptive schema which ordinarily guide awareness can well hinder sensitivity to an "unfamiliar" form and to transformed ideas, by the very fact that their main function is not to promote discovery but to buttress predictability—to provide insurance against the irregular and the unfamiliar. (51, p. 174)

The nature of transformational symbolization and an understanding of the conditions which support its effective integration with representational symbolization must be part of any comprehensive theory of instruction.

Finally, as regards increasing capacity to deal simultaneously with multiple alternatives, Bruner remarks on the great distance between "the one track mind of the young child and the ten-year-old's ability to deal with an extraordinarily complex world" (11, p. 6). He means, of course, the extraordinarily complex *outside* world. We need not detract from the relevance of these observations if we also note, with Lawrence Kubie (56), Ernest Schactel (73) and others, the price that most pedagogical systems exact of children for help in developing this ability to meet multiple demands. It is the price of often forfeiting the ability to make as well as to meet multiple demands, of squaring off and conventionalizing the extraordinary complexities of one's *inner* world.

Bruner may fairly object that the statements chosen here for quotation and criticism were intended by him for psychologists, whose appreciation of their limitations could be taken for granted. My reply is that for every psychologist who reads "Toward a Theory of Instruction" a hundred teachers will not only read it but will try to apply it. Let it be brought to the notice of these teachers, then, that Bruner's is the psychology of alloplastic development, of the forms in which knowledge can best be brought into the human mind and the forms in which it can best be put out again, and of the processes by which we learn to *re*present recurrent regularities in our environments. For a psychology of autoplastic development, of the transformations which take place between intake and output, of the processes by which we *pre*sent irregularities and thereby introduce novelties into our environments, the teacher must look elsewhere. The writings on education of Lawrence Kubie (54, 55, 56), Howard Gruber (32), Ernest Schactel (73), Ulric Neisser (66), Aldous Huxley (35), Paul Goodman (31), Barbara Biber (6, 7), Edith Weisskopf (83), Abraham Maslow (61, 62, 63), Edward Tauber (79), Maurice Green (79), Calvin Taylor (80), Frank Barron (5), and Gordon Allport (3) will do for a start. And let us not altogether forget Alfred North Whitehead (88).

Would that these diverse views, and the observations on which they are based, could be set down in some unified and consistent form, ready for inclusion in a comprehensive theory of instruction. Perhaps, though, it is better that this is not now possible, as such a statement would, at present, probably be as exclusivistic in its own way as the one we have been holding to scrutiny.

In anticipation of a theory of instructed learning that will ultimately coordinate these two psychologies, I want now to take up in some detail the tentative "theorems toward a theory of instruction" which Bruner has advanced, in the hope of underscoring those points at which fruitful coupling of the two psychologies may in future prove feasible. Let me say at the outset that I am aware how much easier it is to qualify another man's theorems than to state a set of one's own, and I am accordingly grateful to my friend for supplying the initiative which makes the following exercise possible.

"A theory of instruction," says Bruner, "is *prescriptive* in the sense that it sets forth rules concerning the most effective way of achieving knowledge or skill. By the same token, it provides a yardstick for criticizing or evaluating any particular way of teaching or learning" (11, p. 40). The prescriptive posture of a theory of instruction does have the decided advantage over the descriptive posture of traditional learning theory in that it squarely faces the unrealism of the "random encounter assumption," as has been noted. There is, however, a disadvantage in the prescriptive posture, which we should not overlook. It implies an image of professional instruction as an applied art or craft. This, of course, is what professional instruction is, but, in our time, the view carries perjorative connotations of impersonality and mechanization. This does nothing to win the confidence of teachers. We may object that the mechanization of teaching is not among the aims that prompt us to formulate a theory of instruction. Nevertheless, we should bear in mind that the prescriptive posture had its origin in modern efforts at curriculum reform, and that the term "teacher-proof" did creep into the early shop-talk of such projects, and remains with us if only as a reminder of past mistakes. Perhaps we should learn from this that it is insufficient to disclaim intentions to exclude teachers from the work of curriculum revision if nothing is done to include them. Admittedly, these reservations apply not to the theory as such but to liaison problems in necessary fields of observation. Such problems can affect methods, however, and methods, we know, can shape theories.

Bruner states:

"A theory of instruction is a *normative* theory. It sets up criteria and states the conditions for meeting them. The criteria must have a high degree of generality . . ." (i.e., it should not be related to the achievement of particular end results [11, p. 40]).

I would add that one of these sets of generalities might well concern itself with how, in fact, the other sets of generalities become actualized in various instructional settings by various instructors. We have rather good anthropologies of mental hospitals, prisons, and industries, but to my knowledge we do not have a decent anthopological study of the classroom. Perhaps this is because in the training of teachers we discourage the research attitude. In any event, we are a long way from enjoying the situation of the physicist and the engineer, in which each is equipped to take up where the other has left off by virtue of a modicum of common training. Unless the backgrounds of teachers and educational psychologists come to include some such common ground, it is unlikely that we shall see the development of the independent form of research

activity which is necessary for the development of a normative theory of instruction. As things stand, psychologists
will continue to work in the hothouses of experimental
education while teachers work the vineyards. This is a
situation calculated to substitute the *improbable* encounter
for the random encounter as the observational base of
our theory of instruction.

A theory of instruction, says Bruner, should be con-
structed around four problems: (1) the factors that predispose a child to learn effectively; (2) the optimum
structuring of knowledge; (3) the optimal sequence that
is required for learning; and (4) the nature and pacing of
rewards and punishments, successes and failures.

As regards the factors that predispose a child to learn
effectively, Bruner chooses to focus attention on the
activation, maintenance, and direction of predispositions
to explore alternatives. Exploration of alternatives, he says,
is furthered by the presence of an "optimal level of uncertainty" (that is, neither routine nor too confusing), by
the benefits exceeding the risks involved, and by indications
that tested alternatives are relevant to achievement of a
goal. A course of instructed learning should make it more
likely that these factors be operative than were the child
to be working on his own. Throughout, the focus is on
the *objective* dimensions of these factors: an optimal level
of uncertainty about a curricular problem, the risk of
obtaining a wrong solution to a curricular problem, the
relevance of tested alternatives to the goal of correctly
solving a curricular problem. When working with children
who are ready and able to be this objective in their schoolwork, the teacher can do no better than to try to follow
these prescriptions. However, it is a fact of a teacher's work
life—especially the elementary teacher—that she must devote most of her attention to those *subjective* factors which

often present both obstacles to and detours toward objectivity.

In suggesting that subjective uncertainties, subjective risks, and subjective goals also be systematically considered in a theory of instruction, I trust I shall not be accused of favoring a return to "the friendly postman." It can only seem so if we confuse those aspects of instructional theory which are of primary concern to curriculum designers with those aspects of instructional theory which are of primary concern to the teachers. As has already been said, the designers of curricula should see to it that the children are confronted with queries and materials which are at once significant, credible and relevant—ready or not. Unless the curriculum maker succeeds in this, there is little for the teacher to do beyond "managing" the class. It is the teacher's responsibility, and this in rather precise proportion to the quality and power of the curriculum, to make the children ready for it. This is, I believe, what we refer to when we speak of the *art* of teaching—what Whitehead, in an earlier time, referred to as its romance and rhythm. I submit that the prime media of this art are no less than the subjective uncertainties, the subjective risks, and the subjective goals which the children can be expected to bring in bewilderingly individual ways to any good curriculum about which they are not yet ready to be objective.

Let me be specific: it is, of course, necessary to know what may be objectively risky to a child as he sets himself to exploring alternative solutions to this or that problem, so that we may help him to assume the risks that pay off, either in the form of rewarding solutions or in the form of informative errors, and to avoid those that attend wasteful random efforts. This, however, is not sufficient for effective instruction. It is also important to know what the *child* perceives to be risky, i.e., what he sees as the

possibilities of being alone and/or helpless with his imagination. *Not*, let us recall, in order to help him avoid all
such possibilities, but, on the contrary to help him to
assume those of his subjective risks which promise a
payoff in creative learning.

I am reminded of an interview I once had with a
twinkle-eyed youngster, let us call her Charlotte, who had
been helping us to test some materials designed by Professor Robert Adams of the University of Chicago for a
fifth-grade unit on the origins of urbanization. Many of
the artifacts were replicas of objects excavated from burial
sites in Nippur by Adams himself. Charlotte and I spent
some ten minutes discussing Abraham Lincoln's eyelash.
She had been much taken by the discovery that most of
what we know of "olden times" was based on the digging
up of old graveyards. And the two of us had been speculating on the differences between old-fashioned graveyards
and modern graveyards. Abruptly, she was reminded of a
story she had read in the third grade. It included a reference to Lincoln's eyelash, supposedly found during the
exhuming of his remains for reburial. She had asked the
teacher if she might skip that story in future because it
frightened her (but she remembered it two years later,
and was telling it to me with relish!). What had frightened
her about the story? Well, the eyelash. What could it
have meant? Well, was Lincoln like Jesus? Had he, too,
risen from the dead; or had the doctor made a mistake
and pronounced him dead before he really was? And how
long could an eyelash last under the ground? And how
could the person who discovered it have been sure it was
Lincoln's eyelash and not someone else's? Anyhow, it was
all pretty scary and she had been grateful not to have
to read the story again.

I was struck by the formal similarities between her

questions and the kinds of questions that Adams must ask of the things *he* finds in graveyards. The point I wish to stress, however, is that Charlotte had been confronted with powerful and significant curricular materials for which she was ideally unready at objective levels. Her responses to these materials, it seemed to me, included some optimal levels of uncertainty, some promising risks, and some worthy goals—all, however, of a decidedly subjective nature. Were these to be viewed as obstacles to objective mastery of the subject, and thus to be avoided? Or were they indices of progress toward creative mastery of the methods and principles of archaeology, and thus to be cultivated? These are moot questions in the case of Charlotte, who was teaching us, and not we her. But they are the kinds of questions with which a theory of instruction should be able to cope. Perhaps not so urgently in respect to mathematics and the physical sciences, where starkly subjective responses are less likely to be immediately useful in assimilating subject matters, but surely quite urgently as regards the humanities and social sciences, where the subject matters are so inherently close to the intimate inner concerns of the children themselves.

Turning to the structure of knowledge, and sequences of learning, Bruner begins with Turing's theorem: any problem that can be solved can be solved by simpler means—from which he derived the rallying cry of the new curricula: ". . . any subject can be taught to anybody at any age in some form that is honest." He proceeds to emphasize that knowledge about anything can be represented in three ways, three parallel systems of processing information—the "enactive" system, in which information is processed by acting on it; the "iconic" system, in which information is processed by perceptualizing it; and the "ratiocinative" system, in which information is processed in terms of a set of verbal-symbolic or logical propositions governed strictly by laws of formation, transformation, induction, and implication.

> What comes out of this picture . . . is a view of human beings who have developed three parallel systems for processing information and for representing it—one through manipulation and action, one through perceptual organization and imagery, and one through the symbolic apparatus. It is not that these are "stages" in any sense, but rather emphases in development: that one in some measure must master the manipulation of concrete objects before there can be perceptual decentration, or in simple terms, that you must get the perceptual field organized around your own person as center before you can impose other, less egocentric axes upon it, and so on. In the end the mature organism seems to have gone through a process of elaborating three systems of skills that correspond to the three major tool systems to which he must link himself for full expression of capacities—tools for the hand, for the distance receptors, and for the process of reflection. (12, pp. 34–35)

It will be recognized that this is the systematic core of Bruner's contribution to the new educational psychology. A profound contribution it is, and one that is presently both little understood and not very readily understandable. This, out of considerations which should embarrass no one. Piaget's investigations of children's learning and thinking processes, upon which these formulations were based, are exceedingly complex; moreover, they translate very murkily into English (despite what can only be called the heroic efforts of John Flavell, of the University of Minnesota) (29). If anyone is equipped to apply Piagetian psychology to pedagogy it is Jerome Bruner.

I am sure, however, that his would be the loudest voice in warning that the application has just barely begun, and that by far the largest part of the effort remains ahead of us.

For my part, I want only to emphasize that the overriding challenge brought to a theory of instruction by Piaget's findings is that of specifying *optimal orchestrations* of the three systems of representing knowledge. It is sometimes assumed, since Piaget's studies show learning to follow a *unilinear progression* from action through imagery to ratiocinative organization, that all effective learning follows a similar progression. It should be stressed that most of Piaget's observations have concentrated on the earliest and most rudimentary forms of adaptation in time and space. In respect to later forms of learning, it would seem more likely that the three systems of representing knowledge become involved in *multilinear configurations of progression and regression,* and that optimal orchestrations of the three systems will vary as a function—at least—of subject matter, degree and quality of previous experience with the subject matter, and individual style. For example, retrogression from ratiocinative to iconic representation may serve to obscure the subject matter at certain distances from closure, or within certain cognitive styles, while at other distances from closure or within other cognitive styles, the same retrogressive maneuver may serve to clarify. Billy's retrogressive shift from the ratiocinative "infinity" to the iconic "box of Cream of Wheat" was a potentially clarifying thought, but it is easy to conceive how at another time or in another context it could obscure.

Conversely, the assumption that the three systems are parallel, in the sense that each can be pursued without interfering with the others, may only hold after some threshold of learning has already been passed. At prior stages, relations of mutual refraction between the systems may be characteristic. We have often observed, for example, that premature verbalization can inhibit or even preclude iconic representation. On the other hand, it is sometimes striking how some children are best aroused to enactive and iconic involvements by the possession of as yet meaningless words for things.

In short, as we pursue questions of optimal orchestration in regard to the three systems, we will probably do well not to overgeneralize two assumptions: the *unilinearity assumption*, which may be specific to *early* stages of learning; and the *parallelism assumption*, which may be specific to *late* stages of learning.

One further thought concerning optimal orchestrations of the several systems of representing knowledge: It is in light of the recurrent controversy over whether or not teachers should include among their responsibilities both dispensation of knowledge and the cultivation of conviction that the differences between the problems of teaching the physical sciences and the problems of teaching the social sciences may take on proportions of a quantum leap in pedagogy. The enactive and iconic referents to which the symbols of the *physical sciences* apply are ultimately *objective* with respect to the child's ego. The enactive and iconic referents to which the symbols of the *social sciences* apply are ultimately *subjective* with respect to the child's ego. Ultimately, therefore, the grounding of these two branches of knowledge in the roots of childrens' self-interests may be seen to be qualitatively different. If so, it means that the roles of enactive and iconic skills will be different in the two instances, and therefore that the parameters of "success" and "failure" will also be different in the two instances. Success in the physical sciences is more likely to lead to experiences of discovery, and failure, to experiences of helplessness. In the social sciences success is more likely to lead in experiences of revelation, and failure, to experiences of isolation.

Pedagogy, across all subjects, has traditionally been oriented toward the discovery-helplessness axis, and it is for this reason that our attempts to introduce social science curricula into elementary education may be doubly revolutionary. For, the latter seek to introduce new substance, substance pertaining to the more valued interests of the self, and by that virtue they press for new methods, methods as pertinent to the values of the learner as to the value of what he learns.

Finally, we come to the matter of "reinforcement." "First distinguish two states," says Bruner,

> One is success and failure; the other one is reward and punishment. By success and failure, I mean the end state that is inherent in a task. The problem is solved or not solved or close to solved. By reward and punishment, I mean something quite different. It relates to the consequences that follow upon success and failure—prizes, scoldings, gold stars, etc.
>
> It is often the case that emphasis upon reward and punishment, under the control of an outside agent such as a teacher or parent, diverts attention away from success and failure. In effect, this may take the learning initiative away from the child and give it to the person dispensing the rewards and punishments. This will be the more likely if the learner is not able to determine the basis of success and failure. One of the great problems in teaching, which usually starts with the teacher being very supportive, is to give the rewarding function back to the learner and the task. (15, pp. 531–32)

As I understand the aim of these remarks, it is to include consideration of Robert White's theory of "effectance motivation" in the planning of pedagogical strategies, thus to bridge the gap that has too long existed between the psychologies of learning and motivation. (See Chapter Nine.) In the interest of achieving this aim, several qualifications seem to be in order: (1) The parameters of "success" and "failure"—as experienced by the child—may differ qualitatively, as has already been said, as a function of the proximity to the child's ego of the subject matter. (2) The same may be said, for related reasons, of "reward" and "punishment." Reduction of anxiety, for example, is often thought of as rewarding—at least by motivation theorists. It is readily conceivable, however, that one regularly *intrinsic* satisfaction to be derived from the study of man is reduction of anxiety. If anyone cares to object that the element of anxiety-reduction is, in this context, epiphenomenal, that the directly effective cause of the satisfaction is the achievement of insight or control or distance or what have you, then let him defend the position that an invariant sequence relates anxiety-reduction to any of these states. Furthermore, I suspect that on close inspection in classrooms it would be practically impossible to pry apart the extrinsic factors (the teacher's respectful acknowledgement, say, of a child's skepticism) from the intrinsic factors (the motives, whether "libidinal" or "effectance," which may have prompted the skepticism in the first place). (3) From the observation that need-reduction has borne too much of the weight of "motivating school children," and that "effectance" motives have been allowed too little of the weight, it hardly follows that correction lies in reversing the imbalance. White's citation of the precondition of effectance motivation—the relative quiescence of libidinal motives—attests to the intimate relation of these two components of human motivation. To overlook this relation in the teaching of the physical sciences is perhaps not too costly (although there is surely some price), but in the teaching of social studies, in which repeated stimulation of libidinal motives is inevitable, this relation may well prove to be crucial.

In other words, the terms intrinsic and extrinsic, as used by Bruner to modify informativeness and need-reduction in his laudable effort to tailor reinforcement theory to the needs of teachers may inject a false dichotomy into our considerations, which would bode ill for the coordination of our theory of instruction with White's theory of motivation. It seems more plausible that both informativeness and need-reduction have their respective intrinsic and extrinsic dimensions. Much more needs to be known about how people gain information, and about how people gain satisfaction, and of the intrinsic and extrinsic aspects of both processes, and of the interactions between, before we finally axiomize the functions served by success, reward, failure, and punishment, respectively.

A comprehensive understanding of pedagogical authority, for example, would certainly show that more than gold stars and pats on the back are available to teachers as expressions of reward. The answering of questions, the posing of new questions, silence, empathy, understanding, courtesy, good timing, discipline, good humor, bad humor —all, depending on context, may be experienced by the child as *extrinsic* rewards. All, however, are likewise conceivable, depending on context, as steps in a teacher's contribution to the gradual process of giving the rewarding function back to the learner and the task.

Therefore, in the interests of fully appreciating whatever dualities of function may be involved in all of this, I would advance the following as working leads: Success and failure are a function of informativeness; are pertinent to the short-range experience of discovery, and to the long-

range experience of competence—all of which figure prominently in the processes of accommodation, mastery, and
the *attainment* of concepts. Correspondingly, reward and
punishment are a function of need-reduction; are pertinent
to the short-range experience of revelation, and to the long-
range experience of self-confidence—all of which figure
prominently in the processes of assimilation, invention, and
the *formation* of concepts. Appreciated within this perspective, instructional research regarding reinforcement
functions is more likely to seek comprehension of inter-
actional processes than to delineate distinctions only.

   I shall conclude this critique with reference to the so-
called "Washburn hypothesis," since it has piqued the
thoughts on education of both Bruner and myself, but in
separate ways. On the occasion of the one hundredth anni-
versary of the publication of Darwin's *The Origin of
Species*, Washburn and Howell presented a paper at the
Chicago Centennial Celebration, which included the following passage:

> It would now appear . . . that the large size of the brain
> of certain hominids was a relatively late development and
> that the brain evolved due to new selection pressures *after*
> bipedalism and consequent upon the use of tools. The tool-
> using, ground living, hunting way of life created the large
> human brain rather than a large brained man discovering
> certain new ways of life. We believe this conclusion is the
> most important result of the recent fossil hominid discov-
> eries and is one which carries far-reaching implications for
> the interpretation of human behavior and its origins. . . .
> The uniqueness of modern man is seen as the result of a
> technical-social life which tripled the size of the brain, re-
> duced the face, and modified many other structures of the
> body. (13, pp. 124–25)

"This implies," says Bruner, "that the principle change in man over a long period of years—perhaps five hundred thousand—has been alloplastic rather than autoplastic. That is to say, he has changed by linking himself with new external implementation systems rather than by conspicuous change in morphology . . . " (13, p. 125).

Thus, Bruner concludes his definitive paper on "The Course of Cognitive Growth" with the following statement:

> What is significant about the growth of mind in the child is to what degree it depends not upon capacity but upon the unlocking of capacity by techniques that come from exposure to the specialized environment of a culture. (13, p. 153)

In his subsequent writings on education, Bruner has been consistent in reading as the implication of the "Washburn hypothesis" that we should seek to teach from the outside-in, to link children more effectively with their society's tool systems, via language skills, representational and diagrammatic skills, attention-saving skills and strain-reducing skills.

Without wishing to diminish acceptance of these prescriptions for the improvement of education, I should like to suggest that insofar as Bruner offers them in such ways as to exclude pedagogical innovations which seek to educate from the *inside-out*, via *nonverbal symbolic* skills, *presentational* skills, attention-*diverting* and strain-*producing* skills, he does so by himself overlooking the crucial difference between organic and cultural evolution. The morphological increase of brain size as a consequence of tool use was a process in *organic* evolution. As part of cultural evolution, however, tool-use ceases to be antecedent and primary and becomes *subsequent* and *auxiliary*. In cultural evolution, in other words, it is tools which are linked to man and not man to tools.

As an amateur anthropologist I remain as impressed as is Bruner with the discovery that it was not a large-brained hominid that developed human technical-social life, but rather a small-brained hominid capable of tool-use and cooperative social patterns that led to the emergence of large-brained hominids. As an educator, however, I am more impressed with modern man's need to comprehend and master what is *now* his tool of tools—himself. All things considered, what must we understand nature's interest to have been in superimposing cultural evolution on organic evolution, if not that change shall emerge and be regulated from the inside-out, that tools shall be means to the ends of fulfilling human nature, and not the other way around? In this I do not attach anthropocentric significance to evolution at large. I have merely been persuaded by Julian Huxley (36), Weston LaBarre (59), Loren Eiseley (22), and others more knowledgeable in the study of evolution than I, that this is a proper interpretation of the significant difference between organic and cultural evolution.

To be sure, tools and tool skills cannot be used as means to optimal human fulfillment if we cannot teach children to comprehend them, and link themselves to them. And as our technology becomes more intricate—some of it approaching the intricacy of the brain itself—the challenge to pedagogy compounds. Let me repeat, therefore, that it is not Bruner's specific suggestions toward a theory of instruction, nor the specific prescriptions for educational reform that have been derived from these suggestions, with which I have taken exception. Only their exclusivism.

CHAPTER SIX

The Course of
Emotional Growth

A comprehensive theory of instruction should seek to prescribe not only optimal levels of intellectual uncertainty, risk and relevance but also optimal levels of emotional involvement and personal curiosity. Pose the purely cognitive challenge to a fifth grade child of speculating on the absence of social fatherhood among baboons and he is likely to be led to levels of uncertainty, risk and relevance that are either too high or too low to support his best thoughts— depending on what his uninstructed self-interests happen privately to make of it. But find a way to engage his heart in the problem and you are likely to see the child rise naturally to his own optimal levels of uncertainty, risk and relevance. This is but a long-winded restatement of the homily that we learn best when we care most. The hitch in the homily, and the cause of its being more honored in conferences than in classrooms, is that what a child cares most about may also most readily threaten him—or his teacher.

Considerations of personal-emotional factors in a theory of instruction are of particular importance because of a countervailing professional posture traditionally cultivated in teachers colleges which systematically seeks to exclude such factors from the instructional process. Lawrence Kubie refers to this posture as the "conspiracy of silence":

> The child's fifth freedom is the right to know what he feels . . . this will require a new mores for our schools, one which will enable young people from early years to understand and feel and put into words all the hidden things which go on inside of them, thus ending the conspiracy of silence with which the development of the child is now distorted both at home and at school. If the conspiracy of silence is to be replaced by the fifth freedom, children must be encouraged and helped to attend to their forbidden thoughts, and to put them into words, i.e., to talk out loud about love and hate and jealousy and fear, about curiosity over the body, its products and its apertures; about what goes in and what comes out; about what happens inside and what happens outside; about their dim and confused feelings about sex itself; about the strained and stressful relationships within families, which are transplanted into schools. All of these are things about which school must help the children to become articulate in the classroom. (38, p. viii)

It is, of course, for each teacher to decide how far she thinks it best to follow Kubie in this, and how far she is willing and able to do so. A theory of instruction cannot be expected to make such decisions. It should, however, be expected to provide a framework within which the spectrum of human emotions can be conceived in relation to learning in schools. This would at least enable a teacher to make such decisions in a professional manner. Let me offer the opinion, for example, that a teacher has made a proper professional decision who has consciously and in the light of her own articulate conscience decided to avoid the topic of biological paternity as distinct from social paternity when teaching "Man: A Course of Study," either out of consideration for her own feelings or those of some few of her pupils. Whatever silence may then ensue will not be conspiratorial in nature, and will therefore be unlikely to spread to other sensitive areas where she would choose to be more venturesome. Although an understanding of social fatherhood and the domestication of the male is crucial to understanding man as a species, there are other ways of approaching it than head-on, and if the avoidance of the direct approach has been above the board, the children will not take this to mean that other approaches are likewise to be avoided.

We have need, then, of a theoretical frame for considering emotional growth. Hardly a scarce item in psychology at large. But our needs are specific; the frame we choose should: (1) be derived from a developmental theory, (2) have systematic properties which allow it to be coordinated with cognitive and social growth, (3) offer points of reference to the imaginal processes, and (4) lend itself to teachers by way of being readily exemplified in references to classroom encounters.

Only two *systematic* developmental theories have devoted sufficient attention to the subject of emotions to qualify: Freud's and Piaget's. Freud's theory is superior from the standpoint of coordinating emotional and social growth, and Piaget's theory is superior from the standpoint of coordinating emotional and cognitive growth. From the standpoint of offering points of reference in the imaginal sphere, the Piagetian framework has an edge on the Freudian, because of its lavish collection of observations of normal imaginal behavior. From the standpoint of comprehensibility and readiness of application in classrooms,

Freud's theory derives a very decided advantage from having as its modern spokesman, Professor Erik Erikson, whose ability to transform systematic psychoanalytic theory into basic English has already earned the gratitude of many teachers.

We shall proceed with Freud out of Erikson.

Immediately, we face the problem of Erikson's lucidity. Any restatement of his views here would detract from their clarity. On the other hand, were I to quote him directly as extensively as is necessary for our purpose, his publisher would have just cause for complaint. Erikson himself has supplied the solution. He has not been so taken with his artistry as to refrain from providing his readers with condensations of his views in the form of charts and diagrams. I shall therefore begin with an elaborate chart of Erikson's theory, modeled after one of his own, hoping thereby to entice my readers into reading or rereading Erikson. I shall then proceed to take my chances in reformulating the theory for service in a theory of instruction.

The chart says that during early infancy (roughly the first year of life), when the oral, sensory, respiratory, and kinesthetic organ systems are rapidly proceeding toward functional maturity, *while all other organ systems remain comparatively immature*, the child's psychological and social development is structured by the templates of experience provided by this particular state of imbalance. All kinds of incorporative activities become compellingly interesting. From the point of view of the development of cognitive skills, we speak of attention and focusing—the rudiments of what will later become the ability to "concentrate." From the point of view of imaginal development, we speak of themes of incorporation, of swallowing and being swallowed—the lollipop moon, Jonah and the whale, the world behind the looking glass, etc. The examples are, of course, products of "regression" to infantile modes from more advanced stages of organization, it being impossible for us to remember how life was experienced when our bodies were so lopsidedly arranged. Nonetheless we have learned to look, very palpably, to this remote period of development for the roots of the grosser forms of psychopathology: perceptual anomalies, such as hallucinations; disorders of empathy, such as paranoid delusions, etc.—a point of only passing interest to teachers.

Continuing along the uppermost horizontal, the chart underscores the obvious by designating as the infant's significant social circle his mother. It is an observation of seemingly little relevance to teaching, until we find ourselves in pedagogical contexts declaring for or against "spoon-feeding" or "pampering" or "regurgitation" or what have you.

Erikson's special feeling for one-syllable English comes most prominently into play in his formulation of the psychosocial modalities, the generic social skills without which a child cannot qualify for membership in his species, much less admission into school. He means his choice of terms to be understood colloquially. (I "get" you. Do you "take" my meaning? etc.) These are further refinements in the child's social life of the psychosexual modes of incorporation, and refer to the ability to "get" and "take" all forms of ministrations: attention, inspection, affection, discipline, etc.

It is necessary to understand the close cogwheeling of the biological, psychological, and social forces charted in the first five columns, in order to appreciate the systematic properties of the familiar terms which name the nuclear growth crises. Thus "trust" and "mistrust" do not mean here only what they mean in the Bible, in banking circles, or in love pacts—although, of course, they include these.

A	B	C	D
LIFE STAGES	PSYCHOSEXUAL STAGES	COGNITIVE SKILLS	IMAGINAL THEMES
Infancy	Oral-sensory- respiratory- kinesthetic Zones Incorporative Modes	attention observation inspection	incorporation total embracement or absorption "oceanic" proportions
Play Age	Anal-urethral- muscular Zones Eliminative- retentive Modes	affirmation negation exclusion postponement	disappearance reappearance power magic control impotence
	Infantile-genital- locomotor Zones Intrusive-inclusive Modes	investigation contemplation scrutiny reflection	exploration discovery metamorphosis origination
School Age	Latency Period	representation transcription paraphrase metaphorical thought	invention construction achievement
	Puberty and Adolescence	intuition generalization insight individuation	justice revolution reformation utopias
Young Adulthood	Genitality	paradox enigma dialectic	true love
Adulthood	Genitality and Generativity	tolerance preception	generation regeneration
Senescence	Physical and Mental Decline	"ultimate concern"	

E QUALITIES OF RECIPROCITY IN EXPANDING RADIUS OF SIGNIFICANT RELATIONS	F PSYCHOSOCIAL MODALITIES	G NUCLEAR GROWTH CRISES	H QUALITIES OF AWARENESS	I RELATED SOCIAL STRUCTURES
Trustworthy Maternal Persons (implicit faith)	To get To take	Trust and Mistrust	Hope (Drive)	Organized Faith
Judicious Parental Persons (implicit justice)	To hold (on) To let (go)	Autonomy and Shame- doubt	Will (Control)	Law and Order
Exemplary Basic Family (implicit morality)	To "make" (= going after) To "make like" (= play)	Initiative and Guilt	Purpose (Direction)	Moral Law
Instructive Adults (implicit techno- logical ethos)	To turn to To know how	Industry and Inferiority	Skill (Method)	Technology
Confirming Adults and affirmative peers (implicit ideolog- ical verification)	To be (one- self)	Identity and Identity Diffusion	Devotion (Fidelity)	Ideology
Mates and Partners in search of shared identity (implicit social selection)	To share (one- self)	Intimacy and Isolation	Love (Affiliation)	Organized Cooperation and Competition
Progeny and Products in need of generative ingenuity (implicit social mutation)	To let be To make be To take care of	Authority and Self- absorption	Care (Production)	Education and Tradition
New Generation in need of integrated heritage	To face not being To be a has been	Integrity and Despair	Wisdom (Renuncia- tion)	Literature and Philosophy

Systematically speaking, they refer to fundamental residues of outlook or expectancy which are left as deposits, as it were, by the early life work of learning one's incorporative body, following its cues in adapting to one's incorporable world, and carrying these over into viable and unviable dealings with one's mother. To the extent that these inter-weaving forces fashion sequences of experience which hold together, are coherent and predictable, the child learns to invest life with expectations of its being basically trust-worthy. To the extent that sequences of experience are produced which do not hold together, are incoherent and unpredictable, the child learns to invest life with expecta-tions of basic mistrust. *Both qualities of expectancy are fundamental to further growth,* although an overdose of the latter spells trouble. Hence: growth *crisis.* It is often over-looked by users of Erikson's theory that a modicum of mis-trust is essential to normal development in two ways: (1) by providing the raw materials for conversion into trust by the child's own corrective actions and (2) by providing the prerequisite for learning how to doubt. Let it be empha-sized, then, that in its systematic usage the term "trust" should invoke images of sore mouths as well as kind hearts, regaining lost breaths as well as gaining soft breasts; it should conjure scenes of infants at their best and mothers at their worst (and vice-versa), of oceanic nightmares as well as nirvanic dreams, of learning how to get hurt as well as how to get help.

The next column, qualities of awareness, provides the systematic substance for applying the theory to the proc-esses of instruction. The nuclear growth crises, for all their power as theoretical concepts, and despite the simplicity of nomenclature which Erikson has given them, are quite in-tangible. They are not to be "located" in any one sector of a person's being. A ten year old's sense of basic trust, for example, is in his mouth and skin, in memories of his mother, in his nightmares, and his ability to pay attention to his teacher, among other "places"—both consciously and unconsciously. Indeed the growth crises derive their theoretical power from this very holistic property. The qualities of awareness are more specific in their referents, more observable both subjectively and objectively, and therefore more accessible to instructors and instructions. For example, I learned how to cancel fractions quite fretfully, and how to shoot a basketball with confidence and joy. I can still do both but am now less likely to get the ball in the basket than to cancel fractions correctly. Yet, I have more "hope" with a basketball in my hands than with an uncancelled fraction before me—and an observer would say that I approach the one with more "drive" than the other. It is in this sense that it is not only what one knows but how one learned what one knows that determines the conduct of life.

Systematically speaking, "hope" and "drive" are the subjective and objective dimensions, respectively, of the general qualities of awareness likely to characterize the child's conduct of life whether in moments of success, failure, happiness, or unhappiness—as extensions into consciousness of his particular blendings of trust and mistrust.

How a society reaches back into the infancies of its generations to predispose its members—toward what is valuable to attend and what is trivial to attend, what is awesome to imagine and what is forbidden to imagine, what one should hope to trust and what one should hope to mistrust—varies from society to society as a function of particular child-rearing mores and practices. In other words, the contents of social traditions are variable. The *forms* of social traditions, however, are as unvarying as the asynchronous rates of human maturation from which they are

derived and to which they are ultimately attuned. Thus the
social structure predestined by and related to the unique
configuration of biological, psychological, and social factors
which make up human infancy is "organized faith." All
human societies have generated some forms of organized
faith, because all members of all human societies were
once human infants. This is anything but to say that all
systems of organized faith are infantile—as is sometimes
erroneously held to have been Freud's view of the matter.
It is to say that faith, as a formal dimension of collective
human experience has roots—or, if you will, releasers—in
the ubiquities of human infancy.

Moving on to the second row: the child has had his
year or so of more or less exclusive specialization in the
zones, modes and modalities of receiving; and, in concert
with his mother and those who attend her, has made the
most that he could of it.* Genetically programmed maturational currents have been rising—particularly in the smooth
muscle systems—which are about to give another side to the
child's unevenness, and which will make him a manipulator
as well as a receiver of life. The sphincter and small muscle
systems will now proceed rapidly to functional maturity
while all other organ systems continue to languish in states
of comparative immaturity, thus altering the templates
which define the next stage of psychosocial development.
All kinds of retentive and eliminative activities will now
assume high interest value. From the point of view of the
development of cognitive skills, we speak of affirmation,
negation, exclusion and postponement—the rudiments of
what will later become the ability to think logically. Memory, as we know it, is now possible and while the com-

* Fathers are superfluous to trusting and mistrusting infants only to
the extent that they are incapable of mothering, or to the extent that
they are unable to empathize with wives and infants.

plexities of language development defy explanation it is surely no accident that all children begin to speak during approximately the second year of life, when their use of the "organs of speech" (the oral-sensory-respiratory-kinesthetic system) have become "second nature," when their use of the organs of retention and expulsion have become sources of compelling interest, and when that other avenue of interesting commerce with life, locomotion, has not yet become a very palpable reality (a fact which might, I think, have spared the Kelloggs [50] and others who have tried to teach speech to the agile chimpanzee much wasted effort, had it been fully appreciated).

From the standpoint of imaginal development, there emerge themes of disappearance and reappearance, of power and magic, of control and impotence—hidden treasures, Aladdin and his genie, Jack and the Beanstalk, etc. Father, and other restraining and permitting persons, now join Mother in the child's significant social circle, and, following the leads of newly learned retentive and eliminative skills in the physical and psychological spheres, the child begins to develop the social arts of holding on and letting go—of people and of their approvals, disapprovals, persuasions, injunctions, exhortations, and disillusionments, among other forms of discipline and influence.

Out of this bio-psycho-social mix there derives the second nuclear growth crisis: to the extent that this second set of interweaving impulsions—as supported and predisposed by the first—produces experiences of influencing and of being influenced, of causing and of being caused, of controlling and of being controlled, in combinations which seem both sufficient for now and promising for later, the child learns to invest life with expectations of its being capable of inclusion in his sphere of autonomy. To the extent that experiences are produced of being too controllable or too controlling, of getting there with too little too late or with too much too soon, the child learns to invest life with expectations of its being a source of doubt and shame. Again, the seemingly negative elements are important to continued development, and again in two ways: (1) shame, when converted into confidence by one's own actions, makes for the most viable kind of autonomy; and (2) the capacity to doubt will later provide the necessary impetus to take initiative in things, to change, to make, to make over, to take charge, and so on.

Accordingly, the qualities of awareness likely to characterize the child's continued conduct of life, that derive from his particular amalgam of autonomy, shame, and doubt, will be his qualities of "will" when viewed subjectively, and his qualities of "control" when viewed objectively. And the related social structure within which he will define the meaning of his will, by varying degrees of acquiescence and opposition, is his society's system of "law and order."

The child is yet far from schoolable, but the teacher who thinks she can school him later without at least a theoretical frame for reconstructing these pre-school developments would be in the position of a petroleum engineer who knew no more about oil than that it comes from the ground, or an artist who thinks paints originate in tubes. So, let us continue.

The child is somewhere between three and four years of age. Genetically programmed maturational currents have been rising in still other organ systems—the genital and locomotor systems—which are about to add another side to the child's training in unbalanced living. Indeed, it is doubtless the radically asynchronous nature of man's prolonged maturation, per se, which equips him to adapt to the rapidities of change typical of cultural evolution. Consider, for example, that all other animals are fully mature and reproducing by this equivalent time in their lives—excepting a few of the other primates, and they are largely self-sufficient by this time. The human, on the other hand, is just beginning to get around confidently in space. And his reproductive future is still several subjective lifetimes ahead of him.

The locomotor and genital systems will now rapidly proceed to maturity, adding their existential possibilities to those described, while other organ systems—cortical, glandular, and hormonal—continue to lag behind. All kinds of intrusive and inclusive activities now become of absorbing interest—certain differential preferences having been predetermined by sex (39, pp. 39–41). From the point of view of cognitive skills, there are the several facets of curiosity: probing, brooding, mulling, checking, etc.—the rudiments of what will later become the ability to think critically.

From the standpoint of imaginal development, we speak of the classic themes of exploration, discovery, metamorphosis and origination, as expressed, for example, in the myths of Odysseus, Oedipus, Prometheus, and Nuliajik.

The significant social world is now the full family circle and, again following the leads of newly learned intrusive and inclusive skills in the physical and psychological spheres, the child begins his intensive social training in the subtleties of going out, as Erikson puts it, "on the make": encroaching, interrogating, volunteering, courting, pursuing, prying, enticing. Out of these developments emerges the third nuclear growth crisis: insofar as the child learns to exercise choice and discretion in pursuit of the excitements and fulfillments which his more widely ranging body and more deeply probing mind now bring into view, he comes to invest life with expectations of its being subject to his initiative. Insofar as these pursuits lead him into indecision or call forth inconsistent responses of favor and disfavor from his exemplars, he comes to invest life with expectations of its being a source of guilt—whether of the kind that triggers retreat into self-deception or of the kind that leads to quiet resolutions toward self-improvement, depending on his prior earnings of trust and autonomy.

The consequent quality of awareness which is likely to characterize his conduct of life is, when viewed from within, his sense of purpose; when viewed from without, his sense of direction. The related social structure within which his particular purposes and directions will find their composition is his society's systems of moral law.

Roughly between the ages of five and seven, human children show a marked reduction of interest in matters of the body and a marked increase of interest in matters of the mind. To what extent this is a response to social pressures, due to some universal societal awareness that the child is now "educable," and to what extent it is a response to still further maturational developments in the central nervous system is a question about which there are authoritative differences of opinion. Probably both are involved, but for us the question is academic. Man being the cultured animal, there must come some time in his development when biological releasers and social influences become indistinguishable, even for the crude purposes of making charts. This, then, seems as good a time as any to begin speaking of developmental periods rather than of maturational stages. Thus, the "latency period."

All kinds of representational activities now become the foci of time and energy: puzzles, riddles, "moron jokes," makeshift languages and signaling systems, and passwords. In addition, of course, in literate societies, to reading, writing, and arithmetic. Corresponding developments of cognitive skill include theorizing, paraphrasing, metaphorical thinking, hypothesis construction, etc.—the rudiments of what may later become intellectual inventiveness. Corresponding imaginal developments include preoccupations with themes of great doings—Genesis, Theseus, Paul Bunyon, Walter Mitty, etc. The child's social radius now very significantly includes his teachers, and his psychosocial development encompasses all the kinds of "know-how" for which there are familiar bywords in teachers' shoptalk: leadership, followership, group membership, competitiveness, cooperativeness, etc. Insofar as the child learns, under appropriate tutelage, to coordinate his mastery of basic representational skills and tools with mastery of the related social techniques of dividing, pooling, and otherwise organizing his labors, he comes to invest life with expectations of its being an interesting challenge to his sense of industry. Insofar as he does not master these tools, skills, and social techniques, or is unable to coordinate his mastery of them, he comes to invest life with expectations of its being a source of defeat and inferiority.

Teachers hardly need reminding that children develop their competence as much from their correction of failures as from their successes. And counselors, guidance personnel, and school psychologists will recall how often the areas of a teenager's previous inferiorities may enter into the formation of his identity—whether constructively, as in the case of the student who becomes enamoured of theoretical mathematics as a neat way of transcending old handicaps in arithmetic; or destructively, as in the case of a student who thinks he sees in a psychiatric career a way of getting around past deficiencies in commanding the confidences of people.

The emergent quality of awareness is a prevailing sense of skill; and the related social structure is his society's systems of technology.

It may seem at this juncture that we have slighted that line in the chart which speaks explicitly of "school age" and "instructors." It will not seem so to the reader who understands the epigenetic nature of Erikson's theory. In any event, let us pause to review certain of the axiomatic considerations that give the theory its grammar.

Erikson made one change in Freud's developmental theory: he shifted its emphasis as an explanatory system from infantile determinism to life cycle determinism, i.e., he made a "genetic" theory an "epigenetic" theory. When viewed in the context of psychoanalytic theory as a whole, this is a modest enough alteration. There are even purists who insist it was what Freud had in mind all the time, but that is a nicety for historians to brood on. As a matter of record, the notion of infantile determinism was one that Freud pushed to the fore, for whatever reasons. The epigenetic view is at most implicit in Freud; Erikson made it explicit. This was essential if psychoanalytic theory was to be of use to teachers. As long as we were invited to perceive Johnny's reading handicap or his precocious grasp of commutative functions, or his preoccupation with dinosaurs, or his special problem with subtraction as predetermined by his anal fixations and/or Oedipus and/or castration complexes, we were not likely to feel our competence as teachers to be challenged. What was done was done, and might at best be undone. What, in such lights, could a teacher with all possible hope, will, purpose, skill, devotion, love, care, and wisdom do?

In epigenetic perspective, however, to say that the child's development of autonomy, shame, and doubt, and his corresponding development of will, are *phase specific* to roughly the second and third years of his life, is not to say that these issues were uninvolved in previous developments nor that they will be uninvolved in later developments. The term "phase specific" in Erikson's theory connotes only that these issues are stage center during this period, likely to occupy the focus of the child's thoughts, fantasies, and repetitive behaviors, due to the particular confluences of maturational and social pressures which are universal in this phase of human development. These developments did not spring fully formed from nowhere— any more than the sphincters and muscles which provide their functional models suddenly appeared from nowhere. They had their *precursors* in the preceding phase of development in the following specific ways: at the psychosexual level the anal, urethral, and muscular organ systems were functioning in auxiliary capacities—immaturely so, but functioning; and the oral, sensory, respiratory, and kinesthetic organ systems could and did perform retentive and eliminative functions—secondarily and perhaps awkwardly so, but significantly so. At the level of the psychosocial modalities, the child had all along been learning rudimentary forms of holding on and letting go of his mother's ministrations, and his mother had all along been bringing her influence and styles of discipline to bear upon him as a part of these ministrations. Normally, however, neither party is inclined, during a child's first year, to make these coincidental matters into big issues. The point is that by the time they become big issues they have already been partially shaped in precursive stages. At the levels of the nuclear growth crises and qualities of awareness, it is self-evident how "autonomy," "shame," and "will" must evolve from "trust," "mistrust," and "hope," respectively.

Nor will the developments of later phases be independent of *derivatives* from this second phase. The confidence and style with which a two-year-old learns to affirm and to negate, for example, will surely have a part in shaping his special fortes and failings in the later development of more intricate cognitive skills. Similarly, the particular balances of autonomy, shame, and doubt, upon which the two-year-old comes to pivot his expectancies in matters of conflicting interests, will obviously shape and color his later expressions of initiative, competence, identity, intimacy and so on. Again, it is self-evident that the qualities of purpose, skill, devotion, and love, which will develop over the extended span of the child's life will not be independent of the qualities of will which centered its second and third years.

The second phase of the life cycle has been singled out for illustrative purposes only. Each phase of the cycle could be similarly specified in terms of its phase specific and auxiliary issues, and in terms of the precursors and derivatives of these issues. Erikson has done this for the adolescent period in his "Identity and the Life Cycle" and I refer the reader to that monograph for a more finely worked illustration (25).

For the purpose at hand, it suffices to note that the elementary schooler's comparative preoccupation with industry and skill is hardly an observation on which a teacher, disinclined to confront emotional issues, can rest easily. For, not only will the child be moved to approach, avoid, enthuse, postpone, hedge, fudge, and imagine his own ways into his development of industry and skill, as inclined by his previous developments of hope, will, and purpose (and the respective root systems of these in his body, his family, and his attitudes of trust, mistrust, autonomy, shame, doubt, initiative, and guilt); but he will also be moved to do all this with a searching eye toward staking new claims in previously disputed developmental territories. What may, for example, have seemed hopeless and outside the spheres of his will and purpose in the area, say, of assigning separate and multiple causes to a mother's outbursts, may, with the dawning development of skill in logical thinking, suddenly appear in more promising lights. What was unpredictable and inconsistent, and therefore unmanageable, may now become predictable and consistent, and therefore manageable. Anxiety can be converted into mere irritation—or even tolerance. If, then, the child chooses for a time to devote his newly gained logical capabilities to themes and problems of family discord, what teacher would want to discourage it? Better, what teacher would not try to *encourage* it—to the extent, perhaps, of highlighting the topic of family discord when it is relevant to a lesson?

We may now say with more precision what we mean when we describe the theory as *epi*genetic, and when we cite as its explanatory modus the principle of life cycle determinism. We mean that all of the psychological and social developments which are specific to each phase of the life cycle are, to a degree, predetermined by certain precursors in and certain derivatives from preceding phases of development; *and are also, to a degree, educable by virtue of the new possibilities for reorganization offered by each succeeding phase of development.* Therefore, whatever aspect of a child's psychosocial development may concern us, we may assume that it has a preadaptive history which can be read in phase specific forms; and we may also assume that it has readaptive potentials which may be realized in instructable contexts.

This, I submit, is a theory that commends itself to teachers—particularly to teachers interested in exploring new possibilities. The principle of life cycle determinism, for example, is practically identical with Gordon Allport's concept of the "functional autonomy of motives" (2) and with Andras Angyal's concept of "personality as a time gestalt" (4), both of which have proved popular among teachers because of their intrinsic optimism. However, Allport saw it necessary to advance the idea in opposition to psychoanalytic theory, and Angyal advanced it independently of psychoanalytical theory, both theorists thus losing advantage of the systematic developmental concepts and observations which are the prime strengths of psychoanalytic theory. The principle of life cycle determinism, as formulated by Erikson, however, is strictly derived from psychoanalytic theory and can therefore readily employ and/or deploy such seasoned systematic constructs as "infantile sexuality," "fixation," "regression," "ego defense," and "ego synthesis," which were previously associated—rightly or wrongly—with Freudian pessimism. In other words, psychoanalytic theory may now be used not only post-dictively to chart how a person's past has determined his present; *it may also be used predictively to chart how a person's present may both determine his future and redetermine his past.*

We must not neglect the other side of the principle of life cycle determinism, which is to be seen in Erikson's concept of *mutuality*. We may say that the instructional leverage on psychosocial development discussed so far is *intra*-generational. The significance of this or that skill, attitude, or quality of awareness, we have said, will vary as a function of its position *within* the child's life. We will see that there is a kind of leverage on psychosocial development which is *inter*-generational, wherein the significance of this or that skill, attitude, or quality of awareness varies as a function of its position *between* the child's phase of development and his teacher's phase of development. However, we can best appreciate the concept of mutuality from the vantage of the total life cycle, and we left the child poised at entrance to "junior high." We move on, then, to the fifth row of the chart.

Biologically speaking, this is no longer a "child." Genetically programmed glandular and hormonal maturations either have brought or are about to bring the individual's reproductive system to maturity, with all of the dramatic physical and emotional consequences that come with puberty. However, as though conspiring to protect the individual from a too rapid weaning from the unbalanced states to which he has become accustomed, all public-schooled societies oppose childbearing among adolescents, thus joining the issues which are of prime interest and concern during this period: dependence and independence, conformity and rebellion, membership and individuality. Intuition, generalization, insight—the rudiments of what may later become creative thinking—now come into prominence; and in the imagination, themes of justice, revolution, reform, and utopias become compelling.

The significant social world now includes not only home, school, and local community but the world scene— especially those figures on the world scene, present and past, whose values and views can be joined or opposed in shaping and sharpening one's own values and views.

The social skill to be learned during this period, and it is very much a *social* skill, is to be one's self, to stand for and against things consistently and expressly, in ways that make one recognizedly one's own man, in private and in public. To the extent the young man or woman succeeds in tempering his renewed concern with his body and sex with the ability to think and dream on grand scales, and to recognize and make recognizable that he has put the stamp of individuality on his particular blending of these, he comes to invest life with expectations of its being distinctive. We say he develops a sense of ego identity. To the extent he is unable to subordinate his capacities for the reproduction of life to his capacities for the reproduction of mind, or cannot make social graces of his essential loneliness, he comes to invest life with expectations of its being something one can get lost in. We say he develops a sense of ego diffusion. It is as ill-advised here to think of identity "versus" diffusion as it is to engage in either-or thinking in respect to the other growth crises. The word is still "and." What a poor thing would intimacy be, for example, to one who could not feel lost without his love.

The quality of awareness which is heir to adolescent development is devotion or fidelity. The related social structure is his society's systems of ideology.

Our terms now give trouble. Where along the life stages shall we place college students? In some ways all of them are adolescents; in some other ways many of them are young adults. To settle on experience with sexual intercourse as a criterion would hardly help matters. Any college teacher who has earned the requisite confidences can attest that there are adults and adolescents among those students who have "gone all the way," and adults and adolescents among those who have not. Let us therefore hedge the point, and say that most people may be classified as young adults before they graduate from college, and proceed:

We need speak of maturation no longer. *Culturally* programmed expectations have been rising—particularly in the area of *what* one will do with his life—which now convince the person that life must forever be a contrary thing; for, while he can admit to the practicality of the question, what interests him most is *with whom.* Indeed, all matters of insemination and inception, and other intimacies, are what appeal the most to young adults. They would eschew classes for seminars, office hours for after-lecture happenings, professors for mentors, etc. The effective college teacher learns to trade on this affinity for the intimate by discouraging the merely knowledgeable in favor of getting to the hearts of matters. The cognitive skills specific to this phase involve coming to grips with the paradox, the dialectical, the exception that proves the rule, the enigmatic. Imagination has by now either become so much a part of hopeful planning that we need not treat it separately, or it has become so hopelessly a part of the person's neurosis that it must, alas, be "treated" separately. In either event, it deals in extremes of intimacy —the one and only love, realized in the one and only way, for the one and only purpose. The significant social circle recenters around the partner, and the social modality to be mastered is that of empathic sharing, of being oneself with and for the other.

To the extent the person learns to share, and to be shared, in recognizedly privileged ways, he comes to invest life with expectations of there being times of intimacy. To the extent the person learns there are sides of self which he and his partner cannot share, he comes to invest life with expectations of there being times of isolation. Both will have parts to play in molding subsequent attitudes of authority.

The quality of awareness derived from the normal crises of young adulthood is love. The related social structure is society's kinship systems and other traditions of organized cooperation and competition.

We come now to the seventh phase of the life cycle, adulthood, where we may presume to locate teachers. Perhaps nature's design in all along requiring the growing person to find continuity in discontinuity may reveal itself at this juncture. For, as we approach the time when we might pursue self-indulgences more ably than ever before, we tend to lose interest in ourselves in favor of the interests of progeny. Not some of us, mind, but all of us. Each in characteristic ways, but all of us. I make this a point of emphasis in order to highlight an essential property of the theory. The phases of the life cycle are to be conceived as universal, being manifestations of nuclear maturational and social forces that are distinctive of the human species. The chart, in other words, is misused when employed, as it often is, as a scorecard for rating one's "maturity." The adolescent who is "absorbed in himself" can be a happy creature, because to be "absorbed" in oneself in the context of life that is peculiar to human adolescence feels inherently right. It feels inherently right, because it *is* inherently right. Correspondingly, the adult who is absorbed in himself must be an unhappy creature, the unhappiness deriving precisely from the common inner sense that to be absorbed in self in the context of life that is peculiar to human adulthood is inherently wrong—not morally wrong, although that is a meaning that may be given it, but *developmentally* wrong, i.e., out of phase.

Thus, all humans who reach adulthood experience a very palpable shifting of interests from self to progeny, even if only by default. In this sense, we may say that the adult is moved to take special interest in children—his own, those of others, and his brain children—be these theories, paintings, books, bridges, crops, engines, or customers.

The cognitive and imaginal skills specific to this phase center around tolerance (for ambiguity, for diversity, for alternation), and generativity—the rudiments of what may become "wisdom."

The social modalities specific to adulthood are the modalities of service: to make be, to let be, to cultivate growth. The concept of "mutuality" may now be made articulate by refracting these modalities into their respective components of intergenerational relations: to tend and to minister those who are learning to get and to take; to influence and to discipline those who are learning to hold on and to let go; to be an exemplar to those who are on the make; to instruct those who are learning how to know how; to confirm and oppose those who are learning to be themselves; and to legitimize the privileges of those who are learning to share. Opportunities to engage in all of these mutual arrangements in support of growth are important in the development of attitudes of authority —the alternative being to spend one's tendencies to serve progeny on oneself or one's possessions. Thus the growth crisis of adulthood: the investing of life with expectations of its being capable of generation and stagnation.

Erikson calls the corresponding quality of awareness "care." The related social structure is the society's systems of education.

We may now address the special problem of authority as generated in schoolrooms: it is the problem of defining authority with respect to the relationships of mutuality that derive systematically from the overlapping of life cycles. Consider the relationship of an adult who possesses a piece of knowledge and a child who does not. Which is more important to an understanding of the problem of authority: the child's skill in attending and "getting" the knowledge, or the adult's skill in tending and "serving" the knowledge? The question is meaningless unless taken further: If the child skillfully attends and the adult skillfully tends, then the piece of knowledge is passed along and there is no problem of authority. If the child is deficient in "getting" the piece of knowledge, then the problem of authority resides in the challenge posed to the adult's skill in serving it. If the adult is deficient in "serving" the piece of knowledge, then the problem of authority resides in the challenge posed to the child's skill in "getting" it. If both are deficient in their respective phase specific skills, then the problem of authority resides in the interlocked growth crisis which must normally follow: the crisis over mistrust in the child, and the crisis over self-absorption in the adult. It is not the simple case, then, that one possesses something that the other does not. Rather, it is quite literally the case, as inexorably determined by the facts of overlapping human life cycles, that both possess something that the other does not. At some risk of over-simplifying what from concrete instance to concrete instance can be a study in highly complex human interaction, the concept of mutuality states that while children need, adults need to be needed, and that both needs are of like urgency within their respective developmental contexts. Perhaps I belabor the obvious. But I have been much impressed with how often in teachers' conferences and psychologists' seminars it is exclusively the needs of the children that come into discussions of how to improve learning, when it should be obvious to all that the needs of the teacher are as germane to the problem.

As in all developmental matters, style is an important dimension of individual difference. Every adult will fashion his own style of authority, and each style will be more effective with the learning styles of some youths and less effective with the learning styles of other youths. This is the basis of the second—intergenerational—side of the principle of life cycle determinism. We said that a person's past not only predetermines his present, but that a person's present may redetermine his past. This is what we called the intragenerational expression of life cycle determinism. We may now add that the instructability of a person's present varies as a function of the qualities of mutuality that characterize his relations with his instructors. This is an equation that submits of considerable variance, posing considerable challenges to students and teachers alike, and enlarging by that extent the scope of any theory of instruction.

It would gnaw at this writer's sense of closure were we to omit the eighth and last phase of the life cycle, the age of integrity, despair, and wisdom. But, being unqualified to speak with authority of these matters, I fear I would but mouth Erikson. Therefore, permit me to conclude by quotation:

> . . . If the cycle, in many ways, turns back on its own beginnings, so that the very old become again like children, the question is whether the return is to a childlikeness seasoned with wisdom—or to a finite childishness. This is not only important within the cycle of individual life, but also within that of generations, for it can only weaken the vital fiber of the younger generation if the evidence of daily living verifies man's prolonged last phase as a sanctioned period of childishness. Any span of the cycle lived without vigorous meaning, at the beginning, in the middle, or at the end, endangers the sense of life and the meaning of death in all whose life stages are intertwined.

> Individuality here finds its ultimate test, namely, man's existence at the entrance to that valley which he must cross alone. I am not ready to discuss the psychology of "ultimate concern." But . . . I cannot help feeling that the order depicted suggests an existential complementarity of the great Nothingness and the actuality of the cycle of generations. For if there is any responsibility in the cycle of life, it must be that one generation owes to the next that strength by which it can come to face ultimate concerns in

its own way—unmarred by debilitating poverty or by the neurotic concerns caused by emotional exploitation.

For each generation must find the wisdom of the ages in the form of its own wisdom. Strength in the old, therefore, takes the form of wisdom in all of its connotations from "ripened" wits to accumulated knowledge and matured judgment. It is the essence of knowledge freed from temporal relativity.

Wisdom, then, is detached concern with life itself, in the face of death itself. It maintains and conveys the integrity of experience, in spite of the decline of bodily and mental functions. It responds to the need of the on-coming generation for an integrated heritage and yet remains aware of the relativity of all knowledge.

Potency, performance, and adaptability decline; but if vigor of mind combines with the gift of responsible renunciation, some old people can envisage human problems in their entirety (which is what "integrity" means) and can represent to the coming generation a living example of the "closure" of a style of life. Only such integrity can balance the despair of the knowledge that a limited life is coming to a conscious conclusion, only such wholeness can transcend the petty disgust of feeling finished and passed by, and the despair of facing the period of relative helplessness which marks the end as it marked the beginning. (26, pp. 133–34)

The uses to which the view of the human life cycle described in the foregoing pages might be put are several: To the social scientist, it affords a perspective within which to order the cogwheelings of Man's nuclear distinctions in evolution: his prolonged and distinctively programmed neuro-physical maturation, his distinctive development as a symbolizer, and his distinctive reliance on social organization and tools as instruments of adaptation.

To the humanist, it affords a tentative schedule of criteria for the evaluation of institutional forms and contents. Thus a religion is a "good" religion which provides beliefs, and means of articulating beliefs that are viable vehicles of "faith" throughout the life cycle: to a child seeking to coordinate a growing sense of purpose with a mother's waning sense of will; to a father seeking to bring both confirmation and opposition to a daughter's heterosexual devotions; as well as to an old person searching death for hope. Whereas, a religion is a "bad" religion which offers institutional forms for the expression of faith during some of life's phases at the expense of others, thus reducing, for example, devotion to will, love to purpose, or care to skill.

To the healer, there is afforded a view for seeing health in sickness, as well as sickness in health, without losing sight of etiology either way.

I trust the desirability of considering emotional growth in schoolrooms against so versatile a background is not obscure. It is similar to the desirability of enjoying the colors in a painting with an alternate eye to enjoying the painting's composition. A single yellow leaf in a somber scene of early winter will be entertained by the viewer in quite different ways than the same yellow leaf embedded in a rich Cezanne forest. Similarly, love, hate, pride, embarrassment, joy, envy, or any other point on the spectrum of human emotion will be experienced in quite different ways depending on the various compositions in which the course of a life embeds it. Thus, what can be thought, imagined, or done to *control* this or that emotion; what can be thought, imagined, or done to *express* this or that emotion; what can be thought, imagined, or done to *use* this or that emotion—will all vary as a function of developmental phase. It is here that the chart lends itself to service in systematizing a teacher's professional thoughts concerning her endless and ever-varying encounters with emotions—not, of course, in the heat of such encounters, where she is far better advised to consult her own emotions than to be mentally scanning charts, but in the more thoughtful moments of lesson planning, evaluation, and such occasional "post-mortems" as she may find herself conducting between classes, over the kitchen sink, or while falling asleep.

In the next chapter we shall consider how, specifically, a teacher may use this framework for mapping plans in respect to her pupils' emotions. First, however, it is important to recall the distinctions we previously made between psychotherapy and education. This, because professional approaches to emotions have, in our time, become so thoroughly identified with the therapeutic arts that anyone who seeks to professionalize his posture in respect to people's feelings must overcome the tendency to emulate the doctor. In the case before us, this would lead teachers to confuse ends and means. Doctors, in their special ways, seek to avail patients of their emotions the better that they may learn to express them—or, at least, to control them. Teachers, in ways yet to be as well devised, seek to help students to control and express emotions *the better that they may put them to work in their studies.* To lose sight of this distinction is, for a teacher, not only to risk unwarranted invasions of privacy; it is to lose touch with her own professional identity.

Take the case involving Ann, a Negro youngster, in a fifth-grade class which was helping us to test a unit of "Man; A Course of Study." The unit referred to the Kalahari Bushmen. The lesson plan had two objectives:

to introduce the children to a Bushman family via film and slides, and to develop observational skill (things one can see, usually not see, and never see—in photographs).

The lesson proceeded:

Teacher: "What's one thing you *can* see in the picture?"
Student: "Bushmen."
Teacher: "What's something you can*not* see, but would like to learn more about?"
Student: "What's inside the ostrich egg?"
Teacher: "What's something you could *never* see in a photograph?"
Student: "What kind of a person he is."
Teacher: "All right, now see how many things you can put in each of the three columns: (1) can see (2) can't see (3) could never see.
(Children are divided into groups, teachers moving among them, guiding the activity)

Teacher: "All right, now I'd like to hear some of each group's entries in each column. First, what can be seen?"
Student: "Bushmen."
Student: "Shelters."
Student: "Bows and arrows."
Teacher: "Do these things tell us anything else about the Bushmen?"
Student: "They kill animals."
Student: "They make their own weapons."
Teacher: "What else *can* be seen?"
Student: "Trees."
Teacher: "What are the trees used for?"
Student: "For food."
Student: "To hold up shelters."
Student: "For wood for bows and arrows."
Teacher: "What else?"

Student: "Ostrich eggs."
Teacher: "What's their use?"
Student: "To carry water."
Teacher: "Anything else?"
Student: "To make beads."
Teacher: "What else *can* be seen?"
Student: "A baby."
Teacher: "What do you see about the baby?"
Student: "She's wearing a necklace too."
Student: "They have little clothing."
Teacher: "What does that tell us?"
Student: "It's hot."
Teacher: "Next group, what *can* be seen?"
Student: "They're natives."
Teacher: "Can you tell that from just looking at the picture?"
Student: "*Yes, because they have black skin.*"

Ann, ordinarily a spirited leader of discussion, is visibly startled, looks straight ahead, remains tight-lipped and expressionless through the rest of the lesson. The boy who had made the observation also withdraws, visibly embarrassed. The teacher later reported she had all she could do not to look at Ann, and wished inwardly from that moment on only to get through and over the lesson. With this outlook, she was unable to exploit the instructional opportunities later offered her by the children who were clearly not only ready but eager to confront what was obviously uppermost on the minds of everyone: Ann's feelings of exclusion and their own feelings of regret and embarrassment.

Teacher: "What could you *never* tell from a movie or a slide?"
Student: "Their *feelings*."
Student: "Their names."

Student: "You can't see them thinking."

Student: "It's hard to see if they love each other."

Student: "You could if someone was on top of someone else, or next to each other or holding hands."

Student: "*You could tell how someone was feeling by the way they looked* . . . if they're happy, or sad, or smiling."

Teacher: "We have a difference of opinion: (1) can see feelings in a picture; (2) cannot see feelings in a picture. Shall we leave it in the "can see" column or not? What do you think?"

Student: "Leave it in."

Student: "No, you can't see feelings."

Student: "Yes, you can—by expressions on faces."

Student: "*Someone doesn't have to be crying for you to tell they're sad.*"

Teacher: "All who believe a picture *can* show feelings, raise hands!" (eight hands raised)

Teacher: "All who believe a picture can*not* show feelings, raise hands!" (six hands raised)

Beating retreat behind outward gestures of democratic procedure was not characteristic of this teacher. She supposed later that it was an awkward attempt on her part to reassure Ann that negative views of black skin were not held by all. But the gesture reassured no one and the lesson had been a loss. Little had been learned about Kalahari Bushmen, much less had there been any development of observational skills (at least not those that were planned). What else might she have done? Was she to have brought the whole thing into the open? This she couldn't even have contemplated. She had felt so awful for Ann that she could hardly bring herself to look at the girl much less think of how her plight might be deployed for pedagogical purposes. It was just one of those unlucky breaks that teachers have to live with. "Perhaps the Bushmen materials should be skipped when Negroes are in the class." In any event, she was now for letting well enough alone.

A second teacher, feeling that the class would lose if Ann were not helped to return to her normally buoyant ways, wished to have a go at solving the problem. The children seemed to mistakenly equate "native" not only with "black skin" but with "primitive." If she could clarify the semantics of the unsettling issue, perhaps it would resolve itself. Next morning she went to work as follows:

Teacher: "What do you think, have these people in the film lived elsewhere, or were they born in the Kalahari Desert?"
Student: "They might have migrated there from somewhere else."
Teacher: "No, as it happens, the Bushman family we saw yesterday were born in the Kalahari. What are people called who were born in the place where they're living?"
Student: "Natives."
Teacher: "Yes. Who here was born in Newton?" (six hands)
Teacher: "So, you are all natives of . . . ?"
Students: "Newton."
Teacher: "Yes. Where were some of the rest of you born?"
Student: "Boston."
Teacher: "So we say you are . . . ?"
Student: "A native of Boston."
Teacher: "Yes, who else?"
Student: "My family came from Quebec, but I was born in New Hampshire, and now we live in Newton."
Teacher: "And so . . . ?"
Student: "My father and mother are natives of Quebec, and I am a native of New Hampshire, and if we have any more children they will be natives of Newton."
Teacher: "Very good."
(From the start it was clear that Ann had been accepting the apologies being covertly extended. She finally acknowledges:)

Ann: "My whole family was born in New York, so I am a native of New York, but my uncle is a soldier in Germany and they just had a baby, so I guess you'd say I have a cousin who is a native of Germany."

Ann was back, and, the tension of the previous day having eased, the class proceeded to a lesson in the diagramming of kinship systems.

My reputation as "the emotions man" had caused me to be invited to this second class. Afterward, the teacher, making no attempt to hide her pride, asked me what I thought of how she had dealt with Ann and the "native problem." Alas, I should like to have enthused unreservedly, but it was, I thought, a clever gesture of courtesy, and no more than that. Ann had gotten the point, had accepted it, and had ceased her withdrawal. All well and good—for Ann. But what of the subject matter? Might not the emotional tides of the previous day been ideal ones to ride toward deepened comprehension of some of the species differences and culture variations the children had already studied? Do baboons ever feel isolated? Resentful? Embarrassed? If so, what about, and how do they show it? Why is it that humans feel embarrassed by so many things? Why are humans concerned with appearances more than other animals? What might embarrass a Bushman that would not embarrass us? And vice-versa? What are some of the ways that animals exclude each other? What are some of the ways that humans exclude each other? Does anyone know what *prejudice* means? What's the difference between avoiding a person because he has a cold and avoiding him because of prejudice? So, what else does it mean when we say that humans are more complex than baboons, besides that we have language, use tools, etc.?

The children had shown themselves ready to take up such questions, would even have preferred them, judging from the quickened tempo of their responses the previous day when their feelings had accidentally been engaged. ("Someone doesn't have to be crying for you to tell they're sad.") What's more, Ann would have received a more effective aid to her mental health, not as the result of a parenthetical sub-lesson designed exclusively and not very subtly for her benefit, but naturally and inclusively between the lines of bona fide instruction in the subject matter, and designed for the benefit of all.

Let us enter it as a fundamental rule, then, that cultivation of emotional issues in classrooms, whether by design or in response to the unpredictable, should be means to the ends of instructing the children in the subject matter. This not only for the reason that resolution of emotional issues, when integral to learning, tends to deepen the learning; but also for the reason that in the setting of a schoolroom emotional issues cannot be optimally resolved until they become relevant to educational objectives.

Consider the matter from the other side: patients go, or are sent, to clinics to be treated—not taught. Any attempt to teach a patient, when not clearly intended as subordinate to the objectives of treatment, should be viewed with suspicion, because that is not part of the agreement that brought the child to the clinic. Conversely, students go to school to be taught—not treated. Any attempt to treat a student, when not clearly intended as subordinate to the aims of teaching, should likewise be viewed with suspicion. Not that there would be anything wrong in attending to a student's mental health as such, if this could be done effectively. The point is that unless an explicit agreement has been made (as, for example, at Summerhill or the Devereaux schools) prescribing that pedagogical and therapeutic ends are to be simultaneously pursued, mental health needs cannot be optimally served in classrooms *except* as a means to improved teaching. May not Ann's feelings of rejection, for example, have been compounded to some degree by the very procedure designed to relieve her of them, precisely because the lesson was designed to serve this purpose and no other?

Let there not be misinterpretation of these qualifying remarks. They are not a rationale for avoiding emotional issues in classrooms. The qualification only states that if the confrontation of emotions in classrooms is not made in the primary interests of achieving instructional objectives both the means and the ends may suffer.

In illustration of the instructional process when these means and ends are well coordinated, let us look in on another fifth grade class, this one in New York City's PS 113. The teacher, Mrs. Florence Jackson, is preparing to begin a four month unit on the origins of city life. The designer of the unit, Professor Robert Adams, had included among its objectives:

1) Tolerance for partial solutions to problems.
2) Ability to weigh alternative explanations to problems.
3) Awareness that in human societies the sequences of cause and effect are generally multilateral.
4) Increased ability to recognize general patterns of human behavior.
5) Growing awareness of the universality and the inevitability of social change.
6) Consideration of the nature and importance of our prevailing urban environment.
7) Appreciation of the emergence of urban civilization as one of the handful of major turning points in human history.

A large order, befitting a "new" curricular unit in the social studies. Mrs. Jackson, sensing she would need every bit of motivation she could find—or make—in order to get her pupils (even though selected for their high intelligence) from their present conceptions of city living to the conceptions of urbanization prescribed in Adams' objectives, decided not to leave the arousal of emotions to accident. Instead, she chose to devote several introductory sessions to two starkly humanistic questions, which she hoped would provide leverage on issues that she knew her Harlem pupils cared deeply about: (1) What reasons do people have for living together? (2) What problems do people have in living together?

The first discussions led to this summary on the blackboard:

REASONS WHY PEOPLE LIVE TOGETHER

progress
religion
education
specialists
experts
discovery

PROBLEMS PEOPLE HAVE IN LIVING TOGETHER
Disagreements

About leadership
About scarcity (food, land)
About religion
About confusion

WHAT MAKES PEOPLE DISAGREE?

Jealousy
Difference of opinion

> Selfishness
> Stubbornness
> Laziness
> Greed
> Childishness
> Spite
> Wrong information

The children had offered some concrete examples from their daily lives in their discussions but had avoided any but respectably abstract entries in meeting their formal assignments. Therefore, so there would be no mistaking the value that the teacher placed on emotionally charged items, Mrs. Jackson made a special assignment: "Write a brief account of a time in your life which involved disagreement."

Here is a verbatim sample of the children's responses:

DISAGREEABLE

People annoy me when they clean the walks with shovels and they scrape them against the walk. People also annoy me when they grit their teeth. I am disagreeable when I argue with my sister and try to fight her, but I always lose. Because when people clean the walk with the shovels and scrape them against the walk, it gives a funny feeling inside of me. I feel like breaking it into pieces. I think I should start giving up, because all I'm doing is getting beat up and it isn't worth it.

MY COUSIN

My cousin makes me mad when he takes things that don't belong to him and blames me for doing something that he did. Once I was in the front room and he *screamed* out

loud. And the lady that lives with us said, "Stop scream-
ing." And he says, "That wasn't me, that was Gail." So my
aunt fusses at me and I feel like bopping him in the mouth.

Once my father was in the room with me and my
cousin gave a piece of tissue to our dog and he tore them
all over the house and my father saw it all. Then my aunt
came in and said that I did it; my father and aunt had an
argument. My dog is a bad one too. Every time I come
home from school I can't get in the house without him
jumping on me and knocking me down. But I love both my
cousin and dog, even though they do all those things.

A DISAGREEABLE TIME

Once my friend and I had a disagreeable time. His name
is Johnny. He is so disagreeable in so many ways. Once we
were going to go to the movies. And when Saturday came
he wanted to go to Rockaway Beach. He is so choosy, but
when it comes to plotting schemes he is a genius. Once he
planned a way on how to get fifty cents by not even working, and you don't call that a genius?

CAN'T WE PLAY IN PEACE?

Around 111th Street there is only one good side to play on.
There is one big space on that side and that's where Mr.
and Mrs. Cranky (their nicknames) are. There is a park to
play in but can you play Slug and Rope in the park? No,
every time we play, zing, out comes the noise, and good-bye
to the Rope game, and boy, are they touchy, don't touch
anything or they will have ten fits. They have the best place
to play Slug and Donkey but will they let us play? No!

WHEN I WAS DISAGREEABLE

I was disagreeable when I went to the store for my mother.
She wanted a small loaf of bread. It usually cost 19 cents

but they had raised it to 25 cents. I told him, "Just yesterday it was 19 cents. Now today it is 25 cents." He said, "What is six cents?" I said, "Six cents is a lot of money when you don't have it." He said, "Are you going to buy it or not?" I said, "I am certainly not."

Here, then, were controlled and shared expressions of the particular qualities of hope, hopelessness, will, defeatedness, purpose, confusion, love, loyalty, anger and indignation, which these children could readily locate in their own lives, lived, as they have been, in the particular settings of faith and faithlessness, law and lawlessness, morality and deceit that are typical of their own estranged society. Confronted with the poignancy of these statements, their reflections of lingering good humor in surroundings of entrenched social illness, it would be understandable if Mrs. Jackson might rather practice preventive psychiatry than teach social studies. Or, if she chose to give up teaching altogether, and took up professional picketing instead, who would point the finger? But Mrs. Jackson has her own tastes in matters of generation and care. She is a teacher, an authority in her profession, the first to test ESI's elementary social studies materials in Harlem. She makes no secret of her dissatisfaction with many of the lessons she is asked to test, and rightly insists on tailoring them to the skills and interests of her pupils, but she is committed to their stated objectives, and to the ultimate benefits that may extend to her pupils if she can help them to achieve those objectives. So, she proceeds to lay the groundwork for eventual comparison of an Iraqi village to the seminomadic life of the Netsilik Eskimos— now sure of conveying to the children that she means them to involve themselves in the comparison, i.e., to *use* the feelings and images they had already controlled and shared.

We return to Mrs. Jackson's class, one week later:

Teacher: "I'm going to give you each a story about family life in an Iraqi village called 'D-A-G-H-A-R-A.' While you're reading it, try to remember our discussions of why people live together and the problems they have in living together. After we've finished reading, we'll just sit and think for a while. Then we'll discuss the story and try to answer the questions I have appended to it."

FAMILY LIFE IN IRAQ

The home is the center of Iraqi family life. The house must be large enough for your grandfather, your own parents and brothers and sisters, and all your aunts and uncles and their children. This means that a home is often a series of houses built together in one unit. The grandfather is the head of the family. He alone has final control in all economic affairs. He takes care of all business matters, selling extra produce and buying small items for the home and farm. He also furnishes the money which enables his sons to marry. Under this system his sons and their families as well as any unmarried daughters live with him until he dies. Then the sons make up their own families and have their children and later grandchildren living with them. This doesn't always happen to be true, but most families follow this pattern.

Although boys and girls have a great deal of fun with their families, their families decide a great many things which children in other parts of the world decide for themselves. Children are not given an opportunity to say what they want to do. "Children are to be seen and not heard" is very true in Iraqi families.

Another custom is that people will say to the father of a newborn baby girl, "I give you tears." The neighbors do not offer congratulations because they believe that family reputation depends upon how a girl behaves when she grows up. A girl is an extra responsibility. The neighbors rejoice if the baby is a boy. He can help his family when he grows up and become a leader in the community.

QUESTIONS

1. How does the number of people in an Iraqi family compare with our families?
2. Why would the families continue to live together after the grandfather dies?
3. How do our families feel when a baby girl is born into the family?
4. How would you react if your parents made the decisions on everything you wanted to do?

Here is a sample of the ensuing discussion. Note two things about it: (1) The lightness of touch with which the teacher was able to lead it, and (2) The ready candor which the children brought to it.

Student: "We don't have the whole family living with us like they do."

Student: "The girls there can't get married until the grandfather dies. That's different from us."

Student: "I agree with Sylvia. My whole family doesn't live together."

Student: "Here it's different about the boys and girls. Here girls learn faster and are smarter, and the mother enjoys having girls around because the boys are just rough."

Student: "I disagree. Boys do just as much around the house as girls."

Student: "I want to disagree about Jeffrey's statement that the girls there couldn't marry until the grandfather dies. The paper doesn't say that. It's not so because the son could immediately take over."

Student: "In the other paper it says that the custom is to marry the first cousin."

Student: "Sometimes men can sew better than women. Also the chefs in restaurants are usually men."

Student: "Boys and men are built more rugged."

Teacher: "Therefore?"

Student: "I read a book about the frontier days. When the mother and father died the son worked all his life to help the sisters and brothers grow up and get educated."

Student: "Boys don't change the baby's diapers."

Student: "In Puerto Rico I had to work in the fields and the girls could stay home."

Student: "Mrs. Jackson, I want to defend my statement. Because it is less work to hunt and to fish than it is to prepare the food, so the woman works harder."

Student: "Men have stronger constitutions than ladies."

Teacher: "Therefore?"

Student: "I had to teach my mother how to run the sewing machine."

Teacher: "The time is running out and we ought to discuss the next question."

Student: "Oh no!"

Student: "If it weren't for ladies, men wouldn't even be born."

Student: "How come they say 'It's a woman's world?' "

Student: "I disagree with the girls who say that girls are better, because if you put a girl in a cage with a bear she would just cry."

(laughter)

Student: "Men must be jealous of ladies because I'm reading in the newspapers all the time about the men that kill their wives."

Student: "No it isn't always that way. I read in the newspapers sometimes where ladies kill their husbands."

By way of showing the headway that these children were making toward the achievement of Adams' objectives, which at first seemed impossibly out of reach of fifth graders, consider the following:

The idea of the continuity of the generations, and the mechanisms of inheritance. For example: "When they said that the girl couldn't marry until the grandfather dies, that's not so because the son could immediately take over." "Maybe the families stayed together after the grandfather died because they want to remember him and do what he would have wished."

The idea of biological and individual differences. For example: "Boys and men are built more rugged." "Men have stronger constitutions than ladies." "I had to teach my mother how to run the sewing machine."

The idea of division of labor and specialization. For example: "Sometimes men can sew better than women." "Sometimes men can cook better than women." "The girls can help inside, and the boys can help outside."

The idea of the human life cycle. For example, the repeated references to birth, death, marriage, and violence.

The idea of the influence on social organization of natural resources and cultural heritage. For example: "Maybe the people stay in the same place after the grandfather dies because they already have the resources there, and it would be foolish to move on where they have to make it all over again." "Just because the grandfather dies, that's no reason why everyone should break up—the ones who are still living know each other and are used to each other's ways."

I submit this lesson as one more verification of Bruner's dictum that it is possible to teach anything to anyone at any age in some form that is honest and interesting. But I would emphasize that it was Mrs. Jackson's use of the curricular materials, not the materials themselves, that made the lesson honest and interesting. To be honest, myself, I should admit that I am not sure if Mrs. Jackson ever studied Erikson or Bruner. But I would still advise other teachers, not sharing Mrs. Jackson's native talents, to study Bruner *and* Erikson.

Unfortunately, for reasons having more to do with funding research than with improving education, Mrs. Jackson's talents had soon to fend for themselves. And so I cannot bring this report to its promised conclusion. The politics of curriculum research notwithstanding, however, Mrs. Jackson and Professor Adams had started something that developed a momentum of its own. And so I may at least report on how it went with these children in response to the first film in the Netsilik series: (Note the evidence of continuing progress toward Adams' objectives.)

Teacher: "Last Friday some of you said that you would like to visit Daghara village. It's too bad we can't take you there by film. But, today you will be seeing another people on film. I won't tell you who they are or where they live because you'll know that as soon as you see it. I'd like you to compare the people you see in this film with the people that you learned about in Daghara village.
(Several of the children ask if they can take notes and are given permission to do so.)

Later:

Student: "I liked the part about catching the fish. It was excit-ing. I was impressed with their skill."

Student: "They do so many things for themselves—to help themselves—and to get what they want—like skinning that turkey." (sic)

Student: "They ate their fish raw—and the way they used the tools! They are very expert with tools! Also the dog eating the fish head, but I don't think that they should eat the eyes."

Student: "I liked best the men building the houses. If I had to be in the wilderness and build myself a shelter I wouldn't know how to do it. They must feel very good that they can do all that."

Teacher: "How did they learn?"

Student: "It was probably handed down by their ancestors, but even so, to be that skillful shows that they must be pretty smart." "Because if I hadn't seen this film I wouldn't know how to do it."

Student: "They're also very smart to build a dam to slow down the fish so they can catch them."

Student: "I like the way they did the fishing. It's faster that way than with a pole."

Student: "Sharon said the food didn't taste good. But she's not eating it; *they* are. Maybe it tastes good to *them*."

Student: "What would they do if they wanted to buy some-thing, if they had to go to work? I mean, the way they make their own clothing and skin the fish and all? How do they get those skills? Were they handed down?"

Teacher: "How do *all* people get skills?"

Student: "Their ancestors hand the skills down and then people learn certain ways and they get accustomed to them and so they stay that way."

Teacher: "What did you think of the little boy?"

Student: "He was playing at fishing and he'll get better and better so that when he is a man he'll be as good as his father."

Student: "I disagree. I don't think those skills were handed down from their ancestors completely. If that was so, they wouldn't get better and better. These people are doing very well, so they must have improved on what their ancestors did."

Teacher: "What makes people want to progress?"

Student: "They get tired of the way they're living. They do the best thinking that they can, and then they ask other people to join in, and if they're determined enough they just do it."

Student: "They want to make it better for their children who are coming on. It isn't just to keep up with the Joneses. I'm sure our parents are not just trying to keep up. They're trying to make it better for us."

Student: "How come some parts of the world have seasons like us and other parts do not? Like Daghara is always hot and this place is always cold."

Student: "How deep is the water where they were fishing?"

Teacher: "Just a few more minutes. Do any of you have any other questions?"

Student: "When the lady was fixing her hair and put a stick in her hair she could have knocked herself out. Why does she do that?"

There was a small genius in this class, and I should not end this report without relaying his notes on the Netsilik film, which I borrowed from his desk after class.

ROBERT GRIFFIN—DAGHARA IN COMPARISON WITH ALASKA

The difference between Daghara and Alaska is encountered beyond the actual facts of life in both places. Daghara seems to be so much more mature and progressive than Alaska. In the film we saw that Eskimos are used to doing things for themselves. In what we have learned so far about Daghara it seems that many of the people there are tired of doing things for themselves. They want to be modern and have all the conveniences. In Alaska it seems as if the people are saying: 'You go your way and I'll go mine.' Maybe *we* can get a lesson from both peoples.

CHAPTER SEVEN

Toward a Complete
Theory of Instruction

The rationale for cultivating emotions in schoolrooms is thus the reverse of the rationale for cultivating emotions in clinics. In clinics, issues which are known to be emotionally charged are raised for the purpose of creating conditions under which emotions can come to be controlled and expressed. In schoolrooms, conditions are created which invite expression of controlled emotions for the purpose of imbuing curricular issues with personal significance. The power of emotion to generate interest and involvement in subject matters which would otherwise find children uninterested and uninvolved lies in their deep personal familiarity—such familiarity being a consequence of emotion having been integral to every phase of personal development from infancy on. The value of emotional involvement in the learning process thus lies in its potential for aiding assimilation of new or remote experiences in idiomatically illuminating ways.

This potential is carried by more than merely associative connections. The emotions are intimately interrelated with certain symbolic functions known to be central to creative thinking. The symbolic functions which regulate all human experience have been classified into three systems: conscious, unconscious, and preconscious. Conscious symbolic processes are predominantly verbal, thrive on repetition, and serve primarily the communication of ideas. Unconscious symbolic processes are predominantly nonverbal, also thrive on repetition, and serve primarily to *prevent* communication by disrupting connections between conscious symbols and their referents. Unconscious symbolic processes are ultimately traceable to childhood experiences in which attempted communication led to situations of being alone and helpless with *pre*conscious experiences. Preconscious symbolic processes are predominantly analogical and therefore serve primarily to diversify the relations between conscious symbols and their referents. This is why the preconscious has become the focus of so much theorizing among investigators concerned with "creative thinking"—especially its so called "incubative" and "illuminative" phases (83).

Human mentality would not be possible without both the conscious and the preconscious processes—and their interaction. So we cannot be accused of taking a perjorative view of the conscious system if we note, with Kubie, that in most instances it consists of a biased sampling of the "preconscious stream" (57). For example, I wish to concentrate at this moment on communicating in English a rather fine distinction pertaining to human mental functioning. I can very palpably sense the rush of enteroceptive, exteroceptive and proprioceptive activity just below the threshold of consciousness. I am sure that a polygraph would indicate at this moment that I am in a state of emotional arousal. Yet, I am not aware of experiencing any particular emotion; rather I am aware only of concentrating on a line of thought. That is, I am automatically ruling out any emotion or attendant image which might divert me from my chosen line of conscious thought. In other words, I am biasing my sample of preconscious mentation for the sake of communicating something I already know. If, on the other hand, I should conclude that I am not as much in command of what I know as I thought I was, or that to communicate effectively I must refresh it, see it from another angle, or relate it in this instance to some otherwise disparate thought, then it would be clear what I should do: go for a walk, take a swim, play tennis, read a novel, or entertain some fantasies that would probably not bear reporting. That is, I should need to stop concentrating in the hope that a less biased sample of my preconscious vagaries would supply what was lacking.

In a sense, then, we often choose to be unimaginative in order to be effectively conventional, and we do so by remaining aloof from the collateral and emotional references which orbit preconsciously around our conscious lines of thought. This is obviously all to the good; nothing less than civilization depends upon it. The trouble comes when the vague sense of choice wanes and we find ourselves being unimaginative for no very good purpose. I need hardly add that people are as frequently miseducated into this dilemma as they are not educated out of it. This, because most teachers—I should say most teaching methods—place a tacit premium on remaining aloof from emotional references in subject matters not only when there is a good reason for doing so but also when there is not.

Since I have been personalizing my point of emphasis, I shall give a personal illustration: Over the past several years, incidental to my work with ESI, I have perforce learned a great deal about the Kalahari Bushmen. Among the many things I thought I knew about the Bushmen was that they are a "resourceful people." I put that in quotations because it is the way I now realize that I learned it:

"The Bushmen are a resourceful people." Recently, in a seminar with a group of teachers who were preparing to teach some trial units of "Man: A Course of Study," I shared the viewing of a film sequence which I had not previously seen. It shows a very dusty, elderly man looking very uncomfortable in the afternoon heat. He motions knowingly to an adolescent boy who routinely pulls his loin cloth aside and proceeds to urinate in the sand at the man's feet; whereupon the man lies down and distributes handfuls of the moistened sand over his body with unmistakable expressions of blissful relief. The ladies and I were the pictures of controlled emotion. No sound emitted during this part of the film, and in the discussions that followed there was a very deft steering around certain topics. It was one of those situations in which the quality of control was made uncertain, however, by not knowing who would be the first to mention the subject that was obviously the focus of everyone's inner tensions. My own uncertainty was made the more acute by the knowledge that this was exactly the kind of situation to which I should rise with some professional flourish, in order to demonstrate at first hand what it had become expected of me to espouse at second hand: the usefulness of openly confronting emotionally charged issues. But for ten minutes after the conclusion of the film, my training and convictions could get only so far as to remind me that here was an opportunity I should be taking, and wasn't. Truth to tell, I had never before shared with a group of lady school teachers the view of a man urinating, much less the view of pleasure in handling excrement, and, as I recall it, I spent the ten minutes feeling alternately embarrassed, abashed that I should feel so, and angry at certain members of the staff, who, I thought, should have alerted me to this part of the film, so that I might have come prepared for it.

Fortunately, out of the sounds at my ear's periphery came the word "resourceful." The seminar was discussing the Bushmen's resourcefulness in the hunting of warthogs, but the word saved the day for me in a very different connection. I knew that the teachers expected me to make some capital of the "urination scene." I also knew that if I had no more to say than that the scene offered opportunities to engage children's emotions concerning the "anal-urethral" phase, and related issues of holding on, letting go, shame, etc., I would raise doubts concerning my own rule that the confrontation of emotional issues in instructional settings should be means to educational ends and not ends in themselves. But during those ten minutes I just could not see the relevance of the urination scene to the pedagogical objectives of "Man: A Course of Study." Out of this unspoken emotion-filled dilemma, I learned, I say, in a very illuminating way, that the Kalahari Bushmen are indeed a very resourceful people: What could be more resourceful in an environment which offers precious little water, but which regularly offers afternoon temperatures of 115 degrees, than the trick of turning a young person's urine to an old person's refreshment? And wasn't this a superb stimulus for getting children to ponder the distinctive resourcefulness of "Man"? Immediately, contrasts and similarities lined up for inspection: the rigid hierarchies that govern access to waterholes among various other species; the implicit rules among non-human primates which govern grooming behavior; the gaming partnerships among the Eskimos in winter camp, through which are resolved so many unplayful conflicts of interest; the Roman baths, and the unparalleled engineering of the viaducts that made them possible; modern Western plumbing, and the training it affords in private enterprise—so central to so many other values of industrial technology. Fortunately, the people who made the film were not thinking of pedagogical objectives; only of honestly recording how the Kalahari Bushmen actually live their lives. And so I was given an opportunity to observe with my own eyes how really human the Bushmen are, evidenced by their ingenuity in adapting environments to themselves rather than themselves to environments, by means of cooperative social patterns!

Subsequently I was able to meet my responsibilities to the seminar. I might add that the teachers were as relieved to confront the emotion-charged issue, as they were enlightened as to how it might be turned to pedagogical account. On the one hand, they had been wondering whether they could ever bring fifth-grade children to care about such weighty abstractions as were involved in Man's distinctively technical and social means of adaptation. On the other hand, they had been silently resolving to skip this particular film for fear of provoking unmanageable tensions in their pupils. Now secure in the knowledge of the film's relevance to *curricular* objectives, several of the teachers were eager to show the film.

The point to be emphasized, however, is still the personal one: I knew before that "the Bushmen are a resourceful people," but in no way that warmed me to them. Indeed, this piece of knowledge was probably as drab to me as it was, because, unlike the children, I was very much at home with the relevant abstractions—too much so, perhaps. I am confident, for example, that I shall never observe a specimen of human behavior that is not somehow distinctively resourceful—in comparison with the other animals—by virtue of its being symbolically processed, and related to some aspect of technology and social organization. So, of course, the Bushmen are resourceful, because the Bushmen are people. Hardly a very assimilated thought. Now, however, I have personally assimilated a particular facet of Bushmen resourcefulness as a vivid case in point of human resourcefulness. And I know that I shall never forget it.

To what can we refer as the source and process of this illumination? All that I had observed was that I was feeling embarrassed and ashamed—very familiar feelings—and that the man in the film was feeling contented and blissful—also very familiar feelings. Being momentarily unable to resolve the contradiction, I was reduced to feeling inferior in my work. Now recall the distinction previously made between "insight" and "outsight." I can say that some of the ten minute interval was spent in trying to achieve insight into my unwanted feelings, since I have learned that this is as good a first step toward professional competence in situations of this kind as any. Whatever success I may have had in achieving insight, however, could not have sufficed to meet the demands of the situation I was in. For that I needed the *outsight* which the word "resourceful" triggered. The rest came in a flash. All of the images contrasting and comparing Bushmen with African mammals, baboons, Eskimos, Romans, modern bathrooms, and systems of private enterprise, simply presented themselves in an instantaneous array of outsights. I had, of course, viewed such images before, but not in relation to the resourcefulness of Bushmen on hot afternoons. In that specific relation the images were preconscious. What had enabled them to become conscious, and so to make personally vivid a piece of knowledge that had previously been taken all too impersonally for granted? It was the prior decision to find some way to confront the emotionally charged issue and not to avoid it. Otherwise, the preconscious images would certainly have remained outside of consciousness in respect to this particular subject matter. It is even conceivable, had my situation in the seminar deteriorated into feeling alone and helpless, that the images would have become unconscious in this connection and thereafter served to disrupt rather than to illuminate my knowledge of Kalahari Bushmen.

We should not leave this incident without speculating on what I did *not* observe in it. Our theory proposes that much else transpired preconsciously during the intervening period, which remained below the threshold of my awareness for want of appropriate employment, but which was crucial to providing the images that did emerge into consciousness with their integrative power. Presumably, at speeds which computers cannot match, and with the economies inherent in analogy, a life cycle-encompassing review of memories relating to embarrassment and contentment had occurred. Such that, had I been on an analyst's couch instead of in a seminar, the conscious sample of my preconscious orbitings might have included images contrasting and comparing the existing situation with previous ones involving episodes of small muscle control—both successful and unsuccessful; of power and manipulation fantasies—both anxiety allaying and anxiety provoking; of various attempts to hold on to and let go of social influences—both satisfying and frustrating; and of the gamut of other memories, fantasies, feelings, and sensations that have gone into my capacities to draw from life experiences of willfulness and experiences of shame. Had the situation been one in which achievement of insight were the appropriate objective, and had that objective been as well achieved as the one reported, the instantaneous flurry of images might well have included a different order of waterhole, other kinds of grooming, more clandestine "partnerships," and private enterprises of a less mutual nature. As it is, all that can be observed of this alternate preconscious course, of which I remain unaware, are the evidences of parallel themes in the manifest contents of the images that did become conscious.

I think it important to have included these latter speculations because of what I have found to be a typical first error made by many teachers who become persuaded that psychoanalytic principles can improve their teaching skills. Not content to lead their students to confront emotionally charged issues, they rush to *interpret* them in ways that are all too readily available in psychoanalytic case histories, overlooking that these are insight-oriented, not outsight-oriented, and therefore run contrary to the manifest purposes of teaching. Imagine the impact on my moment of creative outsight concerning the Kalahari Bushmen, for example, had someone interpreted my momentary loss for words as reflecting a mental block rooted in early ambivalences on the toilet! Remember, however, that the interpretation would probably have been valid, its rudeness residing not in remoteness from truth but in remoteness from relevance.

We may at this juncture seek to clarify a point of typical obscurity along the topographical dimension of psychoanalytic theory, namely the distinction between unconscious and preconscious symbolization. Freud successfully precluded our venturing fruitlessly into notions of differential cortical locations in these matters. But when he came to formulate the more general distinction between the primary (metaphorical) and secondary (literal) symbolic processes he did not say in so many words how he conceived it to coexist with his earlier tripartite formulation of conscious, preconscious, and unconscious symbolization. Kubie gave the clarification: in both preconscious and unconscious symbolization the primary process is dominant, but the former seeks conscious reception, elaboration, and communication, whereas the latter is refractory to con-

sciousness and appears to "seek" deception and miscom-
munication.

However, in his enthusiasm to trace creative behavior
to preconscious symbolization and neurotic behavior to unconscious symbolization, Kubie allows another misconcep-
tion, one that can be particularly misleading to teachers
who usually can only effect commerce with either of these
potentials through conscious channels: the notion that the
difference is fundamentally intra-psychic or "in the head."
Thus creative persons have more preconscious symbols at
their disposal and neurotic persons are afflicted by more
unconscious symbols. There is some nosological truth in
this way of putting the matter, but it is a truth of little
service to teachers whose concerns are less with what is
already in students' heads as with what they can help the
students make of it.

The truth of the matter, let us call it the operational
truth, is that the primary process is rendered preconscious
in its functioning by the *psychosocial conditions* which define it and give it value. These conditions are the same that
we emphasized earlier: (1) the subject matter should be
significant and believable (or make-believable) and (2) the
approach to the subject matter should be such that *all*
emotions and images are welcomed and sought after and
assumed to be ultimately relevant to the educative process—
not shunned and belittled or assumed to be threatening to
children. When these conditions obtain, neurotic persons
are capable of creative behavior; when they do not obtain,
creative persons are capable of neurotic behavior. The fluid
condition, in other words, which our previous considerations of community-aloneness and mastery-helplessness an-
ticipated.

Moreover, these are conditions which find their impetus less in a teacher's methods than in her attitudes, for

they are less subject to permission or arrangement than they are to authorization. Finally, for all their predetermining effects on non-conscious processes, they are conditions which begin and end in consciousness.*

Consider the following illustration of the same points involving less dramatic materials in a more familiar setting: one of the subunits of "Man: A Course of Study" includes a lesson based on slides depicting certain behavior patterns of the herring gull. One slide shows a predator in the vicinity of nests containing newly hatched young. Another slide shows the starkly white adult gulls in flight. Another shows the grey-brown chicks almost perfectly camouflaged, crouching motionless in the nests. Another shows a juvenile gull assuming the headdown position of subordination in the presence of an adult. The immediate objective of the lesson is for the children to grasp how the invariant instinctual responses of herring gulls adapt them to their niche. A long range objective is to supply points of contrast which the children can use to appreciate the increased flexibility of human adaptation due to the ability to learn new responses and to modify old ones.

On the day I observed this lesson it proceeded as follows:

Teacher: "Why don't the big gulls stay with the young on the nest?"
Student: "The fox could see them there and eat them up."
Teacher: "Why don't the chicks run from the fox?"
Student: "The fox could easily catch them and eat them up. If they don't move, maybe the fox won't see them—even if foxes have color vision, which I think they don't."

---

* An observation which is being given perhaps its broadest evidential base in the drugless experiments in consciousness expansion being conducted at California's Esalen Institute.

Teacher: "If the chicks had the same white color as the adults would crouching silently like that be of any use?"

Student: "No, then it would be better if they all ran away; some would be eaten, but others would get away, and at least the race would be saved."

Teacher: "How do herring gulls know that behaving in these ways would enable them to survive? Were they taught?"

Student: "No, they act by instinct, not by thinking."

.

And so on—with the teacher asking the questions and the children giving the answers—until the very last minute when, in order to make a point in time:

Teacher: "In this last slide you see one of the juvenile gulls crouching in that particular position of submission. They do that to keep from being attacked by the bigger gulls."

Student: (*incredulously*) "You mean they attack their young?"

Student: (*uneasily*) "How long before they can fly away?"

Student: (*annoyed*) "How long do they have to do that? When could they fight back?"

Student: (*anxiously*) "Do they . . . *hurt* . . . their . . . *own* . . . young?"

The bell rang and although I thought the teacher fielded these last questions rather poorly ("Well, I guess gulls can sometimes be pretty mean") it ill behooved me as a guest to mention it.

It happened, however, that I was then conducting an in-service seminar on the subject of emotions in teaching for another group of ESI teachers, and, to check on the progress of my own teaching, I asked them what they thought of these questions and what they might do with them.

Student: "Perhaps the children are associating their own experiences of being attacked with the young gull's pose."

Student: "There was a marked shift in cognitive mode there, from responding to questions by the teacher to initiating the intrusive mode themselves. That could be the tip off to be on the alert for feelings of excitement or guilt."

Teacher: "You mean you want the teacher to be mentally scanning Erikson's chart as well as her lesson plan?"

Student: "Not at all. She did the best she could on the spot. But she has a whole evening to improvise a lesson plan for tomorrow that might capitalize on the shift."

Teacher: "Such as?"

Student: "Well, she might begin tomorrow's lesson by reminding the children of their questions when they found out that adult gulls attack the young unless they see the posture of submission. Then she might ask them what thoughts they had when they first learned of this."

Student: "They'd only give what they thought you wanted to hear—the convergent thoughts. I would also ask them what thoughts they *might* have had—or some other kinds of kids, say in Russia or China, might have had—to get their divergent thoughts."

Student: "If they responded well you might go further and give them some assignment that encouraged them to express their feelings, both the syntonic ones (what feelings *did* they have) and the dystonic ones (what feelings *might* they have had)."

Student: "But remember these children have had very little experience expressing emotional reactions in school. Wouldn't they at least need to sense the teacher's purpose in giving such assignments? After all, this could get pretty personal."

Student: "If you ask me we're going overboard with all these emotions. After all it was only one slide! I can see the point about not avoiding emotions when they are running strong. But aren't we going to rather ridiculous extremes running a few innocent queries into the ground?"

Student: "That depends. If all we want to do is teach about herring gulls then it would be going overboard. But supposing Patsy is right, that the children are associating their own experiences of being attacked with that of the young gull. Wouldn't that offer an ideal chance for getting on toward the larger objective: What makes Man human? And with points of contrast that we already knew the kids cared about?"

Teacher: "Let's assume you are right. How would you suggest a teacher might proceed to check it out?"

Student: "That's what you're supposed to tell us!"

Teacher: "And I will, too, if you don't come up with something first!"

Student: "I've got an idea. Assuming they responded well to the convergent and divergent thoughts and the syntonic and dystonic feelings and all (I agree it seems pretty elaborate for an introduction, but maybe the children would need that to get the idea that something really important was in the wind). Anyway, assuming they took to all that, how about following up with a straight down the line lesson plan: 1) What are some ways that humans "attack" their young? 2) What are some ways that human young prevent such attacks? And then, if things look promising, the pay off question: 3) Why do herring gulls have so few ways and human beings so many ways of attacking and preventing attack? If I were the teacher and I'd gotten that far I'd expect to hear not only about instincts and learning, but about language, and tools, and social structures and prolonged childhood, and conscience, and morals, and all the things this course is supposed to be about. Not in so many words, of course, but in terms that I would know meant a lot to the kids—because there wouldn't have been one of them that *I* had not attacked myself, or who I wasn't sure cared to know more about humans attacking their young—whether it was me or their parents or the principal or whomever.

Teacher: "All right, let's try that out here, just to get the feel of it. I'll ask the questions and you give the kinds of answers you think the children in your class would give. Not what you'd like to hear, not what *you* would say if you were in the fifth grade, but what you really think your actual fifth graders would say."

Teacher: "O.K. What thoughts did you have about that last slide?"

Student: "If I behave well I won't get punished."

Student: "Don't herring gull parents love their young?"

Student: "Don't herring gull parents know who their own young are?"

Student: "How do herring gulls perceive their own young—by sight or smell or what?"

Student: "Does the young gull get anything besides not being attacked if he is good?"

Teacher: "All right, what thoughts *might* you have had if you had seen the film on TV or were in a different mood or something?"

Student: "If he's smart he'll keep his head down or get a peck in the pants."

Student: "How long does he have to stay in that position? He'll get a stiff neck."

Student: "If he held his head up, would the big one kill him?"

Student: "Why doesn't he make tracks out of there?"

Teacher: "O.K., what *feelings* would your children have had that they would tell the teacher about?"

Student: "Shock."

Student: "Fear."

Student: "Disbelief."

Student: "Revulsion."

Teacher: "And what feelings might they only own up to *other* kids having?"

Student: "He can make me hold my head down but he can't hear what I'm saying under my breath."

Student: "When I grow up I'll fix his wagon."

Student: "Look at him with his head sticking up. But I've seen it in the garbage."

Student: "Just you wait 'enry 'iggins!" (I really have a child who would say that.)

Teacher: "O.K., all is going well with the convergent and divergent thoughts and the syntonic and dystonic feelings and, as you say, "all of that." So let's continue: What are some ways that human adults attack their young?"

Student: "Spanking."

Student: "Bawling out."

Student: "Ridicule."

Student: "Deprivation—TV, dessert, play, etc."

Student: "Shaming."

Student: "Abandoning—or playing at it."

Student: "Scaring."

Student: "Threatening—to forbid playing with Billy."

Student: "Telling father."

Teacher: "And what are some ways that human young prevent or avoid such attacks?"

Student: "Silence."

Student: "Being respectful."

Student: "Raising your hand in class."

Student: "Imitating."

Student: "Getting dressed by yourself."

Student: "Washing your hands."

Student: "Making your bed."

Student: "Doing homework."

Student: "Practicing the piano."

Teacher: "And now the clincher: Why do you think it is that older and younger herring gulls have so few ways of attacking and preventing attack, and older and younger humans have so many ways?"

Student: "Oh, let's not spoil it. I can really hear my kids saying some of this, but I've always thought of this kind of thing as by-play, chit-chat, diversion. Not as part of a lesson. I want to try it with my own class, and I don't want to spoil it with my own preconceptions."

Perhaps our sceptic was right. Such a lesson might turn out to be heavy handed, and much ado over one slide. But I have seen more heavy handed lessons than I can count, and much done in classrooms about far less. And so I continue to hope that something similar may be tried by eventual teachers of "Man: A Course of Study" when they come to the package that will be labelled: "Man and Animals—Herring Gull."

If, as was implied above, a teacher is ill-advised to refer to Erikson's chart in reconnaissance of *immediate* points of contact between her pupils' emotions and her curriculum's objectives, why was a whole chapter devoted to it? The answer is that in adapting the chart to the needs of teaching I was not thinking of teachers as soldiers but as generals. In other words, the chart is offered as an heuristic for the lesson *planner*—not for the conductor of lessons.

A teacher's workday is almost entirely consumed in meeting the tactical demands of necessarily preconceived lesson plans—not to mention the demands made by administrative procedures, parents' requests, individual needs of students, problems of classroom management, etc. It is a kind of work in which emotionally charged issues, appearing unpredictably as they usually do, are likely to be perceived as disruptive forces, alien to the purposes at hand, and therefore either to be avoided or met with a mind to dispelling them as quickly and summarily as possible. This is natural under average teaching circumstances. Now, if a teacher is temperamentally inclined to regard children's emotions as something to be relegated to extracurricular activities, or chooses, for other reasons, to regard her professional responsibilities as pertaining exclusively to whatever commerce she can strike up between the curricular materials and the pupils' intellects, then that is that. It is the teacher who wants to include the cultivation of childrens' thoughts *and* emotions among her professional responsibilities with whom we are primarily concerned. Such a teacher has usually found ways of responding well to her pupils' feelings during the unpredictable moment to moment encounters of the classroom day, but rarely during the more deliberative times of composing lesson plans. More often than not this teacher has come to regard her skills in "human relations" as just that, and nothing more. That is, she comes to see her responsibilities in these matters as being primarily between human being and human being, and only secondarily as between teacher and student. From the vantage points thus developed over the course of a career it is difficult for such a teacher to perceive her pupils' emotions as opportunities to be exploited in the integral aspects of planning future lessons.

The Erikson chart is offered as a first aid in meeting this problem. It at least provides a conceptual container in which the teacher can store observations of passing emotional encounters between herself and her students and her subject matter for later reference. It remains to be shown how the chart can be employed as an heuristic device to place these passing observations into more lasting perspectives, to raise questions or hunches as to possible reorganizations of lesson sequences, orchestration of materials, offbeat coordinations with other subjects, etc. It is to this usage of the chart that we turn next.

As has been noted, the key to effectively involving emotions in educational endeavors is relevance—to the subject matter itself and/or to its presentation. How, then, may Erikson's conceptual scheme be employed to anticipate relevance? Three interrelated ways suggest themselves: (1) coordination of developmental issues with curricular issues; (2) coordination of cognitive skills with emotional and imaginal skills; (3) coordination of classroom management with instruction.

COORDINATION OF DEVELOPMENTAL ISSUES WITH CURRICULAR ISSUES

The subject is the origin of cities. The children have been emulating archaeologists, speculatively reconstructing from photographs and replicas of the Nippur digs the kinds of people who began the urban ways of life which so profoundly changed the course of human history. Where did these people come from? What did they believe in? How were they governed? What were their rights and wrongs? What did they know? What did they do? How did they pass along to future generations what they knew and did and believed in? Subsequently, Charlotte recalls a fear she felt in response to a story about Abraham Lincoln's eyelash. On the face of things, nothing would seem less relevant to the subject. In the interview situation it quickly became apparent how very relevant this passing memory was, but presumably in a regular classroom situation there would not have been an appropriate opportunity to explore the matter on the spot.

Now let us envision the teacher of Charlotte's class trying to conceive of a teaching strategy that would remedy an acute condition in her class of "cooperation-itis": the children are being helpful; they are well-behaved, following instructions, doing the reading, participating in discussions, and completing assignments. It is clear, however, that whatever interests are being generated are products of relative deprivation. This is new material and the children are grateful not to have to dissemble total boredom; they are also respectful of the teacher's special interests in the material—and who knows but what there may be some surprises yet to come. And it is, after all, rather like playing detective or hide-and-seek and will therefore do until school is out and they can return to things that matter.

The teacher knows she can exploit this condition, can get Charlotte and her classmates to learn something of the rules of evidence and inference that would show up later on examinations, and also something of ancient history. She also knows, however, that if the children come to *care* about any of this, such that they might later pursue it independently, they will have done so without much assistance from her. Moreover, her experience has convinced her that such children are always in a minority. She wants to have a professional hand in the majority of her pupils not only learning the subject matter but also *caring* to learn it.

How can Erikson's chart be of service to her? It can key her into broad areas of emotional import, and therefore of personal significance, which *if made relevant to the subject matter* would provide some children with opportunities for linking insights to outsights, and other children with opportunities for linking outsights to insights—thus rendering the insights more mature and the outsights more meaningful. The insights might be conscious or preconscious, communicated or privately entertained; the outsights might bear directly on the subject matter, or might reflect prior knowledge brought by the children to the subject matter. The processes of mutual enhancement between insight and outsight might surface in expressed forms, or they might remain preinspirational to some as yet unencountered aspect of the subject matter.

How might this teacher turn the unlikely topic of Lincoln's eyelash to such advantages in planning future lessons? She would first ponder two questions: (1) What may be the *developmental* significance of the story and Charlotte's reactions to it, such that all of the children might respond, overtly or covertly, with related personal interests? (2) What dimensions of the subject matter would be most related to subsequent affective and imaginal responses? There is, of course, no compelling need for the aid of a chart in seeking answers to these questions, but it has been known to help beginners. It would remind the teacher in the present instance, for example, that every child in her class is especially concerned with issues of industry and inferiority, that any emotion will gravitate toward these issues, and is likely, therefore, to seek outsightful points of contact with the subject matter which center on matters of technology. This is actually what Charlotte did in the interview, without instruction. With the assistance of the chart the teacher might then go further in the direction of "deepening" her instructions. She might see that there are possible points of contact in this passing incident between concerns the children may recently have shown about matters of trust and mistrust with the intrinsically related facets of the subject matter which center on issues of organized faith; and between the children's fantasies of discovery and rejuvenation with intrinsically related facets of the subject matter which center on systems of moral law. Admittedly, a teacher of mathematics or physics might be hard pressed to locate in the subject matter articulable blends of technology, organized faith and moral law (although Einstein could not refrain from it), but for a teacher of social studies who wants to lead her students to care about archaeological rules of inference and the kinds of people who began urban life on our planet, what an opportunity!

I wish I could go on to suggest a specific lesson plan. I think of some exercise that might find the children wondering what Charlotte's diversion could tell them about what makes Man human (Charlotte, herself, being a valid specimen) and which might then lead them to puzzling how the people who formed the first cities must have conceived related human thoughts and memories. Did these people die? Did they imagine rebirth? What did life mean to them? What did they think of as good and bad? What kinds of laws might they have had? What might they have believed in? How might their beliefs have been different from or similar to ours? What makes us think so? What does all this tell us about how we got the way we are?

This is all too pedantic and would probably fall flat in an actual classroom. Experience has shown, however, that when a teacher senses such ultimate relevance between her students' private worlds and her subject matter, much more plausible lesson plans are usually forthcoming. The behavioral signs of success are always the same: the classroom noise resembles the noise of a workshop more than that of a playpen or a prison. (The professional ears of most teachers know this difference well.) And the answers, when they come, are not only correct but convincing, by virtue of their inclusion of metaphor, allusion, paraphrase, and other signs, that, having found the subject in themselves the children can put themselves into the subject.

COORDINATION OF COGNITIVE SKILLS WITH EMOTIONAL AND IMAGINAL SKILLS

A characteristic position of new curricula advocates is that if we can learn to present school children with man-sized problems in forms appropriate to their age, and can then give them instruction in how to fully use their heads, the involvement of their hearts must inevitably follow. Would that this stratagem, which is valid for some children, were valid for all. Unfortunately, it is based on premises supplied by an exceedingly small number of children—

usually two or three per class. These are always temperamentally contemplative and highly verbal children, who are also unusually facile at resolving emotional conflicts. They are warm, generous, inquisitive, poised youngsters who already exude a sense of personal integrity and style. Over the years, I have found myself informally identifying various experimental classes by the names of these children; no doubt because they were the ones who confirmed what we so earnestly wished to see confirmed, namely that our new social studies materials provided increased opportunities for optimal learning. The others, however, to be truthful, seemed to be no more engaged by these opportunities than by previous ones.

It is at this juncture that the counter-reformational undercurrents discussed earlier can assume obstructive force in experimental education. The vitality of interplay which can develop with minimal teacher intervention between exceptional curricular materials and exceptional children is welcomed and applauded by all, regardless of occupational or theoretical predilection. But the teacher who seeks to avail her whole class of these exceptional materials by intervening on behalf of those children whose styles of learning she knows to favor initial involvement of emotional or imaginal processes is sometimes faced with unaccountably militant resistance by psychologists who have specialized in the study of cognition. I take the liberty of quoting from a "confidential" report addressed by one such psychologist to a group of teachers and curriculum coordinators:

> If you concentrate on teaching children how to think, you will have taught them how to use their feelings appropriately. Whether or not a child is conscious of the appropriate use of his feelings is irrelevant. Whether or not

he is expressing them verbally in a form you find acceptable or suitable is irrelevant.

If you take care of a child's thinking, his feelings will take care of themselves.

But if you try to take care of a child's feelings, his thinking will *not* take care of itself, and you will have been practicing irresponsible pedagogy. Or medicine without a license.

A theory of instructed learning which disregards the normal range of individual differences found in the average schoolroom must devolve into this kind of doctrinairism. A credible psychology of instruction must at the very least be suggestive in respect to three types of students: those who are predisposed to lead with their thoughts, those who are predisposed to lead with their feelings, and those who are predisposed to lead with their fantasies. It has been one of Bruner's major contributions to the new educational psychology that teachers are coming to include within their professional purviews the cultivation of cross-curricular cognitive skills rather than assuming that these can be left uninstructed to maturational processes. I will have it that there are good reasons to be as responsible in respect to emotional and imaginal skills.

Admittedly, one cannot aid in the development of emotional and imaginal skills without reference to their integral cognitive counterparts. But this truism applies from which ever bias one begins. Neither—and this has been obvious since William James—can one hope to effectively aid in the development of cognitive skills without reference to their integral emotional and imaginal counterparts. Admittedly too, appropriateness in schoolrooms lies more often in passions and dreams giving the unobstrusive under- and overtones to the appointed notes of thought, than conversely. But, as surely as the best composed lesson plans are *not* analogous to musical scores, being as conducive to their own displacement by unpredictable opportunities as to their governance of predictabilities, the matter of orchestrating appropriate degrees and forms of emotional and imaginal expression in support of cognitive skills is the teacher's to improvise upon. A theory of instruction should seek to discipline this most sensitive of teaching functions, and not seek to discourage it.

The coordination of cognitive, emotional, and imaginal skills may be left untutored in exceptionally healthy children. For the rest, if exclusive emphasis is placed on cultivating cognitive skills, and development of emotional and imaginal skills is left to random encounters, we run the risk with the child who tends to lead with his head of encouraging pedantry; with the child who tends to lead with his heart of courting anti-intellectualism; with the child who tends to lead with his fantasies of inviting estrangement.

Suppose, for the sake of discussion, we actually were exclusively concerned with cultivating cognitive skills. Instruction in related emotional and imaginal skills would still be indicated. The child who is learning to focus his attention, whether visually, auditorily, or introspectively must find reassurances and intimations of his own style in opportunities to integrate related emotional correlates concerning trust and mistrust, and related imaginal themes of discriminant and indiscriminant incorporation. He *must* find these reassurances and intimations of individuality in such opportunities because these respective cognitive, emotional, and imaginal processes have been intimately related in his previous development, and are, as regards his "ego development," of a piece. We may be sure, then, that he is looking for such integrations, is "ready" for them.

Similarly, in respect to the rudiments of logical thinking, experience in resolving emotional conflicts involving autonomy, shame, and doubt, and the employment of fantasies concerning disappearance, reappearance, power, and magic must work to draw the child's abilities to affirm, negate, exclude, and postpone into the orbit of his synthesis ego. Conversely, the overlooking of these integral emotional and imaginal correlates of logical thinking must work to draw the latter into the orbit of the child's defense ego.

And so on, through the schoolable years of the life cycle: relevant confrontations of emotional issues centering around initiative and guilt, and relevant employment of discovery, exploration, and origination fantasies, must automatically work to humanize the child's growing ability to think critically. Relevant confrontations of emotional issues centering around competence and inferiority, and relevant employment of achievement fantasies, must automatically work to broaden the child's development of representational skills. Relevant confrontations of emotional issues centering around identity and diffusion, and relevant employment of utopian images, must automatically work to inspire creative thinking.

The arrangement of opportunities for these coordinative events to take place in schoolrooms is, of course, work for the teacher's "left hand." To expect these intricacies of ego synthesis to announce their occurrence at every turn would be to overlook that they function, for the most part, preconsciously. Similarly, to expect, much less to require, that the various alignments and realignments of cognitive, emotional, and imaginal skills be as neatly horizontal as our chart makes them appear would be to overlook the epigenetic nature of ego synthesis. (See pages 162–67 above. Also 39, Chapters 3 and 5.)

The teacher's work is actually made simpler by these qualifications. She has only to compose lessons which capitalize on the intrinsic relevance to the subject matter of the various cognitive, emotional, and imaginal skills in any sequence that reveals itself to her—leaving the various, and necessarily idiomatic, integrations of these to her various pupils to engineer in the privacy of their own broodings, brainstorms, empathies, and antipathies.

COORDINATION OF INSTRUCTION AND "CLASS MANAGEMENT"

It had been one of those days when the best of lesson plans and the most cleverly designed of materials must fail because of one child's disruptive claims on the class's attention. Michael had been the "problem child" from the first day of this experimental fourth grade. Unable to subordinate his personal thoughts to participation in instructed activities, and equally unable to keep his thoughts to himself, his contribution to the class consisted of intermittent insertions of irrelevancies. On their face these were innocent intrusions, and Michael's generally infantile ways were otherwise not without endearment. An unverbalized pattern of toleration came to characterize the responses to Michael of both the teacher and his classmates—the discordant remarks being neither openly discouraged nor openly acknowledged. Of late, however, Michael had been taxing the limits of tolerance by stepping up the frequency of his irrelevant remarks, and also by wandering disconcertingly about the classroom. He had privately confided to the teacher that the reason he behaved as he did was because he felt the other children disliked him. The teacher, being concerned that he not reinforce his own fears by jeopardizing what she knew to be her own hope and the desire of the other children to eventually include him, had exacted his promise to at least confine himself to his desk.

On this day, Michael had been impossible, with the result that the teacher found herself devoting almost her full energies to controlling one pupil. Predictably, her influence with the others waned. In the coordinating committee meeting which followed this class, the school principal enumerated the teacher's options in respect to Michael as he saw them: (1) exclude Michael from the program, (2) provide him with special tutoring outside of class designed to engage him in the subject under conditions that precluded his having to compete for a teacher's attention or (3) provide him with a special desk inside the classroom, to which he must retire with one of the assistant teachers whenever he disrupted a lesson, making it clear to Michael that he was free to take his normal place whenever he felt ready to assume normal responsibilities, and making it clear to the class why it was that Michael was receiving special attention.

The teacher, Miss Catherine Motz, was about to choose the latter when she thought of a fourth option: The subject matter for the next week, it so happened, was to be the forms and functions of social organizations among lower primates. This in preparation for eventual comparisons with patterns of social organization among preliterate and modern humans. The children would be informed of the various deployments of baboon troops in response to predators, of the dominance hierarchies which serve to control aggression within the troop, of the special alliances and exceptions to "rules" which facilitate care of the young, and so forth. One of the "structural" differentials which it was hoped the children would come to use in ordering their thoughts concerning their own species pertained to the comparative consequences of isolation in human adaptation and in lower primate adaptation. A baboon who finds himself isolated from his troop because of sickness, injury or aberrant behavior will soon be dead, since a baboon's only effective defense against predators is his troop. Moreover, there is very little a baboon troop can do to "rescue" an isolated member, since its integrity is contingent upon movement from place to place within predetermined time limits—from sleeping trees to foraging grounds to water hole and back to sleeping trees, before dark. By contrast, an isolated human being is rarely in danger of physical harm; if danger exists it is more likely to be psychological: loneliness, boredom, ineffectiveness, apathy, fear, etc. Just as "dangerous," sometimes, by the criteria of human adaptation, but this is danger of an intriguingly different order. On the other hand, humans sometimes *seek* isolation and are the better for it, both as individuals and as community members, having been restored or inspired or refreshed in any of the various ways made possible by our distinctive nervous systems. Moreover, human groups have perfected institutions and supporting technologies for the purpose of regulating isolation in individuals: such as religion, law, medicine, education.

To gain discriminate mastery of the concept of isolation as it is relevant to human and to prehuman adaptation would thus be to possess a conceptual tool with which to comprehend and give order to vast amounts of information concerning social organization in evolution—one of the main objectives of the course. So, approximately, ran Miss Motz's thoughts. And here was a possible opportunity to place at the focus of every pupil's immediate and concerned attention in her very classroom a vivid case in point of human isolation. It occurred to her that she had access to an excellent film on the eating habits of a troop of semi-domesticated Japanese Macaque monkeys in which there are some poignant shots of one monkey who had unaccountably been ostracized; the other monkeys pointedly avoided it, except on occasion to mistreat it. The narrator of the film sees fit to observe that in all likelihood this monkey will live out its days in this unhappy plight. The rough outline of a lesson plan emerged: Show the monkey film. The children would certainly follow with questions and comments about the hapless isolated monkey. Then go right into the core question: "What makes humans human?" Specifically, what *human* situations correspond to the Macaque situation? How do they differ? How to account for the differences? Why do *human* groups sometimes exclude an individual? Are there times when human individuals are excluded forever? When? Why? Are there times when human individuals are excluded temporarily for the purpose of helping them to return as more effective members? If Michael and his classmates, for reasons of tact, chose to leave the local illustration to unverbalized recognition, fine. Their emotional investment in the immediate example of human isolation could not be lost in any event, and its relevance to the subject matter was so obvious that the lesson must gain as a consequence. And, if Michael or his classmates chose to explicate the local parallel? In that event she would note its lack of precision: was avoidance or mistreatment in evidence in the classroom example? It would be interesting and perhaps useful to know if it was perceived so. In any event, Michael's isolation could hardly be made more explicit than the principal's three options would make it, and these lacked the added advantage of directly including Michael in the lesson. Moreover, the children seemed to understand Michael and his problem; at times, she though;, better than she did. They could probably be counted on to respect his privacy. And if worse came to worst? "Well, with such an open line to the subject matter available to me I could simply rule transgressions out of order. After all, the lesson is not for Michael's benefit; it's to help everyone to learn and to think about what makes humans human. And, if anyone thought otherwise, they had better start paying attention!"

Alas, it was the coordinating committee—itself an interesting case of maladaptive social organization—which failed to pay attention. The principal was for the plan, thought it an improvement on his initial suggestions. The psychologist also agreed; if the plan worked it would provide a nice documentary for inclusion in a teacher's manual as regards capitalizing on emotional issues. However, an "educator" noted that the plan ran counter to one of the axioms of almost all instructional "methods" courses, namely that pedagogical and "classroom management" objectives were best kept separate. The psychometrist objected on familiar grounds: the plan smacked of "group therapy." The subject specialist thought it a good idea "on paper," but Michael was diverting enough of the class's attention and this might invite him to monopolize it altogether. The production people were also opposed because there were so many materials to be tested and so little time to test them; if the plan failed it would be time wasted, and if it succeeded even more time might be required to follow it through. And the "researchers" could not see how the plan lent itself to "cognitive skill development." Under these circumstances the teacher was sorry, but this was not an atmosphere in which she felt she could afford to get negative results; she would try it later in her own classroom, if a similar opportunity presented itself.

So much for the advantages of conducting instructional research as a part of curriculum development when the emphasis is on achievement rather than on process!

Ad hoc considerations will, however, serve to illustrate the point intended. It is that instructional and class management objectives need not be pursued separately, and can sometimes be pursued concurrently to mutual advantage. Chronic class management problems such as the one posed by Michael are usually mental health problems. Granted. Thus, we are back to the fine line, previously delineated, which threads its way between instruction and psychotherapy. The same principles hold. Michael was an anxious child, alone and helpless with his imagination, a condition which was being steadily aggravated by the irrelevance of his attempts to reduce his isolation from his classmates. Any efforts to reduce Michael's anxiety which had the effect of distracting the teacher from her primary responsibilities to the other children, and to the curriculum, would have compounded the management problem, and jeopardized the special allowances already made for Michael by his classmates. As regards arithmetic or spelling or physical science, in respect to which the possible relevance of this classroom situation would be obscure, separation of the management and instruction functions would be indicated. However, as regards the *social studies* curriculum, the relevance of this classroom situation to the lesson is so obvious that *not* to utilize it could conceivably constitute a lesson in denial for some perceptive children.

Miss Motz's plan sought to combine the two teaching functions in a way that promised to optimize the effectiveness of each. The class was to be offered an especially credible and relevant (may we say "honest and interesting"?) opportunity to consider the comparative forms and functions of social organization as between man and the lower primates. An opportunity, in other words, for the children to discover these comparisons for themselves. That the children were already emotionally involved in the points of comparison and must, as it were, "double-take" their involvement at the moment of recognizing its curricular relevance would add the factor that is so often lacking in the "self-discovery method," i.e., *self* discovery.

As for Michael, he was to be given a custom-made opportunity to join the class as a working member. The situation he had uncontrollably created by his irrelevancies was to be given the possibility of becoming singularly relevant and controllable. He could be as active or passive as he chose to be in availing himself of this opportunity, but in this one instance his presence could not in any conceivable event be irrelevant. In short, Michael was to be given a chance to become less helpless before his imagination by way of developing outsight. If, in the privacy of his own vulnerable psyche, he should gain an insight or two, or feel less alone with his images of estrangement, so much the better for Michael. Meanwhile, to the extent the plan achieved its instructional objectives, the likeliness would increase of its also achieving management objectives. And, conversely, to the extent the plan achieved its management objectives, the likeliness would increase of its also achieving instructional objectives.

The teacher who has learned to coordinate instructional and management responsibilities in this way deserves to feel, and therefore tends to feel, professional—with the many indirect benefits which then accrue to her sense of presence when engaged in the separate roles of disciplinarian and instructor. She may even hope to earn from her students that rare quality of total respect that children reserve for adults who display not only more knowledge of the world than they have but more knowledge of children than they have.

The epigenetic schedule of psycho-social modalities is particularly pertinent to the development of a teacher's skill in coordinating class management and instructional objectives. The generic modalities which are normally in phase, or coming into phase, during the school years involve the social skills of knowing how, of being oneself, and of sharing oneself and one's knowledge. We speak of classroom behavior which is expressive of these modalities as "mature." The "immature" behaviors, which pose most problems of classroom management are rightly described as such. They are usually expressions of earlier and therefore more practiced incorporative, retentive, eliminative, and intrusive social skills, which have not yet been comfortably realigned in support of the more fulfilling skills of maturity. They may be described, in other words, as *regressive*—either defensively so or strategically so. That is, they are either in defense against anxiety or they are as yet inept attempts to cope with reality—a distinction we shall address in detail in Chapter Nine. In either event, the teacher's best course is the same: to the extent she can bring the behavior in question into relevant commerce with her special province of reality, i.e., the subject matter, she has increased the likeliness that personal development and academic development will come to synchronous terms.

CHAPTER EIGHT

Man: A Course of Study

Relevance, then, is the key to availing the instructional process of emotional and imaginal influences. In emphasizing this point, it has been noted that such relevance is more likely to be found in conjunction with social studies than in conjunction with other subjects in the elementary curriculum. This has perhaps left the impression that as elementary teachers become more knowledgeable about emotional and imaginal development they will automatically appreciate the many points of relevance between the children's self-interests and the lessons and materials of the social studies. Any such impression would be misleading.

On the contrary it has often been the disappointing case in this writer's experience that the more adept a teacher becomes at providing children with opportunities to express their inner lives, the more glaring may be her failures to establish relevant points of correspondence in the subject matter if her own knowledge of the subject matter is shallow. With the result that the children are given insufficient opportunities to *employ* what they have successfully been encouraged to express.

This is less than ironic. As long as "the friendly postman" and "the happy Mexican" could pass as meaningful units in social studies the problem did not exist.

Insufficient mastery of the social sciences poses no handicap in the perpetuation of illusions. As soon, however, as a school system commits itself to a social studies curriculum like ESI's "Man: A Course of Study," which seeks to instruct children in the actual substance of the social sciences, it must face the fact that ignorance of the subject matter on the parts of its teachers will be the rule and not the exception. This for the reason that the course is almost as much a novelty to the teachers as to the children. We do not yet have a generation of teachers adequately schooled in the social sciences.

Let us therefore pause to consider the content and objectives of "Man: A Course of Study." What follows is one man's view. It is a view, however, which has the merit of having been tempered by the exacting questions of teachers who were actively engaged with the exacting questions of children in response to ESI materials.

Since the Endicott Conference, there has been no lack of debate among university scholars over how best to introduce young children to the fundamentals of the social sciences. Some have felt this could best be accomplished as an implicit part of the study of history, that is, by intensive study of certain critical turning points in man's story—the invention of agriculture, the rise of urbanization, the Industrial Revolution, and the invention of representational government. The distinctive nature of man being implicit in these events, it could be expected to become explicit with particular force and timeliness as the children came to understand and to speculate on the causal factors common to these events. There are those, on the other hand, who consider that the children's study of history is best designed to emerge from their study of the social sciences. Among those who hold this view there are two sub-schools of thought. One says that the best way to construct a social studies curriculum is to settle ahead of time on the lines along which the social sciences are best articulated (language, technology, social organization, and the like), and to set these up as the explicit pedagogical objectives, viewing the coverage of such concrete subjects as the Netsilik Eskimo or the Nippur excavations as means to these more general ends. The other contends it is better to teach the exemplary subjects as ends in themselves, assuming that the children will in time extrapolate the broader framework which holds them together.

There have also been differences of opinion regarding the comparative extent to which elementary social studies should seek to instruct the future scholar and the future citizen, respectively. There was a time, for example, in the early phases of ESI's social studies venture, when some feared that emphasis was being placed on the ancient origins of urbanization to such an extent as to divert the children from concerning themselves with the contemporary problems of urbanization. "Nippur is important," as one man put it, "but so are Birmingham and Harlem."

There has been remarkably little disagreement, however, concerning the ultimate objective: a discriminant and disciplined understanding of man *as a species*. If this objective can be realized, then both the future scholar and the future citizen are served. In the one instance the future scholar is instructed in a fundamental set of skills and concepts which will make him a more discerning student of anthropology, psychology, and sociology in the secondary and higher phases of his education. In the other instance it is made possible for the future citizen, during his identity-forming years, to include among his identifications with family, class, race, religion, and nation an identification with the family of man, his species.

Think of the contemporary societal ills that could not

exist if a generation of Americans could be taught to identify—in heart, mind, and stomach—with the human species, that is, if the children's personal sense of identity could be rooted primarily in awareness of the similarities that unite all human beings and secondarily in awareness of the differences that can divide some human beings. Consider, however, that it is precisely the awareness of supervening human similarity that threatens us now, precisely because it questions our present dependence on self definition by contrast with different cultural, ethnic, regional, and national groupings. The goal will therefore not be achieved soon. Nor will it be achieved without meeting resistance. Obviously it cannot be achieved without threatening the children.

Consider further that these objectives presume a curriculum of an explicitly evolutionary cast. Doubtless this will determine, more than any other consideration, the extent to which the new social studies will initially be adopted in the nation at large. Individual boards of education, superintendents, principals, and teachers will vary in their responses to the choice thus posed. The choice itself, however, is clear, undeniable, and absolute. Man's overarching distinction as a species is that he has been the instrument of a qualitative innovation in the proceedings of evolution on this planet, adding to the inorganic and organic systems of producing and regulating change a psychosocial system of producing and regulating change. The various dimensions of man's distinctiveness; his use of language, his use of tools, his social inheritance of acquired characteristics, his cosmologies; all derive their ultimate significance from this observation. There is no way short of self-deception to blink this away. To teach "Man: A Course of Study," for example, while seeking to avoid or even to subdue recognition of its conceptual roots in the theory of evolution would be to teach it in such ways that the "new" social studies would be undistinguishable from the "old" social studies. For example, a lesson or series of lessons on, say, "Man and animals" must devolve into mere biology unless set in an evolutionary conceptual frame. Not that the intricacies of genetics and biological evolution should be gone into in detail at the elementary level, any more than the intricacies of economic history or the symbolizing functions should be gone into in detail at this level. But if a lesson in social studies is not ultimately coordinate with a deepening appreciation of the fundamental differences between inorganic, organic, and psychosocial evolution it will do little to deepen awareness of the overarching similarities that make "a family" of Man.

Take the prospective case that, within the lifetime of children now in school, our taxes will have supported a laboratory of biochemistry in which a form of organic life is manufactured. It will be a lowly form—probably a virus—but it will be a virus that in all aspects of its organicity will not be distinguishable from the natural kind, except that we will know it to be tool-made. In passing, cancer will probably have been conquered by the same tools. Or, take a retrospective case, say, Shakespeare's Hamlet: tool-made from start to finish. Or take the distant prospect of a finished and revised and well-taught social studies unit for the elementary schools. This too will have been tool-made. Or choose from thousands of like examples, but make them sufficiently dramatic to insure some preoccupation with the following questions:

(1) What makes this species so special? What are the distinctive root conditions that are characteristic of man when compared with other animals, from which have followed such events of mastery and relationship? (2) What

were the origins of these distinctive conditions? (3) What are the consequences of these distinctive conditions? What may be their significance? (4) What, finally, may it all be about? Two hundred years ago, there were no answers to the first three of these questions, and only stabs at answers to the last. Now, there are some answers to the first three questions, and at least some more manly postures in respect to the last.

(I) *What are the distinctive root conditions of man the toolmaker?* They are: (1) His preemptive symbolizing capacities and activities. The ability to think in response both to environmental stimulation and in response to his own thoughts and feelings. The ability to invent and communicate languages and systems of mathematics; to order the unknowable by way of mythologies and religions; to express and share individualized experiences in literature, dance, and music; to dream, hallucinate, and play. And, not least, to become, from time to time, self-aware. (2) The extraordinarily large fraction of the expected life span that is preoccupied with "growing up," of being recognized as a full member. (Approximately one-sixth in the most primitive of societies; approximately one-third in the more civilized of modern societies; and in some highly specialized groups, such as the Boston Psychoanalytic Society, approximately two-thirds.) Enter the uniquely human problems and problem solutions involving love, hate, compassion, envy, authority, obedience, independence, conformity, creativity, learning, unlearning, and anxiety. Other animals have met semblances of such problems but only we are required by the amount of time it takes us to grow up to cultivate them. This we have done, and are the more viable for it as a species. Thus we have it, according to Job and Isaiah, that not the least of our claims to evolutionary fame is that we have stood up to God by virtue of being led by little children. (3) The predilection to form social organizations, and the difficulties of reforming them in time: families, extended families, clans, bands, tribes, cities, nations, fraternities, parties, unions, commissions, institutes, gangs, poker clotches, fan clubs, and so on.

These three distinctive root conditions of humanity are, of course, conditioned by the vicissitudes of their interaction—by which we remind ourselves that we intend to leave something over for higher education.

(II) *What are the origins of these distinctive conditions?* It has been one of the most thought-provoking of recent discoveries that although symbolization, prolonged maturation and socialization have for some time been behind man's tool-making, they are themselves the evolutionary products of man's earliest tool-using. Some of our prehistoric ancestors, whose refuse the Leakey's have been digging from Olduvai Gorge, seem to have discovered tools that were as useful for meeting the challenges of their days as are our vaunted computers for meeting the challenges of our days. What they discovered was not much: the utilities of broken bones and sharp stones. When compared to the treasury of meaningful sounds at the disposal of Shakespeare, these are only laughably describable as "tools." Those who mastered them, however, did all that we wish to do: they lived longer and better, and they taught some of the secrets of their achievements to their children. Moreover, they did this with very small brains, and at times on all fours—or so it seems. The rest was done by more time than we are used to thinking seriously of, and by the events of natural selection. That is, the advantages that accrued to those who could apply bones and stones to the problems of hunger, sickness, chance disaster, the needs of other species, and the excessive needs of their own kind were so immense that in the mere span of at most two million years the planet was dominated by the progeny of upstanding freaks with large brains, a new kind of first finger, and a transformed pelvic structure which, incidentally, narrowed the space available for transporting the large-headed newborn out of the womb, thus making it necessary for him to be born in an extremely helpless state. It was these morphological changes, made valuable by the advantages of tool-using, that resulted in symbolization, prolonged maturation, and social organization—or so it seems.

(III) *What have been the consequences, what may be the significance of these three distinctive conditions?* First, our tools have amplified our every native capacity. We sense better (radar, microscopes, aphrodesias). We perceive more (models, theories, codes of ethics). We move more quickly and more comfortably (escalators, jets, shoes). We can remember more (libraries). We can imagine more (LSD). We can handle more sympathy (laws), more pain (anesthesia), more love (contraception), more injustice (democracy), more self-consciousness (psychotherapy). And so on. Second, by virtue of these amplifications, our species has amplified the environment itself, to the extent that we must now seriously ask if we have not altered the very pulse of organic evolution: the principle of natural selection. It would seem, that is, that the issue of survival, at least in civilized societies, seems now to center around our ability to cope with our own inventions much more than around our ability to cope with the natural environment.

What better criterion for the success of a social studies curriculum than to find some students entering college competently entertaining the question of whether the principle of natural selection has become obsolete, and to find them bending their study of anthropology, psychology, sociology and biology to the confrontation of that question?

(IV) *As to what it is all about, we can only make this question more articulate:* We are either the achievement of the planet's purpose, or we are the latest hesitation in the unfolding of that purpose, delaying by our very successes, the ultimate success of our successors. This should keep us all honest after school.

What is commendable to teachers about these questions and answers as guidelines is that they are far too general to be mistaken for anything other than what they are: fundamental conceptual objectives. Obviously they cannot be taught directly: they must be "discovered" or left unknown. Thus a teacher who is using them as they should be used, as criteria for judging which of her daily classroom challenges are worth trying to meet and which are not, will never be caught wanting to give the answer and feeling she shouldn't. Moreover, there is no fixed sequence of how these baseline thoughts should be strung together. Rather, there is an inherent redundancy in them which insures that only the repeated tracing of consequences from causes and causes from consequences will issue into anything like comprehension of what lies between.

In a nutshell, then, these are the criteria to which a social studies teacher—at any level—might well submit her daily decisions as to whether this or that pedagogical strategy, this or that piece of material, or this or that teaching technique is worth exploring:

1) Will it confront the child with his membership in the species that has started a new chapter in the story of evolution—the tool-making species?

2) Will it articulate the child's understanding of the three

distinguishing features of his species: symbolization, prolonged maturation, and socialization?

3) Will it encourage the child to ask how these distinguishing features came into existence, what their morphological bases are, and how these are traceable to prehuman tool-using?

4) Will it enhance the child's appreciation of the evolutionary consequences of man's tool-making achievements? Will it help him to perceive every item of his culture as an amplification either of human capacities or of the environment itself? Will it thus help him to evaluate his culture in terms of its sensitivity to and its usefulness in fulfilling human potentials?

5) Will it serve to build in long-range immunity to swell-headedness? Will it, that is, help the child to evaluate his membership in his species with some sense of the humor involved should we all ultimately prove to have been a very interesting obstacle to the writing of the next chapter?

There has been criticism that the materials of "Man: A Course of Study" have, during the course of their various stages of development and production come to place a disproportionate emphasis on technology at the expense of the other fundamental humanizing agents: language, social organization, cosmology, and education. Perhaps this criticism is merited. I do sometimes sense the influence of a monocular interpretation of the Washburn thesis in these materials. Perhaps, too, a certain technological drift is inherent in producing curricular materials in the first place, since they are themselves tools. At best, however, this criticism misses the point. It is true that a teacher who has not made an intellectual home of her own for these subjects may end up teaching a course on seal hunting, warthog catching, harpoon making, or whatever the materials, taken alone, may suggest, rather than a course on Man. Give the same teacher cross-cultural materials on child-rearing practices, comparative mythology, or the design features of communication systems, however, and she will still not teach a course on Man, but, more than likely, a series of disjointed lessons about "children from other lands," "science and superstition," and "the amazing bee."

On the other hand, let us take a teacher who is herself in the process of mastering the subject of cultural evolution, its continuities and discontinuities with organic and inorganic evolution—a teacher on whom it has perhaps dawned that the single most illustrative case in point of her subject is the manifest presence of she and the children at the apex of seven billion years of ordered change on this planet, engaged in the transmitting and inheriting of what it may all be about. It would be inconceivable to such a teacher that a unit on Eskimo seal hunting might be used as anything but another avenue to the study of psychosocial adaptation in its full and fulfilling complexities, such as how human technology amplifies and redefines the human arm, leg, or sense organs; how the environment itself is thus amplified and redefined as regards its life-giving possibilities. Rather, one would expect to find this teacher formulating lessons in terms of such heuristics as: what kind of an animal is it that fashions an arm that flies like a bird, pierces like a fang, and holds onto its prey like a snake? (See Zachary stalk, decoy and harpoon his seal.) Is it not an animal that fulfills its dreams? And what kind of an animal is it that submits the conduct of its life to imagined versions of prey which nature, in four billion years, never produced? Is it not an animal that dreams some of its fulfillments? And what kind of an animal could so act like its prey as to seem to be one?

Is it not a play-acting animal? And so on: What other tools and rules does this "arm" presume, enable, require? What are the ways that this animal *must* relate and what are some ways that it *may* relate, to others of its kind, as a function of its capacity to develop such "arms"? What are the problems it solves and what are the problems it poses? What are the choices it gives? What are the choices it takes away? And what are some corresponding thoughts about certain contemporary "arms": the one that reaches to Pelly Bay in the overhead projector, or from the principal's office on the P.A. system, or to the moon from Cape Kennedy, or to hell from Omaha?

Such a teacher will also not be embarrassed to entertain whatever the children may choose to believe, or to make believe, that this is all about.

We come now to the point of relevance about "relevance." It was Elting Morison, the former director of ESI's social studies programs, who once said to a group of teachers that they should find ways of "constantly bringing the children to the engagement of intuitive and imaginative powers which reach beyond the data." By "data" he meant the social studies materials being produced by ESI. I hope I have been sufficiently persuasive in previous chapters to remind Mr. Morison that the intuitive and imaginative powers of school children reside in their emotion-toned inner lives. And that, by overseeing the construction of a curriculum which is necessarily isomorphic with the development of these inner lives, he has made it likely that teachers who understand both their subject matter and their pupils will probably succeed in following his directives.

What does it mean that the study of Man is necessarily isomorphic with the development of children's inner lives? One thing it means is that we cannot employ such an outline of the human life cycle as was detailed in Chapter Six without commensurately highlighting the three nuclear distinctions of our species: prolonged maturation (Columns A and B); symbolization (Columns C and D); and socialization (Columns E and F). Moreover, what is Column I but one way of conceiving the parameters of cultural evolution? There is in the social studies and humanities, in other words, a built-in economy which can find the teacher implicitly exercising her comprehension of children while explicitly seeking to comprehend the subject matter, and implicitly exercising her comprehension of the subject matter while explicitly seeking to compre- hend the children.

Another dimension of isomorphism was implied when it was said that children can best discover this particular subject for themselves by discovering themselves in this particular subject. There is more than rhetorical value in this statement. Rather, it follows quite literally from the fact that man's prolonged and singularly sequenced ma- turation *is* one of the three nuclear conditions to which psychosocial evolution can be traced. Thus no lesson in a course of study on Man can be optimally taught without some consideration of its relevance to human childhood. For example, should we want to teach grade schoolers the basic differences between human language and other sys- tems of animal communication we would have to find a way to make the design features of "arbitrariness" (refer- ence to events in ways that are independent of the events themselves) and "productivity" (transformation of events in ways that go beyond direct experience of the events) interesting and meaningful to them. The ablest of teachers, equipped with the cleverest of materials, have found these objectives to be out of reach, because they drew illustra- tions and analogies from the referential field of linguistics alone. The children first needed to objectify more familiar experiences of arbitrariness and productivity, in order to assimilate the highly abstract linguistic connotations of these concepts.

Now, while admittedly the question of the origins of human language is a highly speculative one, and likely to remain so, it is surely not coincidental that the design features of arbitrariness and productivity became fundamental to the communication system of a large-brained animal that spends a large portion of its life span in a state of dependence on its progenitors, and whose survival is therefore contingent on its ability to adapt both to the "arbitrariness" of its protectors and to the "productivity" of its central nervous system. Thus, exercises, lessons, and activities which sought to help the children to objectify and to articulate their homely experiences with parental restraints and with their own worlds of make-believe would be of prime relevance *in the hands of a teacher who understood the subject matter*. Such exercises, lessons, and activities, so far from being mere diversionary indulgences of children's narcissistic whims, as they are sometimes accused of being, might, on the contrary, provide just that angle of pedagogic leverage without which instruction in such abstract matters must be seen as too far for children to fetch.

If, for example, we ask the children to observe that "be" means what it means, and "bee" means what it means, and that "bee-bee" also means what it means, and then ask them what they can infer about human language from these observations, we can hardly expect them to respond with other than a fun-and-games frame of mind, no matter how often nor how ingeniously we repeat the exercise. If, on the other hand, we conjoin such exercises with others that encourage children to observe the shifting conditions of parental control and personal will which govern their young rights to personal pleasure, to personal privacy, to personal safety, and to the redress of personal grievances, and still other exercises that encourage them to observe the forms in which they themselves become rule-makers and rule-breakers in the self-made safety of their fantasies; and if, furthermore, these exercises are embedded in a larger context wherein appropriate comparisons can be made with other species, then I think we might find the children groping toward some dawning sense of the generality of arbitrariness and productivity as distinctive features of human language.

Admittedly, these auxiliary exercises would derive their special interest value from their proximity to the special interests of children. But that is precisely the point to be emphasized: it happens in this particular course of study —Man—that what happens to be especially interesting to the children also happens to be especially honest in respect to the subject. In other courses of study appeals to narcissism may be diversionary in effect. In *this* course of study, however, such appeals are exactly indicated not only as means of motivating the children but as crucial curricular objectives in their own right.

Similarly as regards other fundamental dimensions of any course of study about Man—Man the tool-making animal, Man the teaching animal, Man the ethical animal, Man the self-domesticated (and potentially self-destructive) animal—first orders of relevance must be born to and from the facts of human childhood (the family, the incest taboo, rites de passage, and so forth). It follows that these latter must bear first orders of honesty and interest to and from the immediate experience of being a human child.

C. H. Waddington has nicely revealed still another dimension of isomorphism between the learning of the social studies and the experience of human childhood: the development of conscience. Conscience is of central importance to an understanding of psychosocial evolution, and is also particularly pertinent to the cultivation of children's emotions and imagination in classrooms. "The whole system of human culture," says Waddington,

> is based fundamentally on a mechanism of communication and transmission that requires people to be brought up in such a way that they develop a mental setup which leads them to be ready to believe others. They may not like what they are told; and at some stage they may test it, find it all nonsense, and reject it; but that is a secondary process. . . . As far as I can see, the molding of the newborn human individual into a being ready to believe what it is told seems to involve many very peculiar processes, which can be explained only in terms of such notions as the formation of the super-ego and the repression of the id. Whether notions of this kind are true in detail or not, the molding of the baby into a transmission-receiver seems a difficult and complicated and even slapdash process, and not at all what one might have thought out if one had set out to design this job. A frequent result in the process seems to be that people believe much too much and believe it much too strongly. The process that evolution has provided us for doing the job seems often to lead to considerable exaggeration of the ability to believe.

> However that may be, it seems clear that any social transmission of information must depend on the formation of people ready to receive it. . . . In man this readiness to accept is produced by a mechanism that involves the formation within the mind of a mental system that carries authority and can therefore be believed. Now, the mental system that carries the greatest authority and can be

believed most thoroughly is the set of beliefs and notions we categorize as 'ethical.' The good is that which we regard as having the greatest authority in determining the way in which we should spend our lives.

The point I wish to make is that the appearance within man of ethical belief is a result of the processes that mold him into being capable of acting as a receiver of socially transmitted information. I daresay it might be possible to conceive of molding man into an information receiver in some way other than the particular method by which the process actually occurs in the human race at present. If the psychoanalysts are to be believed, the process we now use is more eccentric than one would have thought possible. But I think that some sort of system by which the mind comes to be willing to believe what it is told is necessary. That means that there would have to be formed within the mind some sort of authority-bearing system. Therefore, any being capable of socio-genetic evolution of the kind that man has developed would also have to entertain ethical or quasi-ethical beliefs.

So I think that there is an absolutely essential connection between human evolution, based on the specifically human socio-genetic mechanism, and the existence of such things as beliefs about ethics and values. That man is an ethical being is an absolutely essential part of the workings of his characteristic evolutionary machinery. (81, pp. 172–73)

It is not necessary for the purpose at hand to dwell on the various refinements and distinctions which comprise the psychology of conscience: the infantile super-ego, the ego ideal, neurotic versus healthy guilt, morality, authoritarianism, etc. What merits our attention once again are the reciprocities of reference between the subject matter of the social studies and the self-interests of the children that are contained in all matters pertaining to conscience. These reciprocities of reference may be emphasized by observing on the one hand that the schedule of normal growth crises outlined in Chapter Six (trust, mistrust, autonomy, shame, doubt, initiative, guilt, and so on) is no less than the most articulate schedule of conscience development that psychoanalytic theory has produced; and on the other hand, that almost all personal experiences which the children can share that involve emotional conflict are potential cases in point of the functioning of human conscience. Indeed, the routine ebbing and flowing of guilt, pride, temper, loyalty, embarrassment, well-being, and other feelings which shape each class-day may be almost literally viewed as cultured microcosmic specimens of this "absolutely essential connection between human evolution, . . . and the existence of such things as beliefs about ethics and values." Specimens, I might add, which by their highly subjective properties must automatically tend to bring the children, as Morison has urged, "to the engagement of intuitive and imaginative powers which reach beyond the data." The problem for the teacher who knows both her pupils and her subject lies not in spotting such opportunities but in choosing between them—and in focusing them with sufficient lightness of touch as to leave their belaboring to the children.

If, as consequences in passing, some children develop personal qualities of conscience which render them somewhat less "slapdash" as "transmission receivers"; which enable them more often to test and reject and less often "to believe much too much and believe it much too strongly"; if, that is, there is a secondary gain in mental health in some instances, I think we should not feel burdened by thoughts of having perhaps practiced medicine without license. On the contrary, the obvious pertinence of all manners of touchy classroom matters to the realities of the subject matter, by way of appreciating the function of conscience in man's distinctive evolutionary machinery, is the best answer to those teachers who most enthusiastically demur from "threatening the children."

CHAPTER NINE

Guidelines

In a rare entry into clinical psychology, Bruner draws attention to a distinction on which I should like to dwell in conclusion, for it points the way toward possible resolution of some of the differences emphasized in preceding chapters. The distinction is between the mental processes of "coping" and "defending."

"Coping," writes Bruner, "respects the requirements of problems we encounter while respecting our integrity." "Defending . . . is a strategy whose objective is avoiding or escaping from problems for which we believe there is no solution that does not violate our integrity of functioning." (11, p. 129)

He continues:

Integrity of functioning is some required level of self-consistency or style, the need to solve problems in a manner consistent with our most valued life enterprises. Given the human condition, neither coping nor defending is found often in pure form. The imperiousness of our drives and the demands of powerful, nonrational, and indocile unconscious mechanisms force some measure of defense. . . .

Yet notwithstanding that there is always a mixture of coping and defending in dealing with life as we find it, I would urge that we distinguish sharply between the two processes. . . .

When early learning is hemmed around with conflict, as it so often is by virtue of being a road to parental approval and love or a weapon in the arsenal of sibling rivalry, with the consequence that it becomes highly charged or libidinized, the affective links that relate concepts and ideas often are powerful and relatively intractable, in the sense that they persist in fantasy and can be found to intrude in the child's thinking in later school settings.

At the unverbalized level, then, the child approaches the task of school learning, with its highly rationalistic and formal patterns, with a legacy of unconscious logic in which action, affect, and conceptualization are webbed together. Feeling and action and thought can substitute for each other, and there is an equation governed by what in grammar is called synecdoche: feelings can stand for things, action for things, things for feelings, parts for wholes. It is as evident as it is both fortunate and unfortunate that these cognitive structures remain in being into adult life— evident in the sense that the structures appear in dream and in free association and, in a disciplined form, in the products of the artist; fortunate in the sense that without such structures there would neither be poets and painters nor an audience for them; unfortunate in the sense that when this mode of functioning is compulsively a feature of a person's life, he is not able to adjust to the requirements of any but a specially arranged environment. . . .

Let me suggest now that effective cognitive learning in school depends upon a denaturing process . . . it involves at least three things. There must first develop a system of cognitive organization that detaches concepts from the modes of action that they evoke. A hole is to dig, but it is also a hole. Secondly, it requires the development of a capacity to detach concepts from their affective contexts. A hole is not just a reminder of a hidden orifice. Finally, it demands a capacity to delay gratification so that the outcomes of acts can be treated as information rather than as simply punishing or rewarding. (11, pp. 129–34)

The "denaturing process" of which Bruner speaks "probably depends," he says, "upon the presence of several conditions in the early history of the child." (11, p. 134) These conditions are as follows: (1) *Stimulation,* or opportunities "to grow beyond enactive representation with its action-bound immediacy and beyond iconic representation with its strong susceptibility to affective linkage. . . ." (11, p. 134) (2) *Play,* or the development of attitudes "in which the child learns that the outcomes of various activities are not as extreme as he either hoped or feared." (11, pp. 134–35) (3) *Identification,* or a development of a willingness to learn as an expression of adherence to adult ideals. (4) *Freedom from excessive drives,* which are seen to result from domination of the learning process by strong extrinsic rewards and punishments.

There are three ways in which this distinction between coping and defending points the way toward possibilities of resolving some of the differences highlighted in previous chapters. First, it comes very close to being an exact reformulation of what, in traditional psychoanalytic circles, has long been referred to as the difference between ego synthesis and ego defense. Thus, a place has been found from which other meetings of mind might be sought by psychoanalytic and academic psychologists, much as Robert White has shown to be possible in his "Ego and Reality in Psychoanalytic Theory"—of which more will be said later.

Second, it does not detract from the importance of the distinction, but rather adds to it, to call into question, in two specific instances, the efficacy of the "denaturing process" on which Bruner suggests effective cognitive learning in school depends. One instance is in the case of children whose defensive specialty is that of excessive intellectualization, i.e., children whose way of avoiding or defending against problems is precisely that of perceiving them in purely ratiocinative forms. These are children who have not grown *beyond* enactive and iconic representation but rather have grown *around* these modes of knowing, and cannot, therefore, return to them for those personal pauses for refreshment which grace the intellectual lives of healthy people. These are children who need to learn in their play not that the outcomes of various activities are less extreme than hoped or feared, but rather that they are more interesting than expected. They are children who can benefit from identification figures whose freedom to live is no less than their willingness to learn. They are children whose intellectual life has grown timid, not because it is too often in a state of overdrive, but because it has lost touch with its stomach for human instincts. In the case of these children the converse of a "denaturing process" is indicated.

The second instance is the case of normal children who, in the course of their schooling, feel inclined to reach beyond the attainment of knowledge to its invention. Here, too, where strategic regressions from the ratiocinative mode of cognition to the iconic and enactive modes of *re*-cognition are desirable, a naturing rather than a denaturing process of instruction is indicated.

Thirdly, Bruner records how, in seeking to remedy psychogenic learning disabilities, psychotherapy alone is less than sufficient. He goes on to describe a form of tutorial treatment which he and his colleagues at the Judge Baker Guidance Center devised, which proved to be an effective complement to psychotherapeutic treatment. An illustration of "tutorial treatment" is reported as follows:

> Take the 11-year-old boy who at one of his first sessions said to the tutor that he was afraid to make an error in reading because his teacher yelled at him. The tutor asked whether his teacher yelled very loud, and, upon being assured that she did, volunteered that he could yell louder than the teacher and urged his patient to make a mistake and see. The boy did, and his tutor in mock voice yelled as loud as he could. The boy jumped. Tutor to patient: 'Can she yell louder than that?' Patient: 'Yes, lots.' Tutor: 'Make another error and I'll try to get louder still.' The game went on three or four rounds, and the tutor then suggested that the patient try yelling when he, the tutor, made an error. . . . After a few sessions, a playful relation had been built up about mistakes in reading, and the beginnings of transference were at hand. Soon the child was able to take satisfaction in the skills in which he was achieving mastery. (11, p. 145)

Thus, these children, whose excessively defensive postures of denial and avoidance had crippled their learning abilities, while being provided with traditional psychotherapeutic help in working through the unconscious factors that originally required such postures, were also being provided experiences that encouraged the replacement of defensive attitudes with corresponding coping attitudes; experiences which "defused" intellectual activity from the demands of immediate action, which suggested and supported the development of playfulness, which provided an adequate competence model, and which encouraged "learning for its own sake."

Here again, Bruner has taken a position that is entirely consistent with that of avowedly psychoanalytic workers in the same field. For example, in one of the reports of a group working under the direction of Dr. Bessie Sperry in the same clinic, with the same kinds of patients, we find the following:

> It had been observed in some cases of psychogenic learning disabilities, that the symptoms proved refractory to prolonged, and otherwise successful, individual therapy. It was as if, prior to and during treatment, these particular symptoms, under pressures characteristically generated in a literacy-oriented culture, formed the nucleus of a secondary neurotic structure. Consequently, the learning functions remained within a conflictful ego sphere, even while the child was experiencing a diminution in severity of primary neurotic conflicts.

> In particular, we came to view arrested development of reading skills as pivotal; being not only pathologic, as a symptom of the primary neurosis, but also pathogenic. A reading handicap is not a symptom that can be "given up" as can the symptoms encountered, for example, in the behavior disorders. While therapy served to liberate these children from earlier determined emotional pressures toward ego restriction, it seemed not to alter the pathogenic attitudes that were being reinforced by ongoing experiences with the printed word of humiliation, fear, isolation, and failure.

> Whether for reasons of time, or of preserving an optimal transference for the resolution of deeper issues, it had not

been found advisable to utilize the therapy hours for as much work with the symptom as seemed necessary. It was also understandable that the usual forms of remedial schoolwork, necessarily focused as they are on the mechanics of reading, were not equipped to alter the highly personal symbolic meaning that the act of reading held for these children.

To meet this special need, a group session was added to the treatment schedule of five boys in which exclusive attention was given to the reorientation of attitudes toward reading as such. There was no attempt to duplicate the children's experiences with either their teachers or their therapists, although the group leader was prepared to combine the roles of both.

Five boys, ranging in age from twelve to thirteen, were invited to join the "Judge Baker Reading Club." All five met the criteria of having worked well in individual therapy over at least one treatment year, and of remaining far below age-level in reading proficiency.

Excerpts from the first meeting leave little room for doubting why reading was something these boys avoided whenever possible:

The leader asked what the boys liked to read for fun. Peter and Brian liked comics. John likes jokes which come in his Children's Digest magazine. Arthur stated he would rather tell jokes. Peter prefers animal books and Brian likes books with lots of pictures. There was some discussion of how to read books; such as, some people read from the back to see how the story is going to turn out. Peter thought this was a sneaky way to read. Brian thought this was no fun because then you would know how everything happened. Peter volunteered a story about Sherlock Holmes called 'The Gold Tooth,' which had to do with a man who was killed and every bone in his body broken; but there was not a mark on his body. It was later learned that this man had been killed by a python. Arthur volunteered that a fellow at camp caught a snake as long as the table around which the group was sitting. Peter then told a story about a guinea pig and a dog which chewed up the guinea pig's skull after it had been preserved, and this made the dog sick. Peter then told about a fire which took place at a riding stable in which twenty-five horses burned to death. They looked like fried meat, only they had bones in them. At this point, John, who seemed to be getting a little uncomfortable at this conversation, asked: 'Ain't it messy to cut animals?' Before Peter could reply, Brian told a story about rabbits which had something to do with their intestines. Arthur then briefly volunteered that he knew a kid who had caught a snake and skinned it alive.

The leader offered himself to the club members as an authority who understood and permitted their avoidance of reading, when necessary, but who also understood and supported their secret desire to become brave readers whenever possible. For example, part of the sixteenth meeting proceeded as follows:

Leader: "Let's start the new book: 'The Wonderful Story of How You Were Born.'"

Peter: "I'd rather eat."

Leader: "Eat all you want. When those are gone, we'll get some more."

(Peter helps himself)

Leader: "The new book is the one you wanted to read, Peter."

Peter: "What is it?"

Leader: "The Story of How You Were Born."

Peter: "I don't want it."

Leader: "We'll start when you're through eating."

Peter: "I'll never finish eating."

Leader: "For a start I'll read to you and you can follow with your eyes."

Peter: "You read it, I'll listen." (Leader reads slowly and Peter interrupts, whistling)

John: "Did you see about the heart which was beating outside the body? It's an operation and the heart gets cut up into little pieces."

Tony: "Okay, John, that's enough."

(Leader continues to read aloud, coming to the part of the story that says that all life begins from a tiny egg)

Tony: "That's queer."

(Leader continues to read)

(Peter interrupts to tell about a baby opossum)

(Brian asks Peter to shut up so the leader can read)

(Leader reads until he comes to a part that tells about the duck-billed Platypus of which there is a picture)

(Peter breaks in to describe an animal he has seen with the bill of a duck, webbed feet, and the tail of a cat. The other boys frown at Peter)

(Leader, with no comment, continues reading)

Peter: "I wish I didn't have to go to school. Oh, what a sad life I live!"

(Leader continues to read)

(Peter again breaks in to tell about a story concerned with buckets of blood)

(At this point in the book there are some pictures of the fetus)

John: "These pictures look like 'the invasion of body snatchers.' "

(Brian adds that the body snatcher killed everyone except himself and his girlfriend, and added that the body snatcher takes people's minds away and makes them disintegrate)

(Leader continues to read as soon as the boys stop talking)

(Peter interrupts to wonder why when you are born and the
doctor slaps you on the rump, you don't slap him back)
(Leader continues to read)
(Brian breaks in to tell about a fight which ended in two
people dying)
(Leader again reads)

The most vivid quality which these boys perceived in the
leader was that of omnipotence, deriving presumably from
their own perception of printed words as deceptive contain-
ers of extraordinarily threatening forces. The leader, as a
special representative of literate prowess, seemed, consequently, to be viewed as a man who knew no fear. It
seemed to us, therefore, and our experience confirmed the
thought, that the leader of such a group does well to represent literacy without apologies; moreover, he does well to
project tacit expectation that the members will come to
view anything less as unworthy of masculine strivings.
There came a time in this group, for example, when the
boys had clearly grown bored with Donald Duck and Super-
man comics, and were even secretly humiliated by their
own persistent requests for these. At this point the leader
announced what was to be a brief weaning period, after
which comic books were simply ruled out as "kid stuff."
Despite surface protests, the boys seemed to welcome the
rule.

The report concludes:

At the outset, these boys had resigned themselves to strict
avoidance of printed words. The dictionary was "nasty"; the
small print "would get you every time," and if there was anything interesting that was not on T.V. they would do without
it. As greater acceptance of reading emerged, it did so in the
form of demanding the "biggest dictionary in the world"

(we secured one that had to be rolled in on a cart), of wanting "the truth," "the facts," and "no made-up stories." The "truth," however, was, for these children, to be found in the adult comic magazine, "Mad," which spoofs intelligence, burlesques rationality, and wryly worships stupidity—all in an intellectually challenging and often sophisticated manner. The reading level was considerably over their heads, but they never tired of tackling it within its "mad" context. "Mad" seemed to afford them an opportunity to look behind their own defenses, while focused outside themselves. It was as if they recognized their own mock stupidity as a defense against brightness, and were, with this assurance, able for the first time to tolerate the "small print." By this medium they were given permission to seek out secrets which are discoverable with persistence, and, with persistence, the secrets were discovered to be not very frightful; here they could vicariously attack and defend, menace and be menaced, sit passively and receive, and at the same time feel free to laugh at the over-definition of their fears. (47)

The language varies, but there is agreement that coping and defending differ not only in degree but in kind, and that it is not sufficient merely to free children whose learning abilities have been crippled by their defenses from the unconscious binds which provoked such defenses; it is further necessary to instruct such children in the arts and skills of coping.

Yet, I find it odd that in documenting this distinction, which shows the way for cooperative research and experimentation by educational and clinical psychologists, and by teachers and therapists, Bruner chooses to refer only to his brief experience with sick children in a clinic, and to leave unmentioned his vastly wider experience with normal children in schools. I suspect the reason for this omission is that, for all his experience with normal children in educational settings, he has not felt free to avail himself of the resulting opportunities to show that the distinction he found to be crucial in the treatment of illness is equally important in the cultivation of health. The suspicion is not an idle one, nor does it lack evidence, and since it may be the prime cause of what I earlier referred to as Bruner's counter-reformational influence—for the curious double-bind in which he places teachers—I shall try to give it substance: "There is," says Bruner,

> a form of pedagogical romanticism that urges an arousal of unconscious, creative impulses in the child as an aid to learning. One would do well to be cautious about such doctrine. As Lawrence Kubie and others have remarked, unconscious impulses unconstrained by awareness and by the sense of play can be quite the contrary of creative. It is too often taken for granted that the processes that lead to effective cognitive functioning are mere extensions of unconscious dreamwork and association. I do not believe this to be the case. . . . (11, pp. 147–48)

He refers to conscious and unconscious processes, and to the cautionary element in Kubie's challenge to experimental education, but not to the conceptual keystone of Kubie's contribution to the psychoanalytic theory of thinking, which forms the provocative element of that challenge: the role of *preconscious processes*. Let us therefore hear Kubie out:

> There is abundant experimental and clinical evidence to indicate that traditional conceptions of how human beings think and learn have started from a natural but totally misleading assumption *that we think and learn consciously*. This is not true. Conscious processes are important not for

thinking but for sampling, checking and correcting, and as tools for communication. The intake of factual data about the world around us is overwhelmingly preconscious, i.e., *subliminal*. This preconscious input consists of an incessant subliminal bombardment, which goes on both when we are awake and when we are asleep. . . .

Second, the bits of information which are furnished to us this way, whether subliminal or conscious, are then processed . . . on a subliminal level. All of this is just another way of saying that most, if not all, of our thinking is preconscious rather than conscious. Here again, the conscious component is only a weighted and fragmentary sample of the continuous stream of preconscious processing of data. . . .

Of this continuous preconscious stream we do conscious spot-sampling; and this is where our symbolic tools enter into the picture. We sample both the input and the preconscious stream by means of combinations of symbolic units. . . .

These then are regrouped into larger generalizations (or abstractions), which in turn are represented by those subtle and flexible symbolic tools, which constitute words and numbers. Words then are grouped into phrases and numbers into equations; phrases into sentences and paragraphs, equations into mathematical models. This elaboration from the elementary building blocks of the sampling process provides us with exciting and magnificent new tools: but it remains a *sampling* process and not a *thinking* or *learning* process. The point is that sampling is not thought. Yet it is this conscious sampling which has always been mistaken for thinking. . . .

The final step is when the sample of the input to which we have given symbolic representation is projected again in the processes of recall, reproduction and communication. . . .

It is clear that what remains cannot be a true representation of the external world, or of what we are trying to learn, or what is processed internally in the learning process, or of what we "create" by recombining units into new patterns. I once put it that unwittingly we distort what we perceive, and then learn what we have distorted. Psychologists, psychiatrists, neurologists, neurophysiologists have erred together in their undue emphasis on the conscious components of mentation. This has misled the educator into neglecting the *preconscious* instrument of recording, processing and of creating. We should learn how to do better than this. The question is how? (56, pp. 76–78)

The complete set of theoretical guidelines recommended by Kubie for pedagogical research, of which Bruner cites but one, is thus as follows:

Where conscious processes predominate at one end of the spectrum, rigidity is imposed by the fact that conscious symbolic functions are anchored by their precise and literal relationships to specific conceptual and perceptual units. Where unconscious processes predominate at the other end of the spectrum, there is an even more rigid anchorage, but in this instance to unreality; that is, to those unacceptable conflicts, objects, aims, and impulses which have been inaccessible both to conscious introspection and to the corrective influence of experience. . . . Yet, flexibility of symbolic imagery is essential if the symbolic process is to have that creative potential which is our supreme human trait. . . . This creative flexibility is made possible predominantly, if not exclusively, by free, continuous, and concurrent action of preconscious processes. (54, p. 38)

Now, despite his seeming aversion to the concept of pre-conscious mentation, Bruner nonetheless says in conclusion:

> What poses the eternal challenge to the teacher is the knowledge that the *metaphoric* processes can, when put under the constraints of conscious problem solving, serve the interests of healthy functioning. Without those constraints, they result in the crippling decline that comes from a specialization on defense. (italics mine) (11, p. 148)

Except that the term "metaphoric" is substituted for the term "preconscious," this conclusion might stand as a paraphrase of Kubie's conclusion—could even be substituted for it. Yet, in context, Bruner has just warned the teacher (in a remark which fails to distinguish between unconscious and preconscious functions—and there is the double-bind) against practicing "a form of pedagogical romanticism that urges an arousal of unconscious, creative impulses in the child as an aid to learning."

We may be justified in concluding that when Bruner warns against taking for granted "that the processes which lead to effective cognitive functioning are mere extensions of unconscious dreamwork and association," his qualms are inspired by ghosts of his own hauntings. In any event, I know of no recent pedagogical research which starts from such an assumption, i.e., which fails to be cognizant of the discontinuities as well as the continuities in the spectrum of symbolic functioning—from hallucinatory, dreamlike *pre*sentations to logical, communicable *re*presentations. The "metaphoric process" whose subordination to conscious problem solving Bruner says "poses the eternal challenge to the teacher" is associatively linked all along the lines of this spectrum. How the metaphoric process may be best supported by pedagogical conditions which are conducive to its subordination, while remaining free of conditions which are conducive to its subjugation, is, as Kubie notes, a pressing problem for research. But the "romanticism" that Bruner fears certainly lurks elsewhere.

It may be thought that too much has been made of Bruner's avoidance of one psychoanalytic concept. He is, after all, a follower of Piaget, and not of Freud. Would that this were the only reason for Bruner's aversion to "romanticism" in teaching! However, he announces the same aversion in connection with his laboratory work, and this in straight Piagetian lexicon. Repeatedly, in his reports and essays on the course of cognitive growth, after distinguishing between the enactive, iconic, and symbolic modes of representation (paralleling Piaget's sensori-motor, concrete, and formal stages of cognitive development) Bruner notes that his singular concern is with the transition from iconic to symbolic representation. And since he is steadfastly true to his singular concern, one looks in vain in his writings for enlightenment as regards the various other kinds of transitional relations which can and do exist between the various forms that human knowledge takes. As a scientist, Bruner is well-advised to pursue his singular concern; unquestionably, psychology as a science is the stronger for his having done so. But a scientist who also becomes a protagonist of action research in an area of pressing social concern should be careful not to allow what to him is a matter of taste to be taken by others as a matter of course. I think Bruner has unwittingly allowed this to happen, much to the detriment of contemporary instructional research.

Let us return to the point at which Bruner and I were last found to be in agreement: In our work with children who suffer from pathological learning blocks, we both observed that therapy was not enough, that a special form of teaching was necessary for the "cure" to take. I daresay we would also agree that this dual form of treatment is a very expensive one, and that if a modification of it appeared to have utility with a wider range of educational problems, ways would have to be found to make it dispensable by teachers, and not only by university professors in temporary residence.

In the preceding chapters I have tried to put the case that curricular innovation, especially in elementary social studies, has posed just such a wider range of educational problems; that in solving these problems neither instruction, as we know it, nor therapy, as we know it, will suffice; that an as yet crudely perceived synthesis of these crafts will be required. A synthesis that respects the fundamental similarities and differences of teaching and treating, as discussed in Chapter Three; that understands and builds on the subtle interplay between anxiety and creative thinking, as discussed in Chapter Four; that is mindful of the course of emotional growth, as discussed in Chapter Six; and its linkages with the parallel courses of cognitive and social growth, as discussed in Chapter Seven; and that is especially prepared to exploit the isomorphisms between the child's self-interests and the interests of the subject matter of the social sciences, as discussed in Chapter Eight. Throughout, I have taken pains to present the emergent problems, and to suggest tentative approaches to their solution, in exclusively pedagogical terms, so as to invite *teachers* to see promise in accepting the challenges involved. For, let there be no mistake about it: it will be neither Bruner, nor Kubie, nor I, nor all the curriculum coordinators and psychological consultants currently at work, or in training, or yet to be born, who will do ultimate justice to these challenges; it will be *teachers*, working alone and in small informal task forces, who will do the job—and, more often than not, with precious little reward for their efforts, save the intrinsic satisfaction of being more competent teachers.

I should like to conclude by proposing that the same four conditions, described by Bruner as conducive to children coping with the problems of their schooling, rather than defending against such problems, will also serve as a set of guidelines for experimentation with new teaching methods that seek to aid children to be *creative* in their schooling—to go beyond mere coping, to mastery and invention. Recall that these four conditions are (1) stimulation (2) play (3) identification and (4) freedom from excessive drive.

With respect to the stimulation of emotions and images in classrooms, it would suffice to say that unflinching standards of intellectual honesty in the classroom would, as a matter of course, provide optimal amounts and range— except that teachers (as presently trained) are known to be capable of extreme inconsistency and contradiction in the face of what they are all too inclined to see as the prospect of "threatening the children." It remains the case, nonetheless, that any lesson in the humanities or social studies which confronts children with the truth of its subject matter—be it family life among the Eskimos, the invention of the steam engine, the Boston Tea Party, the death of Abraham Lincoln, or what have you—will naturally provide effective stimulation of their emotions and fantasies. As has been noted, curriculum designing organizations, like ESI, are forging ahead, regardless—perhaps because they function independently of school systems, and are thus a degree removed from the heat of having to make the best of their own labors. Under these circumstances, perhaps the best that can be suggested to teachers is that they be constantly mindful, as regards this or that fact or film or story or text, that *if it could not threaten* the children *it will not stimulate* them. Conversely, if it is likely to threaten the children, it is also likely to stimulate them. Then, the teacher may make her move: to use or not to use these materials; and, having used them, to look the other way, or to go to work. This will sound crude only to the teacher who has not appreciated the points advanced in previous chapters concerning what it is that threatens children. So, I repeat: a feeling, or image, that cannot be controlled is frightening; a feeling, or image, that cannot be shared is estranging; a feeling, or image, that cannot be put to work is belittling. These conditions do threaten children. But do not blame these conditions, when they exist, on the stimuli. Blame them, instead, on the teacher who lets it be feared that anything transpiring under her guidance could get out of control; or who has failed to create an atmosphere in which the children may choose to share their feelings and private thoughts, free of the illusion that this must lead to acting them out; or, worse, whose command of her subject matter is so shallow as to be unable to see the relevance to it of all possible human feelings and images.

With respect to *play*, it is almost redundant to speak of it in connection with the expression of feelings and fantasies, since playfulness is inherent in these. It is important to speak of it, however, because our educational practices have unfortunately developed intrinsic postures of dourness with respect to what really matters to children—what excites, bemuses, and impassions them. This is why school is typically so boring. What is worse, however, is that the children have come to *expect* it to be so. Thus, the teacher cannot assume that her pupils will immediately respond to her honest and stimulating lessons, even if she is herself confident she can provide conditions which would make them safe, enjoyable, and useful.

In this connection there is room, in my judgment,

especially in the elementary years when children's basic expectations of their education are being formed, for the inclusion of exercises and activities which have as their objectives instruction in emotional and imaginal expression. These need not be conducted independently of the subject matter for all time, but they may well be so conceived for the time being. I am aware that in many schools a portion of the children's time is spent in art, dance, drama, and music classes. I am also aware, however, that these activities are most often intended to serve cathartic functions only, and are likely, therefore, to remain set off in the minds of children from their heavier academic duties. All too often, in fact, such classes are led by visiting specialists with whom the teacher of first authority shares little, if any, professional liaison. What I have in mind is something a little closer to the curricular vest, and conducted by the teacher of first authority, whether in conjunction with art, drama, dance, and music classes, or not.

Let me illustrate by quoting from the reports of one elementary school teacher working in the first grade, Mrs. Elena Werlin.

> The children calmly accept dream-time as they do the pledge of allegiance. If there is too much noise, I insist on quiet, reminding them that it is difficult to remember dreams and that silence will help. . . .
>
> Here are some of the dreams that have been reported recently:
>
> *Robbie:* "This wasn't a dream, but it didn't happen either. My bed turned into a horse.
>
> I was in a plane with my father. He was a pilot. The plane ran out of gas. I landed the plane."

Helen: "My nose was real long. We went on a trip in a car and it stuck out of the window. It touched people's houses."

(It seemed that Helen was delighted with this long nose of hers but was also afraid or ashamed of it.)

Linda: "My two front teeth were very long.

My sister and I put on ghost costumes and scared everybody.

I was in the woods with my father and fell in bushes of prickers."

Steven: "I dreamt of a monkey chasing a nut.

I dreamt that a snake was choking Joe. I was up in an airplane and I came down and killed the snake before it killed Joe."

Brenda: "I dreamt there was no door knob on the downstairs closet, so my father took the door off.

I dreamt that there were two more days until the war. My sister told me that. And then they came and put bricks and gas over us and we died."

Stephanie: "My whole family had four long legs.

My sister Suzy fell into the prickers."

I have tried to make a habit of requesting the children at least four times a week to close their eyes and get pictures to a story, a piece of music, or just in silence. Also, in an effort to loosen up their thought processes, I have been reporting my own dreams, and telling them of the pictures that I see when we listen to music, or just in silence. . . .

I hope that over the year I will be able to help the children use their preconscious thoughts for enriching the way they listen to the music, draw, work with clay, make up stories, dramatize them, or just in classroom conversations. If I can see the preconscious working in those activities then maybe I can figure out ways of spicing up reading, writing, and spelling. But even if this level of thought never shows up in the schoolwork, I feel reassured in getting their feelings out where they can handle them, whether by themselves or with my help.

For example, Steven told a dream about rescuing Joe, who was being strangled by a snake a few weeks ago. One day when he was angry with me and pouting, I said: "I bet if that snake was strangling *me* now you'd have to think twice before coming to *my* rescue." I think this was probably a little too direct because he seemed startled and then made an embarrassed giggle. But that stopped the pouting and later that day I could help him with his spelling without feeling I was sticking my nose in where it wasn't wanted. Or, when David K. (who in the first month of school exploded regularly into ugly tantrums) was angry with me— and the feeling was mutual—I said: "I wish I could send you to that giant you dreamed about. He'd make you behave!" David countered: "If you did, I would kill the giant." Then we threw a few joking barbs at each other and the sun could shine again. I think this helps David to express his annoyance verbally instead of physically. Meanwhile the class hears all this. They know David's dream and can participate vicariously. David and I have shown that we're both bigger than his giant and it makes a nice demonstration to all concerned how anger can be used in a safe way. . . .

The morning started off with Robbie S. getting out of his seat during the time "Hall of the Mountain King" was being piped into the room, and tiptoeing around in time to the music. Others followed and did a pretty good job of following the spirit of the piece. What pleased me most was how tacitly they just assumed I would approve of this and how unselfconscious they all were (especially the boys) as they gave themselves over to the music. The next treat of the day was during snack-time when I asked if there were any dreams. Many, many. . . .

A nice new thing has started. Last week Linda reported a very short dream about a witch chasing her while she was "trick-or-treating." I said this could be the start of a good Halloween story that we might be able to illustrate and put on the bulletin board. All agreed. Monday I brought it up again, telling the children they should think of more things to add to the story. David K. suggested I shut out the lights so they could close their eyes and get better ideas. Most of the children did as he suggested and the ideas the children incorporated into Linda's dream story made Halloween more interesting. . . .

Another helpful new feature is to ask for only certain types of dreams—about me, or parents, or animals. This seems to free certain children to "remember" dreams that would otherwise be too threatening. However, I think I went too far this morning. Robbie S. was being a king elephant who went around "squooshing" cars and people. I asked him what he would do if he was near the school. "I wouldn't step on you because you're my teacher." I said I wouldn't know it if he were an elephant, but he insisted that he wouldn't "squoosh" me no matter what he was. . . .

Still being dissatisfied I tried a different approach. Instead of waiting for the formally allotted time I just threw the idea out when they were in the midst of a puzzle, or book

or drawing: "Stop the work. I know you're busy, but will
you please close your eyes and get a picture to jot down on
this paper? You can get right back to what you're doing
when you've finished. I just want to know what you've got
in your heads now. Thank you."

Connecting the dream-telling with the straight schoolwork
will be a slow process, but I can see that it *is* possible. In
reading, I gave the class the word "bush." It was their first
written contact with it and the climate of the classroom
was humdrum to say the least. I said: "You know, pricker-
bush." Immediately they remembered Stephanie's pricker-
bush dreams, and at last a spelling word was an alive thing
with meaning—not just a word that Mrs. Werlin says we
have to spell. . . .

I have noticed that quite a few of the children's dreams
lately are concerned with their classmates or with me. Here
are two:

I dreamt there was a fight at school. Mrs. Werlin was clubbing everybody and they were clubbing her back with their
heads. Their heads fell off. A big bird picked you (teacher)
up and me up and dropped us in the sea. I sank to the bottom. Under the water I was looking for you.

It was time to go to school. Mrs. Werlin was in her house
and could not make it. I went over and told her it was time
for school. I took her over here. I went in the recess door.
Nobody was here but me and Mrs. Werlin.

I asked the children in the dream circle what *they* would
have done if they were alone with me in the schoolroom:
"I'd play dolls with you," "I'd read with you," "I would run
home."

We may be engaged in a reading or spelling lesson or a
science activity. A related thought, image, or feeling may

come to a child and when his turn comes he just offers it
to the class. Sometimes it's just to embellish a point. Sometimes it's something in need of discussion before we can
move on in the lesson—on a new level with new aware-
nesses. The children seem always to understand. We were
going over the "o" words: mow, throw, go, out, etc. When
Allen's turn came, near tears, he asked if New Mexico was
part of America. It took a few minutes to get to the bottom
of this. He had apparently overheard his parents discussing
his father's impending transfer. We were able to reassure
him at least that New Mexico is part of America and that
fathers are never transferred in less than a week, and usually
longer. It will be sad to lose Allen if he has to leave us, but
at least when he gets to New Mexico he'll know how to
spell it.

Or, we may be learning a new phonogram or the difference
between "sea" and "see." I'll briefly describe each and before I know it the class is bubbling over with their own
awareness of the difference: memories of fun at the sea-
shore, the animals one finds at the sea, talk about seeing,
about seeing the sea—until a hundred connections have
been made, fears and discoveries brought into the open, and
memories revitalized. (84, pp. 234–50)

In these exercises the children are being instructed (1)
that their feelings and images have a place in school (2)
that they are enjoyable (3) that it cannot be told, in advance, when and where they will also serve the learning
process, but that eventually they usually do (4) that they
are particularly effective tools for communication and (5)
that the teacher sees all this, approves of it, and sanctions
it with her authority by providing time for it. Given an
honest curriculum, and a teacher committed to helping the
children master themselves, discipline their tastes, and

deepen their views of the world, such exercises can convince the children that the teacher *means it.*

Several advantages derive from these being *routine*
exercises: (1) the children come to associate their fantasy
life with their work life. This association is, I submit, something more than mentally healthy. (2) The onus of per-
missiveness is removed, and replaced by the more credible
influence of authority. (Children know that we permit them
what may or may not be good for them, but when there
is no questioning the goodness of something, we simply
set aside time for it.) (3) The children can pace themselves;
momentarily useful defenses need not harden for lack of
the right moment to drop them. (4) The teacher can
directly coordinate the products of such exercises to immediately relevant learning tasks, and in less predictable ways
can mediate the children's efforts to understand realities by
constructing them. In short, much of the guesswork is removed from the teacher's task of cultivating individual
discovery.

Given such routine instruction, it is likely that the
children will relate more freely and fully among themselves
and with their instructor when their responses to curricular
matters are particularly impassioned or novel. Of course,
exercises of this kind cannot take the place of honest curricular materials. If a text, or a film, fails to get under a child's
skin it is immaterial what it might have found there. To
the extent, however, that the curriculum does move the
children in depth, it is well for the teacher to have shown
that she is prepared to work with them accordingly.

For example, the most poignant scenes of ESI's film
footage on baboons shows a female dragging her dead infant along for two days with the same front hand that she
needs for walking, obviously unable to leave her newborn
behind, but finding it increasingly difficult to maintain the

brisk pace of her troop which, for a baboon, means death. A potentially more effective means would be difficult to imagine for setting youngsters to comparative thinking about the ties that bind parents to children, and the pros and cons of organized societies—not to mention the advantages of bipedalism. But would the children in most classrooms, much less their teachers, be prepared to respond to these scenes with thoughtfulness? *In most classrooms,* probably not. Dilemmas of this kind must inevitably bring encouragement for the kinds of experimentation reported by Mrs. Werlin.

Dreams are not the only media for such exercises. They merely happened to fit the interests and style of one teacher. Another teacher seeks to press the typically abused "show and tell" period into similar service. Another likes to conduct periodic "wrong answer" sessions, in which merely incorrect answers are tolerated while preposterous ones are applauded. Another likes to make analogy construction a regular part of his examinations. Consequently, his students must prepare themselves to say not only what this or that *is* but what they have made of it. Aldous Huxley, in his "Education on the Nonverbal Level," makes some even more brow-raising suggestions. (35) Such innovations are exceedingly recent, and the room for more of them is large.

As for *identification,* consider that there is nothing a child learns sooner nor more lastingly in school than how to watch the teacher. More than vigilance is in this attitude of watchfulness, and it seeks more than guidance as to the permissible. There is in such watchfulness a quality of readiness for "blind" devotion—exceeded in later years only when falling in love—which seeks beyond what is permissible to what is *possible.* It is not difficult to explain this quality of readiness. Until he enters school, it is the child's parents who define the permissible and represent the possible. Knowing no other world than the one in which his parents live, the preschool child usually finds it sufficiently inviting to merit obedience to parental authority, however restricted his parents' world may in fact be. Upon being sent to school, however, even the children of culturally enriched homes must look back on their parents' world as small in comparison to what their teacher now indicates will be open to them. I sometimes think that there may be no more powerful authority in modern life than that which is carried by first grade teachers in the first week of September. All the submissiveness, the readiness to be led, the eagerness to be shown, which has developed out of that particularly human condition of being relatively weak and ineffective in the proprietary hands of comparative strength and competence, is transferred to the teacher, with—for a while at least—almost none of the ambivalent wariness which is a consequence of these same conditions. Add to this the pull of the future, the new worlds which the teacher symbolizes, and you have an awesome potential for influence.

Now, it happens that in our culture imaginative living is something that is shown rather poorly by parents to children. The parents may themselves have learned to be more or less at home with their more fanciful moments, and more or less competent in ways of enriching their less fanciful ones. But it is ingrained in our child-raising mores that children ought be left to themselves in their play—except for those times when they are supposed to be "getting to know their fathers," or the like. And, too, it is more important to our particular culture's scheme of things that we learn to control our emotions than that we learn to express and share them. Let it be clear that I am referring not to pathogenic parents and their disturbed children—although the stuff of neurosis is nearby. I am referring to normal parents and their normal children. The implications may as well be stated that in our culture it is normal to be somewhat embarrassed by feelings, and to be somewhat guarded against imagination. It need not follow, however, that we view these normal states as desirable. It does follow that we should expect resistance to efforts designed to alter them. ("Don't threaten children." "Don't invade their privacy.") It also follows that teachers of young children, while briefly in possession of their larger-than-home-sized authority, are ideally situated to initiate such efforts. Mrs. Werlin's first graders were discovering not only that their inner lives served safe, enjoyable, and useful functions in a school setting but that Mrs. Werlin also had an inner life which she found safe, enjoyable, and useful to draw upon, and to share in her work as a teacher. Playfulness, warmth, openness, and freedom to entertain the fanciful, then, were not just childish things to be put away some day; they went well with purpose, skill, work, and being in control of things.

One precaution is in order. Children do not identify with teachers' good intentions if these are insecurely plied. By which I mean to suggest that it is better for a teacher, looking to try new methods, to be guided by her sense of comfort before her sense of duty—at least until the two show signs of going together. What could be more erosive of a teacher's projection of presence in her class than to show ESI's seal hunting film, if in truth she could not stand the sight of blood; or to introduce dream telling sessions, if in truth she rarely remembered any; or to experiment with role-playing techniques, if in truth she was inclined towards stage-fright? If ever there were opportunities for innovation in teaching which did not require gallantry, it is those on which this book has dwelled. Opportunities are expendable, to say the least. School is boring, lifeless and long-faced, and the new curricula have only made this more obvious. Any one of the methods described above which seek to make school more interesting and lively by engaging the children's natural feelings and images, if conducted in comfort and with confidence, will make for significant and visible gains. There is no reason to try all of them; indeed there is every reason not to try any of them uneasily.

Finally, as to freedom from excessive drive, I must confess that it is in respect to this matter that Bruner puzzles me most. It is a truism, as old as modern psychology, that states of excessive drive defeat the learning process. But it is as well-known that the best way to create states of excessive drive is to block access to drive-satisfaction. Yet, when I hear Bruner say, ". . . What is crucial is that the child have an opportunity to grow beyond enactive representation with its action-bound immediacy and beyond iconic representation with its strong susceptibility to affective linkage. . . ." (11, p. 134) it occurs to me to wonder if he isn't advocating the creation of just such states of blockage to drive-satisfaction. Since this cannot possibly be so, I must assume that by "grow beyond" he means: in ways and under conditions which favor periodic returns to enactive and iconic representation—what others have called strategic regression or regression in the service of the ego.

States of instinctual drive do exist and are periodically peremptory in all animals. In man, the satisfaction of these drives is regulated, for the most part, symbolically. It is sometimes misunderstood, for example, that Freud referred by the concept of the id to primitive *impulses* to engage in sexual and aggressive acts. This is not so; he referred by this term to primitive *images* (i.e., enactive and iconic symbols) of sexual and aggressive acts—for, in humans, images are the forms impulses normally take. Only in the most deranged human being, whose derangement is precisely that he has lost the capacity for symbolic regulation of his drives, do we ever see the id in action. In other words, in all but the most seriously ill human beings, drives find their satisfaction, and thereby remain free of excess, *by symbolic means*. In quantitative terms, which we can use only roughly in this context, more satisfaction accompanies expression of enactively regulated drives than accompanies expression of iconically regulated drives; and more satisfaction accompanies expression of iconically regulated drives than accompanies expression of ratiocinatively regulated drives.

Admittedly, it is man's capacity for ratiocinative symbolization which has made him the civilized animal, and because ratiocinative symbolization provides the least amount of drive satisfaction, we sometimes find ourselves, in our more civilized moments, at odds with our drives. But, if Freud discovered anything that has never been disputed it is that the way to prevent such excesses of drive tension as can overrule our more civilized intentions is to provide regular opportunities for drive satisfaction in enactive and iconic forms. This is why we take vacations, have hobbies, read novels, drink whiskey, attend plays, paint pictures, and engage other such recreative experiences. A related position, only slightly less well documented, has it that enactive and iconic representations play a vital part in *creative* endeavors as well, i.e., that they inspire, refresh, and, in some cases, *direct* what can only become socially valuable in ratiocinative form: a theory, a poem, a musical score, a lesson plan.

Therefore, we must assume that when Bruner urges teachers to provide children with opportunities to *grow beyond* enactive and iconic representation, he does not mean "grow beyond" to imply "leave behind."

For my part, I have tried to add to Bruner's prescription the reminder that it is not enough merely to *allow* children to remain in touch with these more sensitive of their mental parts; they need instruction in how to *keep* in touch with them fully as much as they need instruction in how to grow beyond them. Furthermore, such instruction ought to be as well-informed, well-designed, and artfully conducted as any other.

But perhaps I have altogether misconstrued the gist of Bruner's meaning when he speaks of the importance of freedom from excessive drives in educational settings. Perhaps he means freedom from drive—period; by which it might be inferred that he means to embrace the recent contributions to motivation theory by Robert W. White, which, while built on Piaget, seek to extend Freud, and therefore offers a nice opportunity for resolving the puzzlements mentioned.

White's position is that the weakness of psychoanalysis in dealing with questions of normal learning is traceable to its insistence on instinctual energy as the *sole* reservoir of human motivation. "How," White asks, "does a creature of instinct come to recognize that the world is there all the time whether he likes it or not, and that it follows laws of its own, whether he likes them or not?" (87, p. 54) Hartmann and Rapaport (72) tried to answer such questions within the bounds of Freud's assumptions by speculating that when a motive did not behave in the peremptory and periodic ways typical of the instincts, it was powered by "desexualized" or "deaggressivized" energy. White puts the convincing case that these speculations are needlessly far-fetched. In their place he postulates an independent source of ego energy (effectance), which differs from instinctual energy in that it stems from the central nervous system itself, rather than from appetitive body tissues, and in that it seeks alterations not in internal organic states but in the environment. Thus a boy may want to become like his father not only because he loves or fears him, and is rewarded and punished by him, but also because he admires the way his father makes things happen in the world. Then if he comes to copy the garbage collector for a spell, we can look upon this as one more instance of his independent admiration of the "big-doers" in life, without being drawn by the need for instinctual explanations into talk of displaced libido, sublimated anal impulses, or similar topics. Similarly, if he later shows an interest in engines, we can comprehend this not only as a possible derivative of his previous concern with garbage collecting by way of internal combustion, but also as a compelling object in its own right for causing interesting changes in the world.

White is careful to ascribe additive rather than replacement functions to his concept of effectance motivation. In a showdown, it is the drives that do the replacing. By definition however, such showdowns must be periodic.

> When instinctual drives are aroused, the activity of the nervous system—the "ego apparatus"—is directed toward instinctual aims. Only when drives are quiet does the system operate in the pure service of feelings of efficacy, and with the breadth and nonspecificity that is most conducive to the growth of varied competencies. (87, p. 85)

This, systematically, is what Bruner must mean when he says in another context ". . . We know that the freeing of instinct is not an end in itself but a way station along the road to competence." (10, p. 117) This statement can be misinterpreted outside its systematic context; the "way station" can come to be understood as one which can or should be left behind, rather than one which can and should offer repeated respite along the winding road from competence to competence.

I have assumed that Bruner would disabuse teachers of such a misinterpretation. And I have said that I would go a step further and have teachers capitalize on those moments of *un*quiet drive states, which, while independent of the effectance motives, are *not unrelated* to them. White enumerates three ways in which effectance motives can be diverted from their normal function of building a sense of competence in a child: (a) "specific obstruction of exploratory play," in which the child is kept out of touch with manipulable objects upon which causative influences might be exerted; (b) "specific obstruction of social efficacy," in which significant adults do not respond to the child's social maneuvers, however skilled they may be; and (c) "generalized obstruction by swamping," in which "spare time is squeezed out because instinctual drives are in a continual state of arousal." (87, pp. 85–92) Nothing could make it more clear that the differences between Bruner's and my emphasis represent a division of labor and not a conflict of interests. Bruner's emphasis on the need in classrooms for actively engageable particulars seeks to free the educative process from the first obstruction. My emphasis on the need for widening the radius of pedagogical strategies to include preconscious functions seeks to free the educative process from the third obstruction. And our respective emphases on keeping teacher-student communication honest, intellectually honest and emotionally honest, seek together to free the educative process from the second obstruction.

There may be a fourth dimension to White's theory that may be suggestive in experimental teaching. Possibly a child's sense of competence derives not only from his being a skillful causer of effects in the *extra*-psychic environment of things and people. Possibly it is further heightened by being a clever manipulator of the *intra*-psychic representations of the drives themselves. I have in mind those times when a child will consciously provoke an arousal of instinct for the seeming purpose of chancing such unpredictable encounters with the inside world as may follow very predictable encounters with his outside world. ("Scare me again, Daddy.") If this is a plausible extension of effectance theory it will remain a good idea to introduce elementary schoolers to replicas of the bones and stones that Leaky is finding at Olduvai Gorge, not only because these are engageable particulars that are likely to lead to fruitful generalizations, and not only because they will provide an intellectually honest invitation to appreciate man's animal origins, but also because they may suggest to the children new ways of stealing a march on their own instincts (21). Similarly, it will remain a good idea to have the children become sufficiently familiar with their dream monsters to introduce them to the teacher—not only because this may be of some general prophylactic value, and not only because it may prevent some transient arousal of instinct from swamping a day's work, but also because the children may learn from it that you can get a familiar monster to put spice into a variety of workaday tasks.

Bibliography

1. Adams, Robert M. "The Origin of Cities," *Scientific American*, 1960, September, CCIII, 48, pp. 153–155+.
2. Allport, Gordon W. *Personality*. New York: Henry Holt & Company, 1937.
3. _____. *Pattern and Growth in Personality*. New York: Holt, Rinehart and Winston, 1961.
4. Angyal, Andras. *Neurosis and Treatment: A Holistic Theory*, ed. Eugenia Hanfmann and Richard M. Jones. New York: John Wiley & Sons, 1965.
5. Barron, Frank, and Taylor, Calvin. *Scientific Creativity: Its Recognition and Development*. New York: John Wiley & Sons, 1963.
6. Biber, Barbara. "Play as a Growth Process," *Vassar Alumni Magazine*, XXXVII (1951), 2.
7. _____. "Premature Structuring as a Deterrent to Creativity," *Amer. J. Orthopsychiat.*, Vol. 24, No. 2 (April, 1959).
8. Boss, Medard. *The Analysis of Dreams*. New York: Philosophical Library, Inc., 1958.
9. Bruner, Jerome S. *The Process of Education*. Cambridge, Mass.: Harvard University Press, 1960.
10. _____. *On Knowing: Essays for the Left Hand*. Cambridge, Mass.: Harvard University Press, 1962.
11. _____. *Toward a Theory of Instruction*. Cambridge, Mass.: Harvard University Press, 1966.
12. _____. "Education as Social Invention," *Contemporary Ed-*

ucational Psychology: Selected Essays, ed. R. M. Jones. New York: Harper & Row, 1967.

13. _____. "The Course of Cognitive Growth," *Contemporary Educational Psychology: Selected Essays,* ed. R. M. Jones. New York: Harper & Row, 1967.

14. _____. "The Growth of Mind," *Amer. Psychol.,* XX, 12 (1965), 1007–17.

15. _____. "Needed: A Theory of Instruction," *Educational Leadership,* XX (May, 1963), 523–32.

16. _____. "The Act of Discovery," *Harvard Educ. Rev.,* XXXL, 1 (1961), 21–32.

17. _____. "Some Theorems on Instruction Illustrated with Reference to Mathematics," *Sixty-Third Yearbook of the National Society for the Study of Education.* Part I. Chicago: University of Chicago Press, 1964, 306–35.

18. _____. "The Growth of Mind," *Occasional Paper No. 8,* "The Social Studies Curriculum Program." Cambridge, Mass.: Educational Services, Inc., 1966.

19. _____. "Myth and Identity," *Daedelus,* CXXXVIII, 2 (1959), 349–58.

20. _____, Goodnow, Jacqueline, and Austin, George. *A Study of Thinking.* New York: John Wiley & Sons, 1956.

21. Clinchy, Evans, and Jones, Richard M. "Bones and Stones." Unpublished memorandum, Cambridge, Mass.: Educational Services, Inc., 1962.

22. Eisley, Loren. *The Immense Journey.* New York: Vintage Books, 1946.

23. _____. "The Lethal Factor," *Contemporary Educational Psychology: Selected Essays,* ed. R. M. Jones. New York: Harper & Row, 1967.

24. Erikson, Erik. *Childhood and Society.* New York: Norton, 1950.

25. _____. *Identity and the Life Cycle.* "Psychological Issues Monograph Series," I, 1. New York: International Universities Press, 1959.

26. _____. *Insight and Responsibility.* New York: Norton, 1964.

27. _____. "The Roots of Virtue," *The Humanist Frame*, ed. Sir Julian Huxley. London: George Allen and Unwin, Ltd., 1960.

28. Frankl, Viktor. *Man's Search for Meaning*. Boston: Beacon, 1963.

29. Flavell, John. *The Developmental Psychology of Jean Piaget*. Princeton, N.J.: Van Nostrand Company, 1963.

30. Getzels, Jacob W., and Jackson, Phillip W. *Creativity and Intelligence*. New York: John Wiley & Sons, 1962.

31. Goodman, Paul. *Compulsory Mis-Education and the Community of Scholars*. New York: Vintage Books.

32. Gruber, H. "Education and the Image of Man," *Contemporary Educational Psychology: Selected Essays*, ed. R. M. Jones. New York: Harper & Row, 1967.

33. Hartmann, Heinz. *Ego Psychology and the Problem of Adaptation*. New York: International Universities Press, 1958.

34. Holt, John. *How Children Fail*. New York: Pitman Publishing Corp., 1964.

35. Huxley, Aldous. "Education on the Non-Verbal Level," *Contemporary Educational Psychology: Selected Essays*, ed. R. M. Jones. New York: Harper & Row, 1967.

36. Huxley, Julian. *Evolution in Action*. New York: Harper & Row, 1963.

37. _____. *New Bottles for New Wines*. New York: Harper & Row, 1957.

38. Jones, Richard M. *An Application of Psychoanalysis to Education*. Springfield, Ill.: Charles C Thomas, 1960.

39. _____. *Ego Synthesis in Dreams*. Cambridge, Mass.: Schenkman Publishing Company, 1962.

40. _____. "The Negation T.A.T.; A Projective Method for Eliciting Repressed Thought Content," *Psychological Test Modifications*, ed. M. Kornrich. Springfield, Ill.: Charles C Thomas, 1965.

41. _____. "The Differential Effects of Negated Word Associations on Ability to Recall Traumatic and Non-Traumatic

Stimulus Words," *Psychological Test Modifications*, ed. M. Kornrich. Springfield, Ill.: Charles C Thomas, 1965.

42. ———. "A Model of Transitional Thought-Organization," *Psychological Test Modifications*, ed. M. Kornrich. Springfield, Ill.: Charles C Thomas, 1965.

43. ———. "The Role of Self-Knowledge in the Educative Process," *Contemporary Educational Psychology: Selected Essays*, ed. R. M. Jones. New York: Harper & Row, 1967.

44. ———. "Some Educational Aspects of Group-Leader Interaction," *Contemporary Educational Psychology: Selected Essays*, ed. R. M. Jones. New York: Harper & Row, 1967.

45. ———. " 'Education in Depth' and 'The New Curricula,' " *Contemporary Educational Psychology: Selected Essays*, ed. R. M. Jones. New York: Harper & Row, 1967.

46. ——— (ed.). *Contemporary Educational Psychology: Selected Essays*. New York: Harper & Row, 1967.

47. ———, Sellards, Ruth, and Lacy, Elizabeth, "Reading Club —An Experiment in Symptom-Focused Group Treatment," *National Institute of Health Research Grant M-826 Progress Report* (May 31, 1958), pp. L-28–L-32.

48. ———, and Friedman, Neil. "On the Mutuality of the Oedipus Complex; Notes on the Hamlet Case," *American Imago*, XX, 2 (1963), pp. 107–31.

49. Kaiser, Hellmuth. *Effective Psychotherapy*, ed. Louis B. Fierman. New York: Free Press, 1965.

50. Kellogg, W. N., and Kellogg, L. A. *The Ape and The Child*. New York: McGraw-Hill, 1933.

51. Klein, George S. "Consciousness in Psychoanalytic Theory: Some Implications for Current Research in Perception," *Contemporary Educational Psychology: Selected Essays*, ed. R. M. Jones. New York: Harper & Row, 1967.

52. ———. "On Subliminal Activation," *J. Nerv. Ment. Dis.*, CXXVIII (1959), 293–301.

53. ———. "On Inhibition, Disinhibition, and 'Primary Process' in Thinking." ("Proceedings of the XIV International Con-

gress of Applied Psychology," IV), *Clinical Psychology*, ed. G. Neilson. Copenhagen, Munksgaard, 179–98.

54. Kubie, Lawrence S. *Neurotic Distortion of the Creative Process*. Lawrence, Kansas: University of Kansas Press, 1958.

55. ———. "The Forgotten Man of Education," *Contemporary Educational Psychology: Selected Essays*, ed. R. M. Jones. New York: Harper & Row, 1967.

56. ———. "Research in Protecting Preconscious Functions in Education," *Contemporary Educational Psychology: Selected Essays*, ed. R. M. Jones. New York: Harper & Row, 1967.

57. ———. "The Concept of Dream Deprivation: A Critical Analysis," *Psychosom. Med.*, XXIV, 1962.

58. ———. "The Fundamental Nature of the Distinction Between Normality and Neurosis," *Psychoan. Quart.*, XXXII (1954), 167–204.

59. LaBarre, Weston. *The Human Animal*. Chicago: University of Chicago Press, 1954.

60. Langer, Susanne K. *Philosophy in New Key; A Study in the Symbolism of Reason, Rite and Art*. Cambridge, Mass.: Harvard University Press, 1942.

61. Maslow, Abraham H. "Deficiency Motivation and Growth Motivation," *Nebraska Symposium on Motivation*, ed. M. R. Jones. Lincoln: University of Nebraska Press, 1955.

62. ———. "Defense and Growth," *Merrill-Palmer Quarterly*, III (1956).

63 ———. "Resistance to Being Rubricized," *Perspectives in Psychological Theory*, ed. B. Kaplan and S. Wapner. New York: International Universities Press, 1960.

64. Mayer, Martin. *Where, When and Why: Social Studies in American Schools*. New York: Harper & Row, 1962.

65. Morison, Elting. Personal communication.

66. Neisser, Ulric. "The Multiplicity of Thought," *Contemporary Educational Psychology: Selected Essays*, ed. R. M. Jones. New York: Harper & Row, 1967.

67. Paul, I. H. "Studies in Remembering; The Reproduction of Connected and Extended Verbal Material," *Psychological Issues Monograph Series*, I, 2. New York: International Universities Press, 1959.

68. Piaget, Jean. *The Origins of Intelligence*. New York: International Universities Press, 1962.

69. ———. *Play, Dreams, and Imitation in Childhood*. New York: Norton, 1951.

70. ———. *The Psychology of Intelligence*. New York: Harcourt Brace, 1950.

71. Pötzel, Otto, Allers, Rudolf, and Teller, Jakob. "Preconscious Stimulation in Dreams, Associations and Images," *Psychological Issues Monograph Series*, II, 3. New York: International Universities Press, 1960.

72. Rapaport, David. "The Structure of Psychoanalytic Theory; a Systematizing Attempt," *Psychological Issues Monograph Series*, II, 2. New York: International Universities Press, 1960.

73. Schactel, Ernest G. "On Memory and Childhood Amnesia," *Psychiatry*, X, 1 (1947).

74. Schwartz, Morris, and Stanton, Alfred H. *The Mental Hospital*. New York: Basic Books, 1954.

75. Shevrin, Howard, and Luborsky, Lester. "The Measurement of Preconscious Perception in Dreams and Images: An Investigation of the Pötzel Phenomenon," *J. Abn. Soc. Psychol.*, LVI, 3 (1958).

76. Silberer, Herbert. "On Symbol-Formation," *Organization and Pathology of Thought*, ed. David Rapaport. New York: Columbia University Press, 1951.

77. ———. "Report on a Method of Eliciting and Observing Certain Symbolic Hallucination-Phenomenon," *Organization and Pathology of Thought*, ed. David Rapaport. New York: Columbia University Press, 1951.

78. Sykes, Gresham M. *The Society of Captives: A Study of a Maximum Security Prison*. Princeton: Princeton University Press, 1958.

79. Tauber, Edward S., and Green, Maurice R. *Prelogical Experience*. New York: Basic Books, 1959.

80. Taylor, Calvin. *Creativity: Progress and Potential*. New York: McGraw-Hill, 1964.

81. Waddington, C. H. "Man as an Organism," *Evolution After Darwin*, ed. Sol Tax and Charles Callender. III, 172–73. Chicago: University of Chicago Press, 1960.

82. Washburn, S. L., and Howell, F. C. "Human Evolution and Culture," *Evolution After Darwin*, II, ed. Sol Tax and Charles Callender. Chicago: University of Chicago Press, 1960.

83. Weisskopf, Edith A. "Some Comments Concerning the Role of Education in the 'Creation of Creation,' " *J. Educ. Psychol.* (March, 1951).

84. Werlin, Elena G. "An Experiment in Elementary Education," *Contemporary Educational Psychology: Selected Essays*, ed. R. M. Jones. New York: Harper & Row, 1967.

85. Werner, Heinz. *Comparative Psychology of Mental Development*. Chicago: Follett, 1948.

86. ———. "Process and Achievement—a Basic Problem of Education and Developmental Psychology," *Harvard Educational Review*, VII, 3 (1937).

87. White, Robert W. "Ego and Reality in Psychoanalytic Theory," *Psychological Issues Monograph Series*, III, 3. New York: International Universities Press, 1963.

88. Whitehead, Alfred North. *The Aims of Education*. New York: Macmillan, 1929.

Index